I0459062

SEPTUAGINT:

EXODUS

SEPTUAGINT, VOLUME 2

SCRIPTURAL RESEARCH INSTITUTE

Published by Digital Ink Productions, 2025

COPYRIGHT

While every precaution has been taken in the preparation of this book, the publisher assumes no responsibility for errors or omissions, or for damages resulting from the use of the information contained herein.

Septuagint: Exodus

Third Edition. October 3, 2025

Copyright © 2025 Scriptural Research Institute.

ISBN: 978-1998636457

The Septuagint was translated into Greek at the Library of Alexandria between 250 and 132 BCE.

This English translation was created by the Scriptural Research Institute in 2018 through 2025, primarily from the Codex Vaticanus, although other Septuagint manuscripts were also used for reference. Additionally, the Masoretic texts, Peshitta, Targums, Coptic and Armenian Bibles, and the Dead Sea Scrolls were used for comparative analysis.

The image used for the cover is "Moses and the Sereph" by Raven Mahikan.

Ebook version: ISBN 978-1998288885

Hardcover version: ISBN 978-1998636464

Audiobook version: ISBN 978-1990289385

TABLE OF CONTENTS

I

TABLE OF CONTENTS

TABLE OF CONTENTS

FORWARD

In the mid-3rd century BCE, King Ptolemy II Philadelphus of Egypt ordered a translation of the ancient Israelite scriptures for the Library of Alexandria, which resulted in the creation of the Septuagint. The original version, published circa 250 BCE, only included the Torah, or in Greek terms, the Pentateuch. The Torah is the five books traditionally credited to Moses, circa 1500 BCE: *Cosmic Genesis*, *Exodus*, *Leviticus*, *Numbers*, and *Deuteronomy*.

It is generally accepted that there were several versions written in Aramaic or Canaanite before the translation of the Septuagint. Fragments of the Torah have been found in four languages among the dead sea scrolls, generally dated to between 200 BCE and 600 CE. During this time, the land of Judea passed from the rule of the Ptolemys in Egypt to the rule of the Seleucids in Syria around 200 BCE. The Seleucids attempted to Hellenize the Judeans, and effectively banned traditional Judaism. This Hellenizing activity was partially successful, influencing the Sadducee faction of Judaism, however also led to the Maccabean Revolt in 165 BCE, which itself created the independent Hasmonean Kingdom of Judea. This kingdom was violently xenophobic and led by a priestly monarchy that combined both the powers of the state and the church. The Hasmonean dynasty attempted to conquer all of the territory that had previously been part of the Persian Province of Judea, and either evicted or exterminated the people that were living there, depending on their ethnicity. When the Edomites were conquered they were allowed to mass-convert to Judaism as they were considered the descendants of Esau, however, most other ethnic groups were not welcome.

The Hasmoneans blamed the Greeks for all of Judea's problems and attempted to forge an alliance with the Roman republic. The Hasmoneans appear to have promoted Yahweh Sabaoth partially to forge closer ties with the Romans, as Iaw (Yahweh) was pronounced very similar to Iove (Jupiter) in Latin. The Romans did not respond well to this, and threw the Jews out of Rome in 139 BCE, as recorded by Valerius Maximus:

> *"Gnaeus Cornelius Hispalus, praetor peregrinus in the year of the consulate of Marcus Popilius Laenas and Lucius Calpurnius, ordered the astrologers by an edict to leave Rome and Italy within ten days, since by a fallacious interpretation of the stars they perturbed fickle and silly minds, thereby making profit out of their lies. The same praetor compelled the Jews, who attempted to infect the Roman custom with the cult of Jupiter Sabazius, to return to their home."*

While the Hasmoneans ruled Judea, they converted the national script from the old Canaanite script, today called Paleo-Hebrew, to the Aramaic "block script," today called Hebrew. As a result, almost all surviving texts found from the Hasmonean era and later are written in the Aramaic script, and it is unclear how much the Hasmoneans redacted the texts when they transcribed them. The scriptures the Hasmoneans left the world were later used as the basis of the Masoretic texts, which are used today by Rabbinical Jews, as well as by Catholic and Protestant Christians.

The God of the *Book of Exodus* is called lord the god (κύριοσ ο θεοσ), or simplified to lord (κύριοσ), or God (Θεοσ), and repeatedly identified as Ōn (Ων) or "god" Ōn (θεοσ Ων). These terms are mirrored in the *Book of Names*, the Masoretic version of Exodus, by Yəhōwâ (יְהֹוָה), Yəhōwâ 'ĕlōhē (יְהֹוָה אֱלֹהֵי), 'ăšer 'ehyeh (אֲשֶׁר אָהְיֶה), or 'ēl šadday (אֵל שַׁדַּי) respectively. The Aramaic sections of Masoretic Daniel that were not translated into Hebrew maintain the term 'ădōnāy hā'ĕlōhîm (אֲדֹנָי הָאֱלֹהִים), meaning the "Lord the gods" where the Septuagint has "Lord the god," however, the Hebrew sections have Yəhōwâ 'ĕlōhîm (יְהֹוָה אֱלֹהִים) where the Septuagint has "Lord the god," suggesting the Greek more accurately reflects the Aramaic source texts than the Hebrew translation. According to the Talmud, this was to repair the damage King Manasseh had done 500 years earlier when he removed the name Yahweh from the Israelite texts, however, no evidence has survived from the era of Manasseh or earlier that proves this name was originally in the text. This suggests it was an attempt by the first Hasmonean High-Priest / King Simon the Zealous to create a national Judean religion with a god having a name similar to the Roman god Jove.

The genealogy of nations in Cosmic Genesis appears to have been written in Aramaic, and is internally dated to between 706 and 715 BCE. The text refers to Kahlu as the capital of Assyria, which places its authorship to before King Sargon II moved the capital to Dur Sharrukin 706 BCE, however, the text also mentions the Ashkenaz people, who first appeared in Assyrian records around 715 BCE, when they helped to defend Urartu from a Cimmerian invasion.

There is also a minor but notable difference in chapter 4 of Cosmic Genesis and Bereshít, where Tobel (θοβελ) is mirrored by Tûbal Qayin (תּוּבַל קַיִן). This is in the antediluvian section of the book, which appears to be a childish simplification of older historical records. This indicates the section of text was likely written in 836 BCE for the seven-year-old Judahite king Jehoash. At the time, Tabal in southern Anatolia was a major power at war with Assyria. Over a century later when the Aramaic translation was made or edited by King Manasseh, it was no longer necessary to clarify that this Tûbal wasn't Tabal, which had been conquered by the Assyrians, and the editor's note "Qayin" was dropped.

Tabal was conquered by the Assyrians in 713 BCE, shortly after the Aramean Kingdom of Damascus was conquered in 727 BCE, and the Samaritan Kingdom of Israel was conquered in 720 BCE. The Samaritan refugees fled to Judah and Tyre, however, the Arameans seem to have mainly fled to the Empire of Kush, and settled in southern Egypt around Elephantine. These Arameans were the origin of the Egypto-Aramean dialect, and included many Israelites. Damascus and Hama had, according to the books of the *1st* and *2nd Kingdoms* (Masoretic *Samuel*), been tributaries to the Kingdom of Israel

4

centuries earlier. There were certainly Israelites within the Aramean community that settled in Egypt, supporting the religion being practiced in the Aramean Federation that ruled Damascus and Hama before the region was conquered by the Neo-Assyrian Empire. As the Aramean people are barely mentioned in the genealogy of nations, it is more likely that it was composed by a Samaritan. The core of the genealogy is a collection of references to Mesopotamian cultures, with Arabs, Egyptians, Greeks, and Persians appearing as extensions of the core text. Another version of the genealogy is found in *1st Paralipomena* (Masoretic *Dibrê-hayyāmîm*), which only includes the core Mesopotamian cultures and the Edomite monarchs, indicating that there was originally a simpler version of the genealogy.

The full genealogy was probably composed in Samaria, after the Assyrians conquered the region. According to *4th Kingdoms* (Masoretic *Kings*) the Assyrians relocated most of the population of Samaria and the conquered Aramaean lands. This was a standard policy for the Neo-Assyrian Empire, and the Babylonian Chronicle ABC1 reports the Assyrians relocated 27,290 captives from Samaria.

According to *4th Kingdoms*, after the Assyrians conquered Samaria they brought in different people to live in Samaria, including people from Sippar, an ancient city in Babylonia. These Sipparites were reported to be worshiping "king" Ŏn (ענמלך) in the Aleppo Codex, and "king" 'Ăna (עֲנַמֶּלֶךְ) in the Leningrad Codex, indicating that the name Ŏn in Exodus likely originated with the Sipparites. These Sipparites are

5

reported to have adopted a corrupted form of the Israelite religion from the Samaritan priesthood, which indicates they interpreted Moses' god as ^{deity}Anu (𒀭), the father of the gods in the Mesopotamian pantheon.

Variants of this name are found in the Peshitta and the Targum Pseudo-Jonathan. In chapter 3, the Targum Pseudo-Jonathan uses 'Ănā' (אֲנָא) as a name in a verse that parallels the Septuagint's use of Ōn. Later in chapter 7, the Peshitta also uses Ånå (ܐܢܐ) as a name in a verse that parallels the Septuagint's use of Ōn. Before the vowel markings that developed in the Medieval era, 'Ănā' (אֲנָא) would have been Ånå (אנא), indicating there was an old Aramaic version of *Exodus* that used the name Ånå (𐡀𐡍𐡀). Ånå is not based on the Greek Ōn, as direct transliterations would be Ōn (ען) and Ōn (ܥ). The Library of Alexandra translated the Septuagint from the copies available in Egypt, indicating that the Egypto-Aramaic version of *Exodus* used the name Ōn (𐡏𐡍). Conversely the Ånå (𐡀𐡍𐡀) variant is only found in texts that would have drawn from the Syro-Aramaic texts. The Peshitta is written in the Syriac form of Aramaic, and the Targum Pseudo-Jonathan with is written in Palestinian Aramaic. The fact that the Masoretes, who were based in Babylon, and spoke Aramaic, added the vowel markings that changed "king" Ōn (ענמלך) to "king" Ana (עֲנָמֶלֶךְ), supports Ana being the Syro-Aramaic pronunciation of the Samaritan and Egypto-Aramaic Ōn.

Another name also appears in parallel verses of the targums: 'Ehyeh (אֶהְיֶה). The word 'ehyeh is also beginning of

6

the parallel verse in the Leningrad Codex, the somewhat whimsical phrase 'ehyeh 'ăšer 'ehyeh (אֶהְיֶה אֲשֶׁר אֶהְיֶה), meaning "I will be what I will be." This is the statement paralleled by the Septuagint's "I am Ōn" (εγω ειμι ο Ωμ). The Hebrew phrase survives mostly intact in the Dead Sea Scroll 4QGen-Exodᵃ, indicating was likely the verse in the Hasmonean dynasty's authorized transliteration of the Torah into Hebrew. The Peshitta has an odd variation on this verse, which reads "I will be Asherah Yahweh" (ܐܗܘܐ ܐܬܪܝܗ ܝܗ), which likely predates the version of the verse using the name Ånå (ܐܢܐ), which no longer exists even though the name Ånå is used later in chapter 6.

One of the oldest indisputable references to the Israelite god Yahweh was found by archaeologists digging at Kuntillet Ajrud, in the Sinai Peninsula near the modern Egyptian border with Israel. On pottery shards dating to circa 800 BCE, is a depiction Yahweh as the calf of Asherah, along with text that reads "Yahweh of Samaria" and "Yahweh of Teman." Temen was the capital of Edom at the time, so this was certainly the Israelite god Yahweh, along with his mother Asherah. This concept of Yahweh having a mother and father was ultimately banned by King Josiah of Judah, circa 632 BCE. Nevertheless, the goddess Asherah also had a son named Yå (𐎅𐎛) in the Ugaritic texts from the late Bronze Age, who was also the son of the god Ba'al, presumable Ba'al Hadad, the storm god of northern Canaan, as the ruins of Ugarit are near Mount Zephon. The Old Samaritan version of *Names* likely included this term "Asherah's Yahweh," as this is consistent with the iconography of the era, however, it is unlikely that this was the original phrase in the late Bronze Age cuneiform verse.

Both the Targum Pseudo-Jonathan and the Targum Jerusalem include an interpretation of the Hebrew phrase "I will be what I will be," followed by a paraphrase of the Septuagint's "I am Ōn." The Greek sentence "I am Ōn" is followed by the phrase "tell the Israelites, 'Lord has sent me to you.'" In the Targum Pseudo-Jonathan this reads as "Tell the sons of Israel "'Ănā', he in proper conduct and in good standing, sent me to you'" (כְּדְנָא תֵּימַר לִבְנֵי יִשְׂרָאֵל אֲנָא הוּא דַהֲוֵינָא וְעָתִיד לְמֶהֱוֵי שַׁדְרַנִי לְוַותְכוֹן). This is paralleled in the Targum Jerusalem with "Tell the sons of Israel "'Ehyeh sent me to you" (כְּדֵין תֵּימַר לִבְנֵי יִשְׂרָאֵל אֶהְיֶה שְׁלָחַנִי לִפְנֵיכֶם). 'Ehyeh is the beginning of the Hebrew phrase "I will be what I will be" (אֶהְיֶה אֲשֶׁר אֶהְיֶה), yet in the Targum Jerusalem it is used as an alternate name to Ōn / 'Ănā'.

The alternate reading of 'Ehyeh (אֶהְיֶה) as a name is probably originated in the transliteration of the texts from cuneiform to the Phoenician script early in the Iron Age. It probably originated as a transliteration of ^{deity}Éa (✳◨𒐊), the Middle Babylonian spelling of the Old Akkadian god Ia (𒂍𒐊), the god of life and fresh water. ^{deity}Éa is the most likely way that Canaanites would have written "Yahweh" in cuneiform. Cuneiform was the script used in southern Canaan during the late Bronze Age to write Canaanite, and therefore if the Israelites were using a Torah, it would have been written using the Canaanite script at the time. Ia was the god that caused the great flood in the Old Babylonian flood narratives, and it was believed he controlled the annual flooding of the Euphrates until the Neo-Assyrian era.

Both 'ĕlōhîm (אֱלֹהִים) and 'Ehyeh are probably derived from ^{deity}Éa, suggesting the Phoenician transcriber used a common pronunciation of the name as Álhym (𐤟𐤆𐤀𐤋𐤀) for most of the text, but left a direct transliteration of Áhyh (𐤟𐤆𐤀𐤀) where the messenger of god announced his name as ^{deity}Éa, as the transcriber recognized that "deity" (✳) was not part of the proper name. The text of *Names* is remarkably inconsistent with the use of words generally translated as "god" and "gods." Three terms are used 'ēl (אֵל), 'ĕlōhē (אֱלֹהֵ), and 'ĕlōhîm (אֱלֹהִים). These words have created a great deal of confusion, as ȧl (𐤋𐤀) was the Phoenician word for "god," ȧlh (𐤀𐤋𐤀) was Canaanite for "goddess," and ȧlhm (𐤟𐤀𐤋𐤀) was Canaanite for "goddesses." This confusion is manifest in various translations, where the gender in the texts shift around elohim, however, the main source texts always agree that 'ĕlōhē is a masculine form in regards to the Israelite god. This is likely because the term ȧl (𐤋𐤀) had become synonymous with El, the patriarch of the Canaanite pantheon by the beginning of the Iron Age, and the other gods were referred to as ba'al (𐤏𐤀𐤋), meaning "lord." Therefore, the Aramaic word ȧlhȧ (𐤀𐤄𐤋𐤀), which means "god," was adopted at some point by the Israelites to denote a generic "god."

The term 'ĕlōhē is generally used to connect texts from the time of Moses to older texts, such as the phrase "god of Abraham, god of Isaac, and god of Jacob," suggesting the Aramaic phrases were added circa 710 BCE, when the texts of

Bereshít and *Names* were standardized under the rule of King Hezekiah of Judah. Unfortunately, in *Names* 'ĕlōhē is used as both the singular "god" and plural "gods."

The form 'ĕlōhîm is found in the older sections of text, and is clearly a word used to denote either a singular god in some verses, or a plurality of gods in other verses. The Masoretic texts generally demark the difference between "God" and "gods" by adding "the" to the beginning of the word, rendering the plural form as hā'ĕlōhîm (הָאֱלֹהִים). This is particularly evident in Masoretic Daniel, where "lord of the gods" is rendered as 'ădōnāy hā'ĕlōhîm (אֲדֹנָי הָאֱלֹהִים) in the Aramaic sections.

These variations of Ōn, Ånå, and 'Ehyeh, as well as the singular interpretation of the word 'ĕlōhîm can all be explained if the original phrase in the late Bronze Age texts used the name ^{deity}Éa (✳𐏓𐎷). Elum (✳) was the Babylonian word for "god," which was pronounced in Neo-Sumerian as ^{deity}Anu (✳𐎡). ^{deity}Éa (✳𐏓𐎷) was the Babylonian pronunciation of the old Akkadian name Ia (𐎡), the god of life and fresh water. The Canaanite version of Ia was Ym (𐤉𐤌), the god of the sea, therefore transliterating ^{deity}Éa (✳𐏓𐎷) into the Phoenician script by Israelites at the beginning of the Iron Age would have rendered it as Ålhym (𐤌𐤄𐤋𐤀), the exact word found in Dead Sea Scroll 4QpaleoGen-Exod[1], which was later transliterated into Hebrew as ålhym (אלהים). This god was certainly not Ba'al Yam, the Canaanite "lord of the sea," and so the generic word ålh (𐤄𐤋𐤀) would have been used,

10

even if it rendered a word very similar to the Phoenician word ålhm (𐤀𐤋𐤄𐤌) meaning "goddesses."

This confusion about the god's name begins with the messenger of god telling Moses that he was previously known by a different name to Abraham. This name is rendered as "god" šaddāy (אֵל שַׁדָּי) in the Leningrad Codex and Targum Onkelos, åylšdy (ܐܠܫܕܝ) in the Peshitta, and "god" šaday in the Targum Pseudo-Jonathan. However, the Septuagint manuscripts uses the name "god" Ōn (θεος Ωn), while the Targum Jerusalem use the phrase "god sky" (אֱלָהָא שְׁמַיָּא). God sky is an alternate way of translating [deity]Ān (𒀭𒀭), the Sipparite king of the gods called "king" Ōn (ענמלך) in the Aleppo Codex, and "king" 'Ăna (עֲנָמֶלֶךְ) in the Leningrad Codex, as Ān (𒀭) meant "deity," "sky", and "star."

The verse in *Names* confirms that the name Shaddai was viewed as being in the pre-Mosaic texts by the author. The term El Shaddai was used 48 times in the Masoretic texts, including 31 times in the *Book of Job*, and 6 times in *Bereshít*, but only once in *Names*, when the messenger says his real name is Yəhwâ (יְהֹוָה). El Shaddai was the supreme god of the Amorites, who they called Bel Šadi (𒀭𒂗𒇉), and who as known as [ilu]Šadi (𒀭𒂗𒇉) by the Babylonians at the time, although the name [ilu]Amurru (𒀭𒈥𒌆) was more common, meaning "western god" as the Amorites lived to the west of the Babylonians.

Both *Cosmic Genesis* / *Bereshít* and *Exodus* / *Names* appear to have been redacted in regards to the names El Shaddai, Ōn / 'Ănā', and 'Ehyeh, as there is no reference to El

11

Shaddai in *Cosmic Genesis*, no reference to Ōn / 'Ănā' in *Names*, and no a reference of 'Ehyeh in *Exodus*. Ōn is used as a Greek translation for both Shaddai and 'Ehyeh in Exodus, while in *Cosmic Genesis* the translation of Masoretic Shaddai is "Omnipotent" (παντοκράτορος). The redaction of El Shaddai from the Aramaic version of *Cosmic Genesis* likely took place under the rule of King Manasseh of Judah, who was reported to have removed the name of god from the Torah circa 700 BCE, as the name continued to be used in Samaritan texts. The substitution of ān (✳) for [ilu]Šadi (✳ 𐤌 ⟨⊖⟩) in the Aramaic version of *Exodus* likely happened around the same time in Samaria. As the original term must have been [ilu]Šadi, the term "god Shaddai" is imported from the Leningrad Codex in this translation.

Unfortunately, the Greek translation doesn't generally distinguish between the singular and plural forms, almost always rendering the term as "the god" (ο θεοσ). However, this does create some confusing concepts, such as the Egyptians worshiping the God of the Israelites instead of their gods. In order to clarify the text, the distinction of "god" versus "gods" are imported from the Leningrad Codex where the Hebrew reads 'ĕlōhē (אֱלֹהֵי), 'ĕlōhîm (אֱלֹהִים), or hā'ĕlōhîm (הָאֱלֹהִים), when not distinguished in the Septuagint manuscripts.

This statement that changed the name of the Israelite god was reportedly made by some fire-bramble, which had hands. While this sounds like either a fever dream, or a jinn tricking Moses, it is repeated in all the earliest translations without

12

explanation, until the High Middle Ages, when Greek translations started dropping the "fire bramble," leaving the impression that Moses was talking to "regular" angel. The various ancient Greek, Hebrew, and Syriac translations are all essentially identical, meaning the translators made sure they had the words translated correctly, and also that they didn't know how to explain the talking fire bramble.

As Moses was the only human present, if one accepts the existence of Moses, he was the only one who could have told anyone that this happened. The existence of Moses is often dismissed due to a lack of historic proof that he existed, and certain impossibilities that exist in some of the translations. The lack of historic evidence for his life is a fairly weak argument, as he is described as being an adopted member of the extended royal family of Egypt, who ran away and spent most of his life in the deserts of northern Saudi Arabia and Jordan. Few of the names of the members of the extended royal families of Egypt have survived from any era, and based on the Septuagint's chronology, he would have lived at the end of the Hyksos dynasty, when virtually nothing is known about the royal family beyond the names of the kings.

This dating was confirmed by the Judean historian Josephus 2000 years ago, who claimed to have been given ancient Judean records from the Temple in Jerusalem when it was destroyed. That he received the records is not in doubt, but what they contained is, as the Temple was only a few centuries old at that point. The records from the earlier Temple of King Solomon had reportedly been stolen or destroyed in the various Egyptian, Assyrian, and Babylonian assaults on Jerusalem over the centuries. Nevertheless, Josephus claimed that Moses had been the last king of the Hyksos when they were driven from Egypt, the historic King Khamudi. This is generally dismissed as wishful thinking on Josephus part, however, the time-frame of the collapse of the Hyksos dynasty does fit the chronology found in the Septuagint, and the strange events of Moses leading the Israelites out of Egypt.

One of the biggest problems in trying to understand the story of Moses historically, is that his name is widely considered unknown. In Greek, his name is spelled as variations of Mōsēs (Μωσης), while in Hebrew it is Mōšeh (מֹשֶׁה). In the Dead Sea Scrolls it appears as Mšh (משה / 𐤌𐤔𐤄) and Mwšh (מושה), while the Peshitta renders it as Mwšå (ܡܘܫܐ). However, none of these variants mean anything in Canaanite. Over 2000 years ago, Greek scholars at the Library of Alexandria proposed that the name Mšh was only half of his name, a transliteration of the Egyptian msỉ (𓄝𓏭), meaning "give birth to," or "created by." Many kings of Egypt were known as the msỉ of a god, including Ahmose (𓇹𓄝𓏭), Amenmose (𓇏𓄝𓏭), Ramses (𓇳𓄝𓏭), Ptahmose (𓁹𓐍𓄝𓏭𓏏), and Tuthmose (𓅝𓄝𓏭). A theory that has been circulating since at least the time of Josephus in the 1st century CE, is that Moses' original name was Hapymoses, meaning the "Nile god created him." Naturally, trying to find evidence that someone existed over 3500 years ago is complicated when you don't know his name.

An alternate, and much simpler explanation of Moses name is that it is the Egyptian phrase mw-šåȯ (☰☷☰ 🔺☰), meaning "beginning on water," which is what the princess states when she names him. However, this non-religious name would not have been used by an indigenous royal family, meaning the princess would have to be a member of the Hyksos regime, or some other Egyptianized foreign royal family.

As most modern interpretations accept that Moses story is set during the Ramesside Period, it is impossible for him to have been a member of the Egyptianized foreign royal family unless he left Egypt some time in the early Iron Age, by which time the Israelite kings of Saul, David, and Solomon had all apparently used some version of his legal code. This is a massive anachronism that causes many to doubt he existed. However, it is based on the fact that the town of Ramesses is mentioned in the Greek and Hebrew texts. This is commonly accepted as a reference to Pi-Ramesses, which was founded sometime between 1292 and 1250 BCE, however, was not commonly called Ramesses until around 800 BCE. As the original text could not have been written in the Bronze Age using an Iron Age script, it stands to reason that the contemporary name would have been used, not an archaic name that no one would have recognized. The city of Pi-Ramesses was built on the historic site of Avaris, the former capital of the Hyksos regime, and the other cities mentioned, Iwnw (𓉺𓏤 / אׄן / Ων) and Per-Atum (𓉐𓏤𓐝 / פּיתׄם / Πιθωμ) were both major Hyksos centers.

Later in Exodus, Moses went up a mountain to speak with something that had landed on the mountain, and then returned to the Israelites with two stone tablets that were written by the "finger of god." While this is generally interpreted literally by religious people, it is also a clear reference to the tablets being written in hieroglyphs. In ancient Egypt, it was illegal to carved hieroglyphs unless one was trained as a scribe as hieroglyphs were considered sacred. The Egyptians called hieroglyphs zh̯åw-mdw-nṯr (𓂋𓏏𓌃𓊹𓏪), meaning "writing god's words." The majority of the population wrote a cursive script known today as hieratic, but known to them simply as zh̯å (𓂋𓏏), meaning "writing" or "painting." Moses had been raised in the royal family, and would have known how to write Egyptian hieratic, however, if he knew how to carve hieroglyphs, it indicates that he would have been educated to become a scribe.

If Moses did write a book regarding his encounter with the talking fire-bramble, it would have been written in Egyptian, and later translated into Canaanite cuneiform after the Israelites had settled in Samaria. While the Egyptians did not have a talking fire-bramble messenger of god, they did have a messenger of god that fits Moses general description: wåḏt (𓇅𓏏), generally rendered as wadjet, also called "the green one." The term wadjet referred to a messenger of god who specifically served several goddesses associated with the sky, dawn, dusk, or the afterlife. Wadjets were generally depicted as flying serpents in Egyptian art, sometimes with hands and legs. A very similar creature was depicted in Old Sumerian art, the muškiĝir (𒈲𒆜), which translates as "snake with dagger." The Akkadians later interpreted this as muškuššu (✕━◁◈▷), meaning "snake with fire." This serpent with a dagger or a fire was depicted as a scaly animal with arms and legs like a lion's legs, talons like an eagle, a long neck and tail, two bovine horns on its head, and a serpentine tongue.

Wadjets were also represented iconographically with the wadjet eyes (𓂀𓂀). There were two wåḏt eyes, the Eye of Horus (𓂀), and the Eye of Ra (𓂀), one represented Venus as the morning star, and the other as Venus as the evening star. Additionally, a wadjet eye represented Sirius during the heliacal rising, which announced the beginning of the flood season. As such, the wadjets were representatives of several goddesses, including the sky cow Hathor, and the goddess of medicine Sekhmet. In Iwnw, a wadjet was the messenger of the goddess Iusaaset, the wife of the creator god Atum. Wadjet's voice was described as being fire, however, she was also reported to be eternally green, described as the "intact one," and her name included the hieroglyph wåḏ (𓇉) meaning "papyrus plant," which would explain where the interpretation of "bramble" came from.

The iconography of the wadjet continued within Israelite art for almost a thousand years, as statues of seraphs were placed inside King Solomon's temple in Jerusalem. Śārāp (שָׂרָף), the word used in the Masoretic texts, means "burning serpent" and the prophet Isaiah described the statues of the seraphs in the temple as having wings shortly before they were destroyed. When they were destroyed, the bronze statue of a serpent on a pole that Moses carved was also destroyed. It had reportedly been moved into the temple at the same time as the box of the covenant, and other artifacts from the time of Moses. This indicates that Moses statue was viewed as a seraph by the time King Solomon had the seraph statues made.

Most of these attributes were also used in the later Israelite texts to describe cherubs, suggesting that muškuššu (𒈲𒁀𒈦) was the Bronze Age cuneiform Canaanite translation of "wadjet," and krwb (𐤊𐤓𐤅𐤁) was the Iron Age Phoenician script translation of "muškuššu." Isaiah used the term śārāp məʼôpēp (שָׂרָף מְעוֹפֵף), meaning "fire-snake that flies" circa 720 BCE, which is a description of muškuššu, the winged "snake with fire" from Mesopotamian beliefs. Šrp (𐤔𐤓𐤐), meaning fire-snake, would have been the logical Phoenician script transla-tions of muškuššu, later updated to krwb (𐤊𐤓𐤅𐤁) under King Hezekiah's reforms, when the seraph statues in Solomon's temple were destroyed.

In the past few decades, several scholars have tried to link the wonders, or plagues, that happened when the Israelites left Egypt to the Minoan eruption, however, most seem hampered by the name of one of the cities the Israelites were living in, which the *Book of Exodus* records as being Ramesses. This name simply was not used in Egypt as the name of a city until around 800 BCE, and therefore has to be viewed as an anachronism, likely a geographical update made during King Hezekiah's reforms.

Scientific evidence places the Minoan eruption at circa 1600 BCE, however, Egyptologists have long disputed this, claiming it happened sometime between 1570 and 1539 BCE. A mean date of 1557 BCE is commonly used by Egyptologist. The reason for the difference is that the Egyptians left a consistent record of the length of king's reigns from the Minoan eruption until the Bronze Age collapse, and the Mesopotamian cultures kept a record of the length of kings' reigns beyond that point until the Classical era. However, there is probably a gap in the Egyptian records during the middle of the New Kingdom era, when the government collapsed. In his biography, King Ramesses III described a collapse of several decades before his father seized control of Egypt. During this time, an atheist from Syria had apparently seized control of the government, and all order collapsed.

While Egyptologists recognize that Ramesses III's father Setnakhte established a new dynasty, they only generally allow for a few years of anarchy since the previous "King" Tausret. Tausret was the wife of a former king, Seti II, who established herself as the "king" after King Siptah died. She was not the daughter of a former Egyptian king, and so neither the concept of "princess" or "queen" apply to her. Her reign is believed to have only lasted for a year before the government collapsed, although ancient sources like Manetho claimed she ruled for 7 years. The interim king, Merneptah Siptah, is believed to have been Seti II's nephew, meaning he did not have his own heir. Siptah was a child when he assumed the throne, and only ruled for a few years before dying, and so also did not leave an heir. When Tausret assumed the kingship there was most likely no remaining male heirs to the royal family, however, Egyptians did not like female kings, and her reign appear to have been short leading to the collapse of the government.

During this collapse, Ramesses III claimed that a Syrian called Arsu occupied at least some of Egypt, however, no other ancient sources reported this happened, and so Egyptologists currently ignore the claim. Ancient historians, like the 3rd century BCE Manetho, based their histories on the ancient kingship records in the various temples around Egypt, as do modern Egyptologists. This Syrian Arsu is not mentioned in any of the temples, however, if he was an atheist, he would not have worshiped any of the gods, and so would not have been recorded in any of the temples. If their was a collapse of several decades in the middle of the New Kingdom, as Ramesses III reported, it would allow the Egyptian records to be synchronized with the scientific evidence from the Aegean Islands.

Regardless of the exact date of the Minoan eruption, in the Septuagint's chronology, there was a minimum of 500 years between the exodus from Egypt, and the era of Samuel, the last judge of Israel before the establishment of the Kingdom of Israel under Saul. King Saul's reign has not been proven to have happened by archaeological evidence, however, based on the length of the later kings of Israel and Judah is generally dated to approximately 1037 to 1010 BCE. Some of the latter kings are recorded in the records of the Assyrians and Babylonians, and so it is possible to calculate when the earlier kings would have lived based on the Israelite records. 500 years earlier than 1037 BCE would have been 1537 BCE, which is within the estimated range of the Minoan eruption. Unfortunately, like the Egyptian records, the Israelite records are interrupted by the Bronze Age collapse, and there is a gap at the end, in between the rule of Samson's father, and Eli, the second last Judge of Israel. During this time the Benjaminite genocide took place, which reportedly killed all Benjaminites except 50. Yet a few decades later, Samuel anointed Saul, a Benjaminite as the King of Israel.

While the gaps in the text make it impossible to date the exodus accurately, the Minoan eruption can be dated to approximately 1583 BCE, based on the radio-carbon dating of King Ahmose I's body. Ahmose I was the founder of the Eighteenth Dynasty of Egypt, who drove the Hyksos from Egypt, and the average carbon date for his death is 1557 BCE. As all dates used in Egyptology before the Third Intermediate Period are relative, as in this king ruled a certain number of years after a previous king, the death of Ahmose in 1557 BCE is used as a base line in this translation. He was 35 when he died, and 20 when he captured Avaris, the Hyksos capital, which would place the capture of Avaris in 1572 BCE. Avaris was captured in the 11th regnal year of Khamudi, the last Hyksos king. Khamudi became the king when King Apepi and his son prince Apepi died unexpectedly, which the Exodus story strongly implies took place in the immediate aftermath of the Minoan eruption, meaning the eruption and exodus took place in 1583 BCE, 11 years before Avaris fell.

In the immediate aftermath of the eruption, the sky darkened for weeks, and northern Egypt was covered in around 2 meters of ash. The government seems to have collapsed as the Tempest Stele recounts a southern Egyptian expedition into the north to survey the damage, and there is no evidence of the northern army trying to defend the country. The Tempest Stele is damaged, however, the surviving text describes the flooding in Egypt which resulted from the rainstorms:

[damaged text]...the gods expressed their discontent. The gods of the sky come with a tempest and it darkened the west. The sky was unleashed without [...damaged text...] more than the roar of the crowd [...damaged text...] was powerful [...damaged text...] on the highlands more than the waterfall at the cataract of Elephantine.

Each house [...damaged text...] each shelter that they reached [...damaged text...] were floating in the water like the barks of papyrus by the royal residence for [...damaged text...] days [...damaged text...] with no one able to light the torch anywhere.

Then his majesty said, 'This surpasses even the power of the great god, and the wills of the divinities!'

His Majesty descended in his boat, with his council following. The east and the west were silent, as they were naked [...damaged text...] after the power of the god was manifested. Then his Majesty arrived in Thebes [...damaged text...] this statue, and it received what it had desired.

His majesty set about to strengthen Egypt, and stop the rain around him, and he provided them with silver, gold, copper, oil, clothing, and with all the products they desired, after which his majesty returned to the palace (life, health, strength).

Then his majesty was informed that the tombs had been flooded, that the sepulchral chambers had been damaged, that the structures of funerary enclosures had been undermined, that the pyramids had collapsed, and all that existed had been annihilated. His Majesty then ordered the repair of the shrines which had collapsed all over the country and the restoration of the...[...damaged text...]

The Theban dynasty began a war against the Hyksos dynasty in the aftermath of the eruption. King Seqenenre Tao, Ahmose I's father is reported to have started it, however, his reign only lasted a few years. Seqenenre Tao's successor was Kamose, Ahmose I's elder brother, who died three to five years into his reign without an heir, leaving the ten year old Ahmose I as the king.

The Theban (17ᵗʰ) dynasty rose up against the Hyksos and seized control of southern Egypt approximately 30 years before the Minoan eruption. This is also when the Targum Pseudo-Jonathan claims that the tribe of Ephraim sent an expedition from Egypt to attack Gath, and lost 200,000 troops. While it is unclear where the author of the targum got this information, it suggests the uprising in the south of Egypt was supported by the Ephraimites. This Theban uprising happened between 5 and 10 years into the reign of King Apepi I, however, Moses had apparently left during the previous king's life, and returned late in the reign of Apepi I.

The succession of Hyksos kings is debated, as the Egyptians later destroyed most of the relics from that era. The 1st century Judean historian Josephus quoted the 3rd century BCE Egyptian historian Manetho's *Aegyptiaca* (Αἰγυπτιακά) in reporting that Hyksos succession of kings were Salitis (Σάλιτις), Bēon (Βηον), Apaǩnan (Απαχναν), Iannas (Ιαννας), Arǩles (Αρχλες), and Apofis (Αποφις). Apofis was the Greek name for Apepi, and Apaǩnan is accepted as the Greek version of Khyan. Arǩles is unknown from the archaeological record, and therefore ignored by Egyptologists, however, records of a prince Yanassi have been found in the ruins of Avaris, supporting the existence of King Iannas, who Manetho reported ruled for 50 years and 1 month. Some Egyptologist dismiss the kingship of Yanassi along with Arǩles, and claim that Khyan was the king before Apepi I. Khyan is an archaeologically proven king, who was a major builder. He was the king who built the defenses of Gath, a major Hyksos fortified city, and the apparent target of the Ephraimites circa 1612 BCE.

Whether it was King Khyan, Yanassi, or Arǩles, who ever the king was before Apepi I was reportedly already treating the Israelites poorly, which was the ultimate cause of Moses fleeing Egypt. Moses is reported to have fled to Midian, where he married the daughter of a chieftain, and then worked as a shepherd for decades before returning to Egypt with his wife and son. The mountains of Midian (مَديَن) are in northwest Saudi Arabia, on the east coast of the Gulf of Aqaba. Over a dozen towns existed in the region during the bronze age, and the name Mdyn (𐤌𐤃𐤉𐤍) has been found in Ancient North Arabian script dating to the early Iron Age.

After living among the Midianites for decades, Moses encountered the wadjet at a place called har hā'ĕlōhîm hōrēbâ (הַר הָאֱלֹהִים חֹרֵבָה) in the Leningrad Codex. This phrase can be interpreted several ways, which has caused some differences in interpretation over the millennia. The Latin translators interpreted this as "Choreb mountain of God" (Choreb montem Dei), which is essentially identical to the Ge'ez "Ǩoreb mountain of God" (ቆሬብ ደብር አምላክ), Coptic "Ǩōrēb mountain of the master the god" (Ⲭⲱⲣⲏⲃ ⲡⲧⲟⲟⲩ ⲙⲡⲭⲟⲉⲓⲥ ⲡⲛⲟⲩⲧⲉ), and similar to the Greek Codex Ambrosiano's "Mount Ǩōrēb of God" (ορος Χωρηβ του Θ̄Ῡ). However, this is only one possible interpretation, the interpretation that assumes Ḥōrēb (חֹרֵב) was a name.

Hōrēbâ (חֹרָבָה) can also be interpreted as "desolation" or "destruction," which could itself be a description of the land, a description of the gods, or a reference to what the messenger was talking about. The authors of the Targum Onkelos and Targum Pseudo-Jonathan interpreted this as the mountain where "Yahweh commanded destruction" (יְקָרָא דַיְיָ לְחוֹרֵב). The translators at the Library of Alexandria, or the translators of the Egypto-Aramaic version of Exodus they used as a source text, simplified this to "Mount Ǩōrēb" (ορος Χωρηβ), which is preserved in most Septuagint manuscripts. The translator of the Peshitta, or the old Syro-Aramaic version of Exodus, went the opposite route and simplified this to "mountain of God" (ܪܟܡܠܟ‍ܐ ܟܝܪܟ‍).

Moses could have simply been stating that the mountain was in the desert, or he could have been referring to the messenger as having come from the gods of destruction, however, the goddesses Wadjet represented were not associated with destruction. A much simpler explanation is that the word ḥōrēbâ (חָרְבָה) was a transliteration of karibu (𒆠𒊑𒁍), meaning "mighty one." The term was applied to the winged messengers of the gods in Mesopotamian cultures. This is believed to have been the source of the word krwb (𐤊𐤓𐤅𐤁), which later became the Hebrew kərûb (כְּרוּב), Greek ǩeroúb (χερούβ), and Latin cherub. If so, the original phrase would have been "mountain of the gods' messenger" (𐤕 𐤟 𐤋𐤓𐤊𐤁𐤓𐤅), which is what it is described as.

The idea that this is a proper name of a mountain goes back long before the Greeks translated the Septuagint, partially because of the later confusion in Exodus chapter 17, where Moses opens a well on a desert mountain with a ḥōrēb (חֹרֵב). The mountain is called Rəpîdîm (רְפִידִים) in the Leningrad Codex, Rafidein (Ραφιδειν) in the Codex Vaticanus, Rpydyn (ܪܦܝܕܝܢ) in the Peshitta, Rapidin in the Vetus Latina manuscripts, and Rafidin (Ⲣⲁⲫⲓⲇⲓⲛ) in Coptic manuscripts, and so there is no question that the old Aramaic and Phoenician texts referred to a mountain that was not named Horeb.

Additionally, this mountain could only be located somewhere south of Canaan, in the northern Sinai or Negev desert, as the Amalekites came south from Canaan to attack the Israelites at Rafidein.

The name 'Ămālēq (עֲמָלֵק) is a transliteration of the ancient Egyptian term åmw-rqỉ (), meaning "Amorite hostiles," which was pronounced as åmw-lqỉ in the Fayyumic dialect. The Fayyumic dialect was spoken in the Faiyum Oasis, as well as the region of the Nile where the canal that carried water into the Faiyum Oasis connected to the Nile. In this region was the Egyptian city of nn nswt (), from which the dialect was likely derived. The name is commonly anglicized as Henen-Nesut, and was one of the capitals of Egypt during the First Intermediate Period, specifically during the 9th and 10th dynasties. The dialect likely became dominant in the Faiyum Oasis during the 12th dynasty, when the Faiyum basin was flooded with Nile flood water diverted via a canal, turning the oasis into a lake the size of Lake Superior in North America. During this era, the Faiyum was colonized by Egyptians and refugees from the rebellion in Amorite-controlled Syria and Canaan. This suggests the inversion of the l and r sounds in this name was absorbed into written Canaanite during this era.

The term continued to be used long after the era, and appears to have been applied to any nomadic group by the Iron Age. The name 'Ămālēq was used in the Israelite texts as a reference to the descendants of Esau, which is mirrored by Amalēk (Αμαληκ) in the Septuagint. Nevertheless, in 1612

BCE, it would have referred to the Hyksos military in Canaan, not random nomads. The name Hyksos is a modern corruption of the ancient Egyptian hqå-kåswt (𓋴𓂝𓈙), which meant "rulers of foreign lands." The first rulers to bear this title were the Amorite kings of the Middle Kingdom era, although it was also applied to Canaanite kings later. The Theban king Kamose derogatorily described King Apepi I as the "Chieftain of Retjenu" during their war. "Retjenu" (𓊃𓂝) was the Egyptian term for central Canaan, the gateway to "Tjenu" (𓈖 𓂝), an ancient Egyptian name for Syria. The concept of the gateway in Central Canaan, likely originated with the Jazreel and Beqaa valleys, through which the Road of Horus traveled between southern Canaan and Syria. This region was strategic, and the location of many battles throughout Egyptian history. It also played a significant role in the Mesopotamian cultures from the Akkadian era onward, as it was near the location where the gods descended to Earth, and where Gilgamesh fought the Humbaba monster.

When Moses caused the water to flow on Mount Rafidein, the Leningrad Codex describes him as "on the rock with" a hōrēb (עַל־הַצּוּר בְּחֹרֵב). If this was a reference to a winged talking snake with legs and horns that breathed fire, someone would have probably noticed, but the story gives the impression that Moses was trying to get their attention. Therefore, it was almost not a reference to messenger of the gods, meaning the obvious reading is that Moses was using a karbum (𒄑𒀭𒂖𒈨𒃶), meaning "heavy plow." Karbums were used to reopen wells in Mesopotamia at the time, and as the

Amorites were a Mesopotamian people, they and their Canaanites subjects would have also had them.

Unfortunately, either the Greeks, or the Aramaic translators that preceded them, chose to translate both hōrēbâ (חֹרֵבָה) and hōrēb (חֹרֵב) as the name Ǩōrēb (Χωρηβ). As variations of this name are found in virtually all ancient non-Hebrew translations, other than the Peshitta, which drops it, it is likely the name ǩrb (חֹרֵע) was already in the first Aramaic version of *Bereshít-Names* prepared during the reign of King Manasseh of Judah.

The choice to transcribe karibu (𒅗𒊑𒁍) as ǩrbå (𐤊𐤓𐤁𐤀) and ǩarbum (𒅗𒅈𒁍𒌝) as ǩrb (𐤊𐤓𐤁) would have to have been centuries earlier, when the first Phoenician script translation was made of the Mosaic texts, likely during the rule of King Saul. During the intervening centuries, the Neo-Assyrian culture became dominant, along with their version of the word karibu (𒅗𒊑𒁍𒌑), meaning "one who blesses." This was adopted as krwb (𐤊𐤓𐤅𐤁) in Phoenician cultures, and the fact that it was descended from the same word as ǩrb (𐤊𐤓𐤁) appears to have been forgotten, as the texts weren't corrected during Hezekiah's Judahite standardization, or Manasseh's Aramaic translation.

The idea that there is a specific Mount Horeb, where God or his talking fire bramble messenger appeared, has caused a great deal of speculation regarding where it was. However, many of the stories related to "Mount Horeb" are also placed at "Mount Sinai" in parallel texts. This has led to the scholarly consensus that Horeb is another name for Sinai. Various attempts to reconcile the twin names have been proposed, such as Rabbi Abraham ibn Ezra's suggestion that there was only one mountain with two peaks, one called Horeb and the other Sinai, and John Calvin's view that Sinai was the eastern side of the mountain, and Horeb was the western side. However, if hōrēbâ (חֹרֵבָה) is ultimately descended from karibu (𒀭𒊏𒁉𒌈), any mountain were a messenger of god appeared could have been referred to as "mountain of karibu," which would explain why both Horeb and Sinai were called the "Mountain of the gods" (הַר הָאֱלֹהִים).

The quest to find this mountain of God has led to many theories, and at some point in the pre-Islamic era, a mountain in Saudi Arabia was named after Mount Horeb: Jabal Harb (جبل حرب) in the Midian Mountains. This name translates as "mountain of war" in Arabic, and is generally accepted as being an ancient name, however, cannot be documented in the Pre-Christian era. Jabal Harab has traditionally been associated with the mountain that Moses encountered the wadjet on, but not the mountain were he caused water to flow, or where the Mount Sinai events took place, as it is too dry for any large group of travelers to camp for weeks.

Few books have generated as many debates about geographical features as the *Book of Exodus*. It describes in detail a series of wonders that the God of the Israelites, performed to cause them to be freed from their slavery in Egypt, and then their trek across the wilderness to a mountain on which God descended and gave them the original Torah. The wonders themselves have been the source of much speculation in the past 2500 years, but the trek across the wilderness and the location of the mountain of God are the real issues most commonly debated, although ironically, not generally by Jews, Samaritans, or Beta Israelites, the three groups that actually try to follow the laws found in the Torah. Most of the speculation about the geography has been by Christian and Islamic scholars, who have tried to retrace the path the Israelites took out of Egypt in order to find the mountain of God, however, many mountains have been found following the places listed along the route, as most of the locations are debated.

Half a dozen mountains have been identified, each with a list of locations along the route that may or may not be the original locations. This doesn't appear to be a new problem, as even the names for the mountain in the Torah and other ancient Hebrew texts changes from one paragraph to the next. This mountain is called both Sinai and Horeb throughout the Torah, and then Seir in the book of Judges, which is widely regarded as being the oldest Hebrew text that has not been heavily redacted.

The question of why Deborah called it Seir has often been ignored by Christians, however, does seem to have influenced the Second-Temple-Era Jewish view of where the mountain was located. The 1st century CE historian Josephus implied it was in the southern Abarim mountains, a region the Judeans had historically called Seir. Josephus claimed to take possession of ancient scrolls when Ezra's Temple was destroyed by the Romans, which is generally considered plausible. From these he drew his information that, among other things, Kadesh Barnea was Petra, and Mount Sinai was in the Roman province of Arabia-Petra.

The 1st century Christian disciple Paul (Saul) of Tarsus also reported the location of Mount Sinai was in the province of Arabia-Petra. As Paul had been a Pharisee before converting to Christianity and quoted several obscure Judean texts generally associated with the Zealot Sect, such as the *Apocalypse of Moses*, it is plausible that he had read whatever Josephus was quoting.

The question of the two names of this mountain is further complicated by the fact that the two names are believed to be derived from opposing gods, Horeb, meaning "burning," derived from a sun-god, and Sinai, derived from the name Sin, the ancient Semitic moon-god. Biblical scholars in the 1800s and 1900s developed the hypothesis that two names are derived from two Torah traditions, one Solar and one Lunar, which were then united into a single Torah under the rule of King Josiah or earlier.

Subsequent theories have suggested the unification of the two Torahs could have taken place later, under the Persian or even Greek rule of Judea, however, it seems unlikely to have happened that late as the Samaritan Torah has virtually identical twin stories about Horeb and Sinai, and the schism between the Jews and Samaritans appears to have happened during the life of Ezra the Scribe, circa 350 BCE. Textual analysis shows the name Horeb is generally associated with Moses, while Sinai is more often found in texts about Aaron, which implies that whatever the origin of the story, two versions had developed before they were harmonized. The Song of Deborah's reference to Mount Seir could then be interpreted as a third version, likely derived from the prophetess Mariam's teachings.

The three versions can be more simply understood as references to the same place if the Mosaic version originated in Egyptian, the Aaronite version originated in Canaanite written in cuneiform, and the Deborah version originated in a sung version which was not written until much later. Deborah's version uses the name "Mount" Sē'îr (הַר-שֵׂעִיר), which matches the Egyptian name "Highland" Sôr (𓈏𓏤𓂝𓈗), the name of a place in the southern Abarim mountains of modern Jordan in Egyptian records from the late Bronze Age.

This region, including the mountains of Abarim, Midian, and the Hejaz of northwest Saudi Arabia, was known as the land of ^{deity}Sîn (𒀭𒂗𒍪) in cuneiform, as it was generally crossed at night. This name appears in the exodus narrative as the "wilderness of Sin," spelled as Sîn (סִין) in *Names* and Ṣin (צִן) in Masoretic *Numbers*. The placement of the wilderness of Sin in the stations of the exodus was in the Sinai peninsula, before the Israelites reached Mount Rephidim in *Exodus*, and before they traveled south to the turquoise mines of the southern Sinai according to *Numbers*. In both versions, the Israelites traveled from Mount Rephidim east into the wilderness of Sînay (סִינַי), which the Greeks rendered as variations of Sina (Σινα), and the Latins transliterated as Sinai. This name, translated back into cuneiform is ^{deity}Sîna

33

(✳️🛏️🗝️), meaning "moon water," indicating that the Israelites were traveling along the Wadi Rum in the Valley of the Moon, a dry region in southern Jordan, with a seasonal river.

Mount Sinai was either in or near the wilderness of "Moon water," depending on the specific text. Based on this interpretation of the Israelite's path from Egypt, the English biblical critic Charles Beke proposed Jabal Ahmad al Baqir in the southern Valley of the Moon was Mount Sinai in 1878. He also proposed that the nearby Jebel Ertowa was Mount Horeb, however, this region is too dry to support a large camp of tens of thousands of humans and animals for any length of time, and there is no geological evidence that this was different just a few thousand years ago. Most scholars identifying the Israelite's path as going through the Valley of the Moon accept Josephus' identification of Jebel al-Madhbah in the southern Abarim mountains as Mount Sinai.

Josephus identified one of the locations along the route, Kadesh Barnea, as Petra, which he claimed was known as Rekem in ancient times. The location of Kadesh Barnea is central to identifying the location of Sinai, as the Israelites went to Kadesh Barnea after leaving Mount Sinai, and both were outside of Edomite territory, which by the 700s BCE included the southern Abarim mountains. Nevertheless, Josephus reported that Petra was part of Midian during the Exodus era, meaning the Edomites were still only in the northern Abarim mountains, east of the Dead Sea. Josephus' claims about ancient Petra being named Rekem have been confirmed by archaeology, as has the fact that the region was not Edomite until after 800 BCE, meaning it could have been Midianite before that, and also could have been Kadesh Barnea.

As the Greek name Petra simply means "rock" it has been associated with the location called Sela, which means "rock" in Hebrew since the Roman era. Jerome translated "Sela" from the Book of Isaiah as "Petra deserti" in his Latin translation of the Christian Bible, the original Vulgate, circa 382 CE. It is not clear if the two locations are the same, as the ruins of Petra are mostly from the later Nabataean capital, built between 300 BCE and 106 CE, which was then expanded after the Romans annexed it in 106 CE.

The Egyptian el-Amarna Letters, written between 1360 and 1332 BCE do mention the Shasu of Sôr, which is trans-lated as the "nomads of Seir," implying someone nomadic was living in the Seir region of the southern Abarim mountains. The el-Amarna Letters also mention the nomads of Rbn or Lbn, Småt, Wrbr, and Pysps, along with the Nomads of Yhwå (𓇌𓎛𓅱𓄿), which is generally accepted as the earliest reference to Yahweh, however, is a toponym, implying a mountain. Some interpret the Nomads of Rbn, as the Tribe of Ruben, however, Småt, Wrbr, and Pysps do not match the names of Hebrew tribes. The Highlands of Småt (𓈅𓄿𓂧) were likely the highlands of Al-Sharat in southern modern Jordan.

If there was a Mountain of Yhwå in Seir, and if it was near Petra (Kadesh Barnea), the mountain was almost certainly Jebel al-Madhbah, which translates as "Mountain of the Altar."

The Mountain of the Altar has been associated with Moses since the pre-Christian era and includes a Valley of Moses (Wadi Musa) and a Spring of Moses (Ain Musa), connected to the events that happened at Mount Sinai / Horeb / Seir. The mountain's summit is covered in rock-cut ceremonial structures and reached by a rock-cut staircase. There are two giant obelisks, carved out of the rocky surface, near a large rectangular promenade hollowed out so the edges serve as benches. The site also included large cisterns for collecting rainwater. It is unclear when this complex was carved out of the rock, as the site was later quarried for blue slate, which archaeologists believed once covered the site. This blue slate was likely what was later identified as sapphire in the Septuagint.

Nevertheless, while some scholars have identified the Mountain of the Altar with the Mountain of God, most instead point to either Mount Sinai, at the southern end of the Sinai Peninsula, or one of several other mountains in Egypt, Jordan, or Saudi Arabia as being the holy mountain. This is largely due to how one interprets the route the Israelites took out of Egypt, however, is sometimes shaped by other concerns. In the 1800s, the idea that the holy mountain was an active volcano was proposed, which would then explain much of what happened at Sinai, including the columns of fire and smoke, as well as the deaths, however, there are no known active volcanoes in the region the Israelites are reported to have traveled through. Nevertheless, the volcano Hala-'l Badr in eastern Saudi Arabia is often suggested. Hala-'l Badr is believed to have been active sometime in the past 10,000 years, and its name does translate as "Full-moon

Volcano," which could then explain the origin of both the names Sinai and Horeb, however, it is not near the route the Israelites took, and they would have had to march right past Midian to reach it.

As Jethro, Moses' father-in-law came from Midian to visit them while they were traveling, they could not have passed through the heartland of Midian. Nevertheless, many notable scholars have endorsed the Hala-'l Badr theory, as it would explain why the Israelites "thought they saw God." While it is a possible explanation for the events at Horeb / Sinai, it does not explain what the wadjet that Moses encountered was, or why it led the Israelites through the wilderness for 40 years, during which they were generally not in the vicinity of the holy mountain.

Most of the confusion about where the mountain is, is derived from the various interpretations of the route the Israelites took out of Egypt, as well as who the Israelites were while they were in Egypt. Some of this confusion was clearly caused by the translation of the Septuagint at the Library of Alexandria circa 250 BCE. The Greek translators used the term Erythraean Sea (Ερυθραν θαλασσαν), which means "Red Sea" to translate the Hebrew term yam-sûp (יַם־סוּף) which simply translates as "Sea of reeds" or "Papyrus Sea."

The Greeks transliterated the name as the "Sea of Sif" (θαλασσησ Σιφ) in the Codex Vaticanus' translation of Judges, confirming that the name Swf was in the Aramaic text they worked from. Both the Aramaic term śwp (סוף) and Phoenician term śwp (𐤎𐤅𐤐) mean "papyrus plants" and were adopted from the Egyptian term ṯwfī (🝰) which referred to "papyrus," "papyrus plants," and "papyrus marshes." The Egyptian term continued to be used into the Classical era as the Coptic words joouf (ϫⲟⲟⲩϥ), ḥonf (ϭⲟⲛϥ), and ḥomf (ϭⲟⲙϥ), all meaning "papyrus." Conversely, the Egyptian name of the Red Sea was the "Sea of Heh" (𓁨), meaning "very large sea." As the Greek translation of Erythraean Sea is anachronistic, the translation of "Papyrus Sea" is imported from the Leningrad Codex.

The Greek term Erythrean Sea, was adopted from the Aramaic Ymå dÅdwm (ʾדומ ימא), meaning "Sea of Red." This was based on the early Iron Age Canaanite name Ym Ådm (אדמ ימ), meaning "Sea of Edom," which specifically referred to the modern Gulf of Aqaba. During the early Iron age, this region was also called ym Ídwmȯ (𓇋𓈖𓈋𓅓𓈘𓈗) by the Egyptians when the Kushites dominated trade with the Edomites for a around a century in the mid-700s through mid-600s BCE. The Edomites controlled the region of southern modern Jordan after they declared independence from Judah in 849 BCE, until they were conquered by the Babylonians in 553 BCE. Earlier, during the time of Moses, and later during the Classical era, their kingdom was smaller, controlling a region at the southern end of the Dead Sea.

While the Greek translators probably did correctly translate the name "Sea of Red" (ʾדומ ימא) found in the Egypto-Aramaic texts they translated, the "Sea of Papyrus" (ים־סוף) was somewhere else. The idea that the Red Sea events took place in the "Sea of Edom" (𐤉𐤌 𐤀𐤃𐤌) would have likely originated in the Edomite branch of the Israelite religion, which is largely lost. *1ˢᵗ Paralipomena* is a relic of the Edomite Israelite sect, but little else seems to have survived. Edom was a close ally of the Kushite Empire, which lost control of Egypt in 673 BCE. The Edomites came under increasing pressure from Arabs after the Kushite Empire fell, and eventually lost control of their port on the Gulf of Aqaba / Sea of Edom. The Peshitta and targums all use ymå dswp (ܝܡܐ ܕܣܘܦ) / yamā' dəsûp (יְמָא דְסוּף), indicating that only the Egypto-Aramaic version of Exodus likely referred to the events taking place in the Sea of Edom.

This mistranslation has unfortunately been carried into virtually all Christian translations as "Red Sea," including those made from the Masoretic texts which do not mention the Red Sea. Ironically, this has even been re-imported to Hebrew, where the name for the Red Sea is now yam-Sûp, making the ancient mistranslation look correct. Nevertheless, ancient Egyptian records that have been translated in the past couple of centuries clarify the location of the event, and it is not in the Red Sea.

The location is identified by the inclusion of the name Beelsepfon (Βεελσεπφων) in the Septuagint, and Bə'êl Ṣəpôn (בְּעֵיל צָפוֹן) in the Leningrad Codex, generally translated as Ba'al Zephon. Ba'al Zephon was a Canaanite god, worshiped by the people along the Syrian coast near Mount Zephon (modern Jebel Aqra) in the 2ⁿᵈ millennium BCE. These northern Canaanites were active at a transshipment town in

Egypt, where their main God according to Egyptian records was Ba'al Zephon, who the Egyptians equated with their god Amen (𓇋𓏠𓈖). This town was at the edge of the marshland known today as Lake Bardawil on the north coast of the Sinai Peninsula. Lake Bardawil is a shallow saline lake, estimated to be about 10 feet (3 meters) deep at its deepest, with a surface area of 147,000 acres (59,500 hectares). It is the only known site in Egypt where Ba'al Zephon was worshiped. The town was the major transshipment center for Canaanite, Minoan, Cypriot, and Achaean Greek trade with the Red Sea port at the north shore of the Gulf of Aqaba. The other major route went from the Nile to the gulf of Suez, however, this was much longer, and involved dealing with Egyptian bureaucrats.

The old name of Lake Bardawil is also confirmed in the *Book of Zephaniah*, which must have been written between 626 and 612 BCE based on the prediction that Nineveh would fall to the Chaldeans. Zephaniah specifically referred to a sea along the coast of the Mediterranean south of the Peleset-controlled regions, which could only be Lake Bardawil. The Septuagint's version of *Zephaniah* calls this the "sea of reeds" (σχοινισμα της θαλασσης) while the Masoretic version of *Zephaniah* and Dead Sea Scroll MurXII called it the "sea of rope" (חבל הים), and the Targum Pseudo-Jonathan called it the "sea of scroll" (סְפַר יַמָא). All of these are clearly alternate versions of the Sea of Papyrus (יַם־סוּף), which rope and scrolls were made from.

The region of Lake Bardawil was known throughout Egyptian history as a quagmire, where entire armies had been swallowed by the sea. The Greeks had ancient myths about the place, in which it was known as the Serbonian Bog (Σιρβωνίδος λίμνη), or Lake Sirbonis (Sirbonis Lacus) in Latin, which had a deceptive appearance of looking solid because sand would blow onto it, but was a bog that swallowed people that tried to pass over it. The description is essentially one of a massive lake of quicksand that formed after a sandstorm. The high salinity of the water may have helped slow the rate at which the sand settled, although the phenomenon has not been recorded in the past century and likely points to the specific time when the event happened.

The Greek myths were established during the Greek Dark Age, which was approximately the same time as the Third Intermediate Period in Egypt, but later identified as Lake Bardawil when the Greeks ruled Egypt. In the Greek myths, Zeus' ancient enemy, the monster Typhon lay at the bottom of the Bog. As Typhon was the Greek version of the Egyptian god Apepi, also called Apophis in Greek, this myth helps identify the Egyptian king in *Exodus* as Apepi I, one of the last Hyksos kings, who Egyptologists report died around the time of the Minoan eruption.

The Minoan eruption was the volcanic explosion of the island of Thera, modern Santorini in the Aegean Sea, which covered most of the Minoan civilization, based in Crete, with several centimeters to a meter of ash. It also rained ash across northern Egypt, which allows Egyptologists to date it to the end of the Hyksos era. Aegean Prehistorians disagree on the dating, placing it decades earlier, but, whenever it was, a Pharaoh named Apepi I was the king ruling from the Hyksos Dynasty's capital of Avaris in the Nile Delta, which would later be rebuilt as Pi-Ramesses, and then simplified to Ramesses. While Avaris was razed when the Hyksos dynasty fell, the location was a strategic trade port with docks capable of serving over 300 ships concurrently. The docks and shipyards of Avaris continued to be used until the Classical era, and were still called Avaris when the Greeks ruled. Nevertheless, most of the city was not rebuilt until the Ramesside period.

At the time of the Minoan eruption, the Hyksos dynasty was at war with another dynasty in southern Egypt, which had rebelled from Hyksos rule 20 years earlier. The so called Theban dynasty revolted at the same time the Targum Pseudo-Jonathan claims the Ephraimites attacked Gath, and had been in open rebellion for decades, yet had not captured much territory. The Thebans were very limited in their trade, as neither the Hyksos to the north, or Kushites to the south recognized the independent Theban kingdom. Some Egyptologists have debated whether the Kushites rejected the legitimacy of the Thebans, however, most Egyptologists believe the Kushites were also trying to take over southern Egypt. Thebes was able to trade on the Red Sea, with Punt in modern Eritrea, and the Arab nations across the sea, however, their economy was minor at the time, while the Hyksos dynasty was at it's economic peak, controlling the major trade routes between the Mediterranean and both the Euphrates and Red Sea.

Based on the carbon dating of King Ahmose I's remains, the Minoan eruption would have happened in approximately 1583 BCE. The Minoan Eruption was a massive volcanic eruption on the Greek isle of Santorini, which ejected approximately 60 km^3 (14 miles^3) of debris that fell across the eastern Mediterranean, and covered some parts of northern Egypt in 2 meters (6 feet) of ash. The sky was darkened for weeks and the crops and livestock died in the fields. Southern Egypt was also affected, as reported by the Tempest Stele, a stone tablet erected during the reign of the Theban Pharaoh Ahmose I, who conquered northern Egypt and drove the Hyksos dynasty out of Egypt after a three-year siege of the Hyksos dynasty, the city of Avaris.

Dating the exodus to the end of the Hyksos era does fit the timeline reported in the Septuagint's books of *Exodus, Joshua*, and *Judges*, if one uses the Minoan eruption for the date of the exodus. As both the Egyptian king-lists and the span of the Israelite judges time in office are relative, it doesn't matter the exact year that the events took place, and so 1583 BCE is used as the starting point. This is based on the eruption taking place 11 years before Ahmose I conquered Avaris, his being 20 years old when he conquered Avaris, and his death at 35, which is carbon dated to approximately 1557 BCE. As both the Egyptian records and Israelite records break down during the Bronze Age collapse, it is not possible to use either record to establish exact dates by working backwards, however, many of the significant dates recorded in the Israelite records do align with the history of Egypt before the collapse, when the date of the exodus is aligned with the Minoan eruption.

In this interpretation, the king at the beginning of *Exodus*, whose daughter or niece adopted the infant Moses was likely Yanassi, although could have been Arǩles, as Egyptologists are not sure of the sequence of Hyksos kings. The Egyptian records are unclear of how long Apepi I ruled, some stating 35 years, and others 40 years. This would have been either 1618 BCE or 1623 BCE relative to the 1583 BCE Minoan eruption. This discrepancy, combined with the Theban revolt of 1612 BCE, and the Ephraimite attack on Gath in 1612 BCE, suggests the kingship was disputed between Apepi I and Arǩles, and Apepi I did not firmly establish his reign until five years after Yanassi had died.

Assuming Manetho was right, and Yanassi reigned for over 50 years, he should have had multiple adult children when he died, and a dispute for the throne would not have been uncommon in that scenario. If Arǩles did dispute Apepi I's kingship, it would explain why there are no artifacts associated with a prince Arǩles found in the archaeological record, as Apepi I would have erased all records of him during the dispute. The rebellion in Thebes and southern Canaan just 4 years after Apepi I defeated Arǩles, suggests that Arǩles survived the dispute and fled to another country to raise an army.

For some reason, one of Apepi I's sisters appears to have moved to Iberia during her life. Princess Ziwat is documented in the ruins of Avaris, and also from artifacts found in Spain, which suggests that she was married to an Iberian king. There was a significant cultural trade between the Iberians and the Hyksos, as cuneiform was introduced to Iberia during the era. Iberian cuneiform was simplified during the late Bronze Age into something similar to Ugaritic cuneiform, and then continued to be simplified until it was similar to the Mediterranean alphabets of the Iron Age.

This suggests that Arkles was the source of the Greek myth of Ēraklēs (Ηρακλης), later called Hercules, who also traveled to Iberia in the Bronze Age. The Classical Greek philosophers believed that the story of Ēraklēs had been imported from Canaan during the Bronze Age, but could not find a close parallel in Canaanite mythology. Ēraklēs was associated with fighting snakes including the giant river snake Akelōios (Αχελωιος), while Apepi I was named after the giant river snake Apepi. In the myths, Ēraklēs had a twin brother named Ifiklēs (Ιφικλης), which, if this is based on the story of Arkles and Apepi would explain why there was a dispute over the kingship.

As Moses is described as leaving Egypt before the reign of the king when he returned, it suggests he was not part of this dispute between Apepi I and Arkles, but had left earlier, during the reign of King Yanassi. This would make his original flight from Egypt sometime before 1623 BCE, meaning he must have been over 50 years of age when he returned to Egypt after talking to the wadjet. When Moses had run away from Egypt, he could not have gone into Canaan, as the Hyksos ruled southern Canaan, and so he went to the Midyan Mountains of northwestern Saudi Arabia. He returned after hearing that the former king was dead during the reign of King Apepi I, who based on the Minoan eruption happening in 1583 BCE, must have ruled between 1618 and 1583 BCE.

The "wonders" reported in *Exodus*, and the "plagues" reported in *Names*, can, to some degree be linked to the effects of the Minoan eruption, including the fire, hail, and ash falling from the sky, the blisters that broke out on the people, and the darkness that lasted for days. Some of the other wonders do not appear to be related to the eruption, such as Aaron turning his wand into a snake or the sudden appearance and disappearance of the frogs and locusts. The massive environmental shifts the eruption caused could explain the winds that brought locusts into the land, and blew them away, but not why there were so many so fast.

Additionally, the last plague does not appear to be related to the eruption, the deaths of all the firstborn. It's possible that the wonders were embellished, however, the concept that the Lord wants all the firstborn sacrificed to him is embedded deeply within the laws of *Exodus*, and is difficult to dismiss as a later addition. Additionally, the *Wisdom of Solomon* retells a somewhat different version of the *Exodus*, in which the Israelites sneaked out of Egypt under the cover of the plague of darkness while the messenger of death was slaughtering the firstborn. This is certainly different from the *Exodus* version of the story in which the king kicked them out of Egypt, and then changed his mind and pursued them to the sea where he drowned, although the king in *Wisdom of Solomon* also chased them to the sea when he found out they'd run away. The fact that there were two different versions of the plagues in the Era of Ezra's Temple implies that the story was not firmly established in the eyes of the general population. It is clear that the Judahites and Samaritans had slightly different Torahs in the era of Ezra's Temple, and there had been an Edomite Torah, however, these were quite similar.

The exodus described in the *Wisdom of Solomon* is clearly from an Israelite community not effected by the reforms of kings Hezekiah and Josiah. Unorthodox Solomonic literature was generally associated with the Beqaa Valley in modern Lebanon, which was under the control of Zabah at the time. According to *2ⁿᵈ Kingdoms* (Masoretic *Samuel*), King David defeated the land of Souba (Σουβα) / Sôbā' (צוֹבָא) and made it a tributary of Israel in around 1000 BCE. This Aramean kingdom is known from the archaeological record as controlling the Beqaa Valley at the time. It is recorded in *3ʳᵈ Kingdoms* as becoming independent again when Solomon became king, however, Solomon's kingdom continued to control the southern regions of the Beqaa Valley and the neighboring Mount Hermon. Solomon is recorded as building a palace on Mount Hermon, and some Solomonic literature claims Solomon built a temple in the Beqaa Valley. This is likely a reference to the major temple at Baalbek, in the southern Beqaa Valley. That temple was mentioned in the Ugaritic text from the late Bronze Age, so, like the temple in Jerusalem, it long predated Solomon. Solomon probably did renovate the temple at Baalbek like he renovated the temple in Jerusalem, however, it was rebuilt in the Greco-Roman era and so little from the early Iron Age remains.

This region came under the control of Damascus after the Israeli-Judean civil war split the country, and was annexed by King Shalmaneser III of the Neo-Assyrian empire in 841 BCE. The chronicles of Shalmaneser III report that King Hazael of Damascus had built a fortress on Mount Hermon, and while the Assyrians could not defeat Damascus at that time, they did devastate the country, and this is likely when the Solomonic Israelites fled west to the Phoenician colonies in the Mediterranean. At the time, the Kingdoms of Israel and Judah were attempting to appease the Assyrians, and Egypt was weak and poor, divided between multiple dynasties, and the Solomonic literature does not appear to have generally been translated into Aramaic.

The path that the Israelites took when they left Egypt has been a source of debate for thousands of years, and there are two different lists of places they camped at in the Torah, one in *Exodus* and one in *Numbers*. The version in *Numbers* is longer, but does not contradict *Exodus*, and so both could be correct. The content of *Numbers* suggests it was part of the Edomite Torah, likely compiled from a Levitical text used in the city of Libnah. If so, the longer list of stops found in *Numbers* may be older than the version that was compiled into *Names* during the late Bronze Age, however, it is unclear why there is a shorter version in *Names*. The longer version does make the Israelites seem more lost, as they wander back and forth across the Sinai Peninsula, and then around in the desert. One of the places they stopped in *Numbers* which was missing from *Exodus*, was the city of Libnah, although this was apparently long before the city became a Levite city. This has caused some debate, and some view the longer list of stops in *Numbers* as an extension of the list in *Names* made by the Levites of Libnah, however, this is far from universally accepted.

There is a difference found in the Septuagint's version of the longer list in comparison to the version of the longer list found in the Leningrad Codex, near the end of the list that may indicate why the list was initially shortened in Exodus. In the Septuagint, the fifth last stop was called the "water course in the rocks" (αχελγαι ἐκ τοῦ πέραν) in chapter 21, but "lands in the rock" (γαι ἐν τῷ πέραν) in chapter 33. In this case the Greek word γαι, which cane be translated as "lands," was probably a transliteration of hā'ay (הָעַי), as found in other places in the Torah, which means "ruins." This would mean the location was likely listed as the "ruins in the rocks," in the Old Aramaic translation of *Numbers*. However, the version of the text in the Leningrad Codex uses the term "well of the Habirus" (עִיֵּי הָעֲבָרִים) in both chapters 21 and 33. If "ruins of the Habirus" was in the original text, it could call into question the origin narrative of the Israelites presented in *Cosmic Genesis / Bereshít*, which claims that 'ēber (עֶבֶר) was the ancestor of Abraham. This suggests that Exodus' list might

49

have been shortened when it was added to *Cosmic Genesis / Bereshít* in the era of King Joash of Judah.

The revolt in Libnah against the authority of the Kingdom of Judah took place under the reign of Joashs's grandfather King Jehoram, and therefore, Libnah would have probably been removed from the list at the same time. Most of the other places dropped from the Exodus list are generally accepted as having been in Edom by the era of Joash, which had declared independence from Judah as the same time as Libnah. This collection of Edomite names, Libnah, and the ruins of the Habirus being removed together supports the edits to the Exodus list being dated to circa 836 BCE, at the beginning if Joash's rule.

The names of the cities in Egypt where the Israelites had been living before the exodus also support the precursor of the Masoretic version being edited by a Yahwist scribe. The Septuagint lists the cities of Pithom, Ramesses, and Ōn ($\Omega\nu$), while the Leningrad Codex only mentions Pithom and Ramesses. 'Ôn (אוֹן) was the Hebrew translation of the name of the Egyptian city of Ỉwnw (𓉺𓏤) used in Bereshít, which was mentioned at the end of Bereshít as the city where Joseph married the daughter of the high priest, implying he became a priest in Ỉwnw. All three of these places were major political or religious sites during the Hyksos era. Ramesses was known as Avaris at the time, the capital of Hyksos-controlled Egypt. Ỉwnw was the southern-most Hyksos-controlled city during the era of Apepi I, and, like Pithom, was one of Egypt's four major religious centers, the other two being Memphis and Thebes, both under the control of the southern pharaoh.

It is unclear why I̊wnw was removed from the Hebrew translation, but the Greek translators certainly had no reason to add an ancient Egyptian city to the list, let alone use its ancient Canaanite name. The most-likely reason for its removal is because it was the same name of the god 'Ôn (אוֹן), however, this may have also been because the Heliopolitan triad of gods as I̊wnw was very similar to the Heliopolitan Triad at Baalbek, and almost certainly very similar to the triad of Ba'al, Asherah, and Adonai from King Solomon's Temple.

Both I̊wnw and Baalbek were renamed Heliopolis by the Greeks, meaning "Sun city," because towns were dedicated to the worship of the sun. In Egypt's Heliopolis, many ancient sun-gods had temples, including Ra, the sun god that flew the celestial barge; Atum, the sun god who created the universe; Aten, the solar-disk became the national god under Akhenaton; and the scarab-beetle god Khepri who rolled the sun into the sky each morning. Among these sun gods of I̊wnw, was a moon god named I̊o̊hw. The word I̊o̊h (⌒) was the Egyptian word for the moon, however, when treated as a god, it was modified to I̊o̊hw (𓇋𓏏𓎛𓂝𓅱), influencing the development of the dual pronunciations of the name Yah (𐤉𐤄 / 𐤉𐤀 / יה / Ιαω) and Yahweh (𐤉𐤄𐤅𐤄 / 𐤉𐤄𐤅 / יהוה / Ιευω).

Even if one were to accept the idea that the Greeks inserted the name Ōn (Ων) into Exodus, along with a note explaining that city had been renamed Heliopolis, when they listed the cities the Israelites were enslaved in, as opposed to another scribe dropping it, the city was already mentioned at the end of *Cosmic Genesis* and *Bereshít*, which means it already had significance within the overall story. In *Cosmic Genesis*, after Joseph was freed from slavery for interpreting the Pharaoh's dreams, he was married to the daughter of a high-priest of Íwnw. This would make him a priest at Íwnw, and likely place him in line to be a high-priest. The question is "which god was he a priest of?" Given the options for an interpreter of dreams are a number of sun gods, and a moon god, Íȯhw seems like the obvious choice.

The meaning of the word Pithom has been debated for at least 2500 years. The Septuagint has variations of Pitōm (Πιθωμ), while the Leningrad Codex has Pîtôm (פִּיתוֹם), and Dead Sea Scroll 4QExod^c has ptm (פתם). This has generally been assumed to be the town of Per-Atum (𓉐𓈖𓏏𓐝), which was the name of two cities located in the Wadi Tumilat at different points in time. The Wadi Tumilat was a seasonal river that ran east from the Nile to the Bitter Lakes in the western Sinai Peninsula, which is the same route Sinuhe took during his flight from Egypt, centuries earlier in the Middle Kingdom era. The ruins of Tel El Maskhuta appear to have been a Hyksos Dynasty city, which bore the name, and is almost certainly the Pithom in question, as it seems to have been abandoned at the end of the Hyksos era, which is the same era the Septuagint places the exodus. The other Per-Atum was also at the ruins of Tel El Maskhuta, but much later, in the 7th century BCE, and appears to have been built by Pharaoh Necho II during his attempt to dig a canal from the Nile through the Wadi Tumilat and Bitter Lakes to the

Red Sea. He wasn't the first to attempt this, and during the Middle Kingdom a canal was dug from the Nile through the Wadi Tumilat to the Bitter Lakes, however, it was never connected to the Gulf of Suez.

It is worth noting that while the Hyksos appear to have built the first city called Per-Atum, the Wadi Tumilat was considered sacred to the creator god Atum since pre-dynastic times, and there were likely Temples of Atum (Per-Atum) in the wadi throughout Egyptian history. The wadi, or something in it, was called pyṭǒn (𓊪𓏏𓈖) in the *Tale of Sinuhe*, which was written centuries earlier in the early Middle Kingdom era, and so the name Pithom may be a corruption of pyṭǒn and not Per-Atum. In the *Tale of Sinuhe*, pyṭǒn was beyond the Egyptian fortifications, and en route to the Kem Wer, the largest of the Bitter Lakes.

It is not clear what exactly the term pyṭǒn meant, however, there were two of them, the one in the Wadi Tumilat, and another in southern Egypt. It is known that the kings of Egypt took responsibility for overseeing them, which suggests they were quite expensive to maintain. The only thing known to have been very expensive in the Wadi Tumilat during the Middle Kingdom Era was the canal connecting the Nile to the Kem Wer. This suggests that pyṭǒn may have been a Middle Egyptian term for "major canal," as there was also a major canal in southern Egypt, at Aswan, where the river was altered to allow ships to pass the first cataract of the Nile.

Atum was one of the sun-gods worshiped at Iwnw, but his cult center was at Per-Atum in the Wadi Tumilat. Atum was also very archetypal to the God of Moses. Atum was the creator of the universe, who created the universe in a series of events somewhat similar to the days of creation found at the beginning of Cosmic Genesis. He was not depicted as the sun when he was the creator, but a god that resembled a man-serpent, who emerged from the primordial waters, and separated the air, called Shu, from the water, called Tefnut. It is unclear when he became conflated with the sun-gods at Iwnw, but at some point, he became a sun-god, specifically the god of the setting sun.

In the Old Kingdom era, Atum was believed to lift the bå (pure psyche without ego) of the dead to the stars, which does fore-run most of the Christian and Islamic teachings of the soul (psyche with ego and superego) going up to the sky after the death of the body. This idea was found in some early Israelite and Judean beliefs, as demonstrated by the Testament of Abraham, but did not become a central belief in Rabbinical Judaism or Samaritanism.

Atum was married to Hathor in the era before the Middle Kingdom, however, this changed during the Middle Kingdom, as Hathor became increasingly associated with Amen. During the Middle Kingdom, Hathor's epithets of Iusaaset and Nebetetepet supplanted her name among the worshipers of Atum, and by the Hyksos dynasty, Atum had two wives with these names. Iusaaset means "she who causes growth," and Nebetetepet, means "lady of the field offerings," so these goddesses represented the fertility aspects of Hathor. They also both inherited another ancient title, "the hand of god." This was not problematic, as a god can have two hands, however, in the original creation narrative of Atum, only one hand was mentioned.

The "hand of god" was also the title of the messenger of God who led the Israelites from Egypt in the Solomonic tradition, in which Moses was not mentioned. In *Exodus*, the Israelites are also led by a messenger of God which appears to them as a column of smoke in the day, and a column of fire at night. This messenger in *Exodus* is also called the "hand of God," indicating a common origin for both the Mosaic and Solomonic exodus narratives. In *Exodus* / *Names* and *Numbers*, the role of Moses is significant, as he is the only one who can speak with the messenger, however, he is also simply a follower, which suggests the Solomonic version of the story descends from another priesthood, whose followers did not view Moses as noteworthy. Several other leaders are present in the *Exodus* and *Numbers* narratives, whose followers are described as not caring much for Moses' perspective on things. The Aaronites are significant, as Moses and Aaron's followers reportedly killed each other by the thousands. However, the leader most closely associated with the phrase "hand of God" was the prophetess Miriam, who credited "the hand of God" with everything in her songs.

In *Numbers*, after the events in *Exodus*, Moses god descends from the sky, and introduces himself to Aaron and Miriam, which indicates that whoever Aaron's calf statue represented, and whoever Miriam's "hand of God" were, they were not Moses' snake god. The event took place at a place called Asērōṯ (Aσηρωθ) / Ḥăṣērôt (חֲצֵרֹות), generally rendered as Hazeroth, which was entirely cut from Exodus. This section of text was clearly unknown by the prophet Micah, who circa 722 BCE proclaimed that God had sent Moses, Aaron, and Miriam to guide the Israelites from Egypt. At the time, Micah was in the Samaritan Kingdom of Israel, shortly before it fell to the Assyrians. He should have access to the *Bereshít-Names* texts, and possibly a precursor to *Words* (the Masoretic version of *Deuteronomy*). *Numbers* does not appear to have been added to the Judahite Torah until after the Levites of Libnah gained control of Judah a century later.

When this god meets Miriam, he also infects her with a disfiguring disease, as she was opposed to Moses divorcing his first wife, and marrying a Kushite woman. The Israelites had arrived in Hazeroth shortly after passing through the Wilderness of Sinai, suggesting a location somewhere in eastern modern Jordan. In between the Wilderness of Sinai and Hazeroth, the Israelites stopped at Kibroth Hattaavah, where they ate so many birds they became sick of them. This was most likely at the Ma'an Oasis, in southern Jordan. The ancient name is not recorded, and the current name is based on the Minaean trade post that was established there in the late Persian era. However, it was the only wetland in southern Jordan at the time, and was only around 40 kilometers from Jebel al-Madhbah, the mountain that was likely the original Mount Sinai.

FORWARD

The time when the Israelites were in Hazeroth was likely around two years after they left Egypt, as the curse that they could not enter Canaan for 40 years was issued shortly afterward, and are reported to have not received this edict until 2 years after leaving Egypt. This would place the event at circa 1581 BCE, two years into King Khmudi's reign in Northern Egypt, and one year after the beginning of Ahmose I's reign in Southern Egypt.

This might be a reference to a marriage alliance with the Theban dynasty, as the Theban art depicts the dynasty as having Nubian features. In Coptic stories, after leading the Israelites for 40 years, Moses left them and moved to southern Egypt or Kush with his wife. If Moses' second wife was a Theban princess, the edict that the Israelites had to wander the wilderness for 40 years makes sense, as they refused to invade Canaan at the time, and 40 years was considered a standard life long service contract in Egyptian society. The Israelites attacking Hyksos-controlled Canaan at the same time as the Thebans were attacking Hyksos-controlled Egypt would have effectively cut off the Egyptians from Syrian reinforcements. However, the Israelites refused to attack the Canaanites, and were not allowed to return to Egypt for 40 years, until Joshua replaced Moses as the judge of Israel. In the interim, the Theban dynasty fought a continuous war against the Hyksos, defeating them at Avaris a decade into Ahmose I's reign, and the Hyksos fortress at Sharuhen around 1569 BCE.

After Sharuhen fell, King Khamudi retreated to Jericho, and then later retreated to Byblos before disappearing into the Mediterranean Sea. One theory that had been around since the Classical Era, is that Khamudi became Kádmos (Κάδμος), the legendary founder of the city of Thebes in Greece, who had moved from Phoenicia in the Bronze Age.

While most Egyptologists dismiss the entire exodus narrative as being 1st millennium BCE fiction, likely written around the time of King Josiah of Judah, and historians generally follow their lead, there is far too much that contradicts the theology of Josiah's proto-Judaism to support this conclusion. Meanwhile, Biblical scholars have obsessed over the route out of Egypt, conveniently ignoring the inconvenient Egyptian gods in the texts.

While the *Numbers* has a longer route than *Exodus*, the beginning of the route is almost identical. The first place mentioned in *Exodus*, immediately after leaving Avaris was called Sokḵôṯ (Σοκχωθ) in the Septuagint, implying the name of a city. It is generally translated from the Leningrad Codex as Sukkot, however, the Greek translators most likely made a mistake that has subsequently been copied by later translators. The Hebrew word sūkkôt (סֻכּוֹת) simply refers to animal corrals or stables. This is already established in *Cosmic Genesis*, and there is no reason to believe that the text wasn't simply stating they went to get their animals from the corrals. The animals were mentioned later, and they could not have kept them in their homes. Traditional interpretations have this as another town in the Nile Delta, although why they'd go to another town is not discussed. Fringe theories have this as a mining settlement in the Sinai Peninsula, which makes no sense in relation to the rest of the route, and there is no mention of a mine in either the books of *Exodus* or *Numbers*.

The next place mentioned was "Otom (Οθομ) on the edge of the wilderness," in the Septuagint, which again implies a town. This is again an error by the Greek translators that was carried forward into later translations, as the Hebrew term 'ētām (אֵתָם), simply means "fortification." The sentence is simply reporting they reached the fortification at the edge of the Nile Delta, where the wilderness began. Sinuhe also reported passing a fortification on his way out of Egypt, which he sneaked past at night. The Israelites apparently weren't concerned with sneaking past the fortification, suggesting the fortification had been abandoned since Sinuhe had passed it during the Middle Kingdom era.

From this point on they were being led by the column of fire and smoke, which some have interpreted as a volcano erupting that they were walking directly towards, however, there simply are no volcanoes within eye-sight of the eastern edge of the Nile Delta. The curvature of the Earth makes this interpretation impossible, so whatever the Israelites were following, it couldn't have been a volcano.

The next stop in the Leningrad Codex was pî hḥîrōt (פִּי הַחִירֹת), which was translated as "the village" in the Septuagint, showing that the Greek translators were not sure about the location, but assumed it was a village. The Hebrew term pî hḥîrōt (פִּי הַחִירֹת) is a combination of the Canaanite p ǩ

(𐤁 𐤓), meaning "mouth of the," and the Egyptian term ḥr-t. The ancient Egyptian word transliterated as ḥr-t meant both watercourse (𓇯𓈖𓈗) and Nile deposits (𓄿𓈖𓈘) depending on context. The term was generally used in the Nile Delta, where the watercourses moved regularly as sediment built up. This was most likely a reference to the mouth of the Pelusiac branch of the Nile River, the ancient eastern-most branch of the Nile.

This 'mouth of the river' was described as being between Magdōlou (Μαγδωλου) and the sea, across from Beelsepfōn (Βεελσεπφων). Again, these read like names of towns in the Septuagint, however, the Leningrad Codex indicates what they mean. The Hebrew term migdôl (מִגְדּוֹל) simply means "tower," likely a reference to the towers built along the coast to serve as warnings of shallow water. Therefore, the Israelites were following the coast, naturally heading east, which would bring them to Lake Bardawil.

The Hebrew word Bə'êl Ṣəpôn (בְּעִיל צָפוֹן) shows that the term the Greeks translated as Beelsepfōn (Βεελσεπφων), implying a settlement, as actually Ba'al Zephon, a Canaanite god. This god was only recorded as being worshiped in Egypt by Canaanites that had settled in Lake Bardawil, the Serbonian Bog of Greek mythology. This means that regardless of the Lord's instructions to not follow the northern road to Canaan, that is what they were doing when the Pharaoh's army caught up with them. The "Red Sea" incident sounds a lot like the mythology surrounding the Serbonian

Bog, beginning with a strong wind that "blew the sea away" in *Exodus.*

The Greek story reported that the wind would deposit sand over the water, which would then look like land, but swallow people, and according to Egyptian myths, whole armies that tried to cross it were swallowed. This is a description of quicksand, a massive lake of quicksand with a surface area of 147,000 acres (59,500 hectares). While there is almost certainly no surviving evidence of a bronze age army being swallowed by Lake Bardawil, as the salt would have dissolved the wood, bone, leather, and bronze, this is what the story in Exodus is about, not something happening in the Red Sea. There are no reports of Ba'al Zephon worshipers in the Red Sea, and there was a major colony at Lake Bardawil.

The fact that the Greek legend of the Serbonian Bog included the story of Typhon, the Greek version of Apophis (Apepi), being at the bottom of it, implies the Pharaoh Apepi, who was named after Apophis, was the Pharaoh whose army tried to catch up to the Israelites, and who ended up drowning in the sea. The Hebrew term yam-sûp (יַם־סוּף), in no way indicates the modern Red Sea, simply meaning "Reed Sea," or "Papyrus Sea," either of which would be an accurate description of Lake Bardawil.

If this story did take place in Lake Bardawil, the details were likely somewhat different than the version in Exodus, although similar enough that the later "authorized version" of Josiah would make sense. If the Israelites were following the northern coast of the Sinai Peninsula towards Canaan, they would have come to Lake Bardawil, and if the wonders / plagues of darkness, ash, and blisters were as a result of the Minoan eruption, then the Lake would have almost certainly have been covered in ash, which would have taken much longer to settle in the highly saline waters than sand. In some regions of northern Egypt, the ash-fall was up to 2 meters deep, which would have formed a type of loose cement on top of Lake Bardawil, which, the Israelites could have passed over if they were spread out as expected of a nomadic horde of people mostly traveling on foot, and herding animals. Pharaoh's army, on the other hand, included 600 war chariots, along with cavalry and infantry, which one would assume were traveling in tight formations. This concentrated weight could have easily broken through the ash layer, shattering it like ice on a river, causing the entire army to be swallowed up, and explaining why the Greeks had a story of a Nile monster (Apophis) being at the bottom of the lake nowhere near the Nile. This story was specifically Greek, and not based on an Egyptian legend, implying the Ba'al Zephon worshiping Canaanites witnessed the event and told the Greeks.

According to the Exodus narrative, the 'princes of Edom and the chiefs of the Moabites' also witnessed the event, and then ran away, presumably back to Edom and Moab, in western and northwestern modern Jordan. These princes and chiefs were not called kings, as Moab and Edom would have been part of the Hyksos' empire, which also explains why they were there. Egyptian armies were advancing from both the Nile and Canaan, trying to trap the Israelites. After the events of the "Papyrus Sea," the Israelites suddenly turned back, and headed toward the Nile Delta, and traveled south to the Bitter Lakes, which the Greek translators did understand, both translating the Hebrew word mārâ (מָרָה) as pikria (πικρια), and transliterating it as Merra (Μερρα). The Bitter Lakes are a group of lakes that are today along the route of the Suez Canal, and in the times of the Ptolemies along the route of the Arsinoe Canal. Aristotle, Strabo, and others claimed that there had been several attempts to dig a canal linking the Bitter Lakes to the Nile, and then to the Gulf of Suez, including attempts by Pharaoh Senusret III in the Middle Kingdom, Pharaoh Necho II circa 600 BCE, and Darius the Great when Persia ruled Egypt.

The Bitter Lakes were known by the Egyptian translation of "Bitter Lakes" since at least the Old Kingdom era, and the Israelites, Persians, and Greeks all translated the name into their own languages, meaning it is fairly certain that these are the Bitter Waters the Israelites traveled to after leaving the coast. The logical reason for turning back was that the Hyksos armies in Canaan had not been destroyed at Lake Bardawil, and while they had fled in terror, they still existed. Therefore, the Israelites would have turned back, and traveled to the Bitter Lakes to cross the Sinai Peninsula following the dry southern route, which ran from the northern coast of the Gulf of Suez to the northern coast of the Gulf of Aqaba. This route was well established by the Middle Kingdom and was almost certainly the route that Moses would have taken from Egypt to Midian the first time he went there.

The next stop along the route the Israelites took was called Ailim (Αιλιμ) in the Septuagint and 'Êlim (אֵילִם) in the Masoretic texts. It was most likely an attempt to translate an Egyptian name that has subsequently been lost. Most Christian and Islamic scholars, following Helena August's divine revelation, believe that Mount Sinai is in Southern Sinai, however, this location was chosen by Emperor Constantine's mother when he founded the Imperial Church in the 330s CE. As a result of Christian and Islamic scholars following the 'revelation' of the Emperor's mother, southern Sinai is covered in locations that are linked to Moses and the Exodus in folklore.

The logical route away from Egypt for a band of runaway slaves, would not have been to head south into the heavily garrisoned southern Sinai, where the Egyptians were forcing slaves to work at turquoise mines, but east across the Sinai following the southern road, towards Midian, where Moses had previously lived for decades. In the middle of the Sinai Peninsula is a town today known as An-Nekhel, which lays halfway along the ancient southern road. Archaeological evidence indicates it was used as a watering hole since Pharaonic times. It is postulated to have been a Canaanite town, founded during the Hyksos era, named after the Canaanite goddess Nikkal wa'Ib, meaning "Great lady of the Fruitful," who was the goddess of orchards. If this theory is correct, then there must have been a settlement with orchards in the region, matching to some degree the Exodus' description of a place of wells and trees. It is also believed a garrison was built in the region by the Thebans after they

64

conquered the Hyksos. The settlement was called Du Mafkat, but its exact location is unknown. Nevertheless, there were watering holes in the areas at the time, which would have made it an excellent place to stop along the southern road.

From Elim, they continued on through the Wilderness of Sin, and according to the Septuagint's *Numbers*, went to Raphaka (Ραφακα), which the Leningrad Codex calls dāpəqâ (דָפְקָה). The difference between the Greek and Hebrew text would have been caused by a Phoenician or Aramaic D (𐤃 / 𐡃) being replaced with an R (𐤓 / 𐡓). In Phoenician, dpqh (𐤃𐤐𐤒𐤄) meant "the pqh," which was a partial translation and partial transliteration of the Egyptian name m-fkȧ (𓅓𓆑𓎡𓏏𓈒𓈒𓈒), meaning "the turquoise." Tȧ-m-fkȧ (𓇾𓏤 𓅓𓆑𓎡𓏏𓈒𓈒𓈒), meaning "Land of the turquoise," was the ancient Egyptian name for the mountains in the southern Sinai Peninsula.

It isn't clear why the reference to the old Egyptian colony was dropped, but the two lists of stops realign at Rafidin (Ραφιδιν) / Rəpîdim (רְפִידִם), where the Israelites were attacked by the Amelakites. The name 'Ămālēq (עֲמָלֵק) is a transliteration of the ancient Egyptian term åmw-rqi (𓄿𓅓𓅱𓋹𓏤 𓂋𓈎𓂝), meaning "Amorite hostiles," which indicates that this force traveled south from Canaan to attack the Israelites at Rephidim.

Exodus includes one strange detail that deviates from the rest of the Torah in that it identifies Mount Horeb as being at Rephidim, a hill or mountain in between the Wilderness of Sin and the Wilderness of Sinai. At this mountain, Moses made a spring flow, as there was no water in the region. The

Greeks translated the Aramaic text as "in Ǩōrēb" (εν Χωρηβ), which is also how the Hebrew bəhōrēb (בְּחֹרֵב) could be interpreted, supporting the Aramaic text as being the same as the Hebrew, and reading as bǩrb (בכרב). Unfortunately, the Greek translation does not make sense, as they were not near either Mount Sinai, nor in Midian at the time.

An alternate reading of the Hebrew and Aramaic translations would be "with a sword," or "with a plowshare," neither of which probably made sense to the Greek translators, and so they opted for Horeb. This appears to be a misunderstanding of the underlying Akkadian cuneiform text, in which the word ǩarbum (𒁹𒊑𒂊𒉺𒆤), referred to a specialized heavy plow used to break up hard dry soil, as opposed to a lighter plow which was used to make furrows in fields. The name of this tool was spelled as ǩrb (כרב) in Aramaic, however, that word also meant any form of plow, sword, or spear. In this case, the messenger of the lord was apparently offering Moses a tool to break up the hard soil and allow the water to flow.

Based on their path through the Sinai Peninsula, the mountain in question seems to be Hashem El Tarif, a mountain in the eastern Sinai along the southern road, just before one would reach the Gulf of Aqaba. Hashem El Tarif would have been one of the markers used by people crossing the desert before paved highways and GPS, as it rose above the otherwise flat horizon, and was near the northern coast of the Gulf of Aqaba, meaning they would have reached it as they left the Wilderness of Sin and reached the sea. Hashem El Tarif is certainly close enough to Midian that Moses could have ventured that far while shepherding Jethro's flocks and is far more likely a locality for the original interaction with the wadjet than the mountains in the southern Sinai peninsula, which were occupied by the Egyptians. Additionally, it is plausible he would move his flock that far west, hoping to hear news from Egypt, which is what ultimately happened.

Hashem El Tarif is somewhat unusual as it did have a spring near the top of it that once flowed down one side, which could have been the source of the story about Moses opening the spring. Additionally, there is the issue of the Amorite rebels attacking the Israelites at Rephidim, which makes no sense in the traditional interpretation of everything happening in the southern Sinai Peninsula, as the Amelakites lived in Canaan, which was north of Hashem El Tarif.

From Rephidim, the Israelites moved west through the Wilderness of Sinai to Mount Sinai, where God came down and gave them the commandments. The Wilderness of Sinai was the final stop mentioned in Exodus. If one accepts Josephus' location near Petra, and Deborah's referring to it as Mount Seir in the *Book of Judges*, then it was the Mountain of the Altar, Jebel al-Madhbah in southwest Jordan. This site has been associated with the exodus story since pre-Christian times and includes a Valley of Moses (Wadi Musa) and Spring of Moses (Ain Musa) that have been associated with the exodus story since ancient times.

This still leaves the question of who were the Israelites? The earliest mention of them is from the time of Pharaoh

Merneptah, circa 1200 BCE, where they are listed alongside the towns of Ashkelon, Gezer, and Yenoam, two of which are known to have been in southernmost Canaan. The location of Yenoam is unknown, with possible locations suggested throughout modern Israel and as far north as Syria. Nevertheless, if the Israelites left Egypt around the time of the Minoan eruption they should have been noted, somewhere. The only group tentatively identified as Israelites before the time of Merneptah, is the Shasu of Yhwå, believed to have been in the Seir Mountains. This identification is debatable, as Shasu is the Egyptian word for nomads, and Yhwå is a place name.

Several other groups of nomads were listed with the Shasu of Yhwå, including the Shasu of Sôr, Rbn (or Lbn), Småt, Wrbr, and Pysps. These names indicate the Seir Mountains, and possibly the Tribe of Ruben, however, even this is speculation. They were mentioned in the el-Amarna Letters, dated to between 1374 and 1357 BCE, which still leaves a 200-year gap between the Minoan eruption and the first mention of the Shasu of Yhwå. This gap is less significant than it appears if one considers that after the Hyksos left Egypt, they also disappeared, entirely. According to the 3rd century BCE Egyptian historian and priest Manetho, when the Hyksos surrendered Avaris, the Egyptians let 240,000 Hyksos families leave, who returned to Canaan. The Egyptians then occupied Canaan a few decades later, and apparently, there were no Hyksos there. If they didn't record where the Hyksos went, why would they record where a bunch of slaves that ran away from the Hyksos went?

Josephus claimed to have found records in Egypt of Moses, which modern Egyptologists have not found. Josephus claimed that the Egyptians did record the flight of Moses, who led a band of lepers out of Egypt, but he did not believe that Moses and those lepers were the ancestors of the Israelites. He believed the ancestors of the Israelites were the Hyksos, and the story about the leper-leader had somehow become mixed up with the story of the Hyksos leaving Egypt. If records about the leper-leader Moses existed, they would have no doubt been destroyed by Christians or Muslims at some point, nevertheless, Egyptologists generally dismiss the claim that they existed.

The fact that the Egyptians called them a band of lepers is irrelevant propaganda, however, Josephus' Hyksos theory has also been refuted by Egyptologists as well as Biblical scholars, as the Hyksos snake-god (Apophis) and a storm-god (Set), is nothing like the Israelite God. While it seems likely the Israelites were in Hyksos-controlled Egypt, they seem more like a band of runaway slaves that escaped during the Minoan eruption than the deposed Pharaoh.

The last Hyksos Pharaoh, Khamudi, fought a series of losing wars until the only region of Egypt he held was the fortified city of Avaris. When he surrendered the city, the Hyksos fell back to the fortified city of Sharuhen in the Negev or Gaza Strip, about 14 years after the Minoan eruption. Sharuhen was then conquered by the Egyptians too, and Khamudi retreated to Jericho and later Byblos before disappearing into the Mediterranean Sea. This is not the story found in Exodus. Even if the Hyksos refugees did contribute to the gene-pool that became the later Israelite tribes, the story in *Exodus* is the story of Moses and his runaway slaves, not the story of the fall of the Hyksos Dynasty.

The Hasmonean Kingdom of Judea had a tenuous alliance with the Roman Republic until General Pompey conquered Syria into the Roman Republic in 69 BCE. Pompey's goal was to liberate Greek-speaking communities in the Middle East that had fallen under the rule of non-Greeks when the Seleucid Syrian Empire had collapsed, and he carved up Judea, and Edom to the east, placing Greek-speaking cities under the protection of the Roman province of Syria. He also liberated several smaller communities that had been occupied by Judea, granting them self-government, including Ashdod, Yavne, Jaffa, Dora, Marissa, and Samaria.

A series of wars including both Julius Caesar's campaigns, and a Parthian invasion led to the weakening of the Hasmonean dynasty, and in 37 CE, the Roman Senate appointed the Edomite King Herod the Great, as 'King of the Jews.' Herod's rule wasn't particularly popular, as he allowed the Romans to establish themselves within Judea, however, he did expand Judea, reintegrating the Greek and Samaritan cities, and annexing Galilee and Edom. When he died, his kingdom was divided between four successors, a situation that ended in 66 CE when the Romans conquered the region. An uprising in 120 CE led to the Jews being exiled from Judea, and the region became a Greco-Roman colony. In the wake of the Jews, the Samaritans rose in numbers, along with the

Christians after Christianity was legalized. Between 529 and 555 CE, the Samaritans revolted and were effectively annihilated, by the Byzantine Empire.

The ancient documents found in the Caves in Qumran, more commonly called the Dead Sea Scrolls, span a large section of Judean history. The fragments of the Torah have been found in ancient Phoenician, Hebrew, Aramaic, and Greek. The Phoenician fragments in the dead sea scrolls have been particularly debated, as they are believed to be the oldest. The current Hebrew script was officially adopted by the Hasmonean Dynasty in 140 BCE, when the first King/ High-Priest Simon the Zealous issued an authoritative Hebrew translation of the Torah. The Hasmonean dynasty paid scribes to replace older versions of the Torah and other non-Hebrew scriptures which were in use, and ordered everyone to bring in their old texts to get the new and improved versions.

The new Hebrew language of Judea was a combination of the old spoken dialect of Canaanite used in the region, which had been written in the Phoenician script, today called Paleo-Hebrew, and the "block letter" version of the Aramaic script. Unfortunately, almost no one in the Kingdom of Judea could read the new Hebrew Torah, and so the Aramaic Targum was also developed to explain what the Hebrew texts said. Before the new Hebrew version was published, there were two versions in circulation in Judea, the Aramaic version used by the Judean intelligentsia, and the Phoenician script

71

Paleo-Hebrew version, which appear to have mainly been used by Samaritans.

Outside of Judea, the Septuagint was the dominant form of Israelite scriptures across the Greek-speaking world, which at the beginning of the Christian era extended from the Roman Empire in the west, to the Indo-Greek Kingdom in the east. The earliest Christian Bibles used the Septuagint for the Old Testament, however, by the 4th century some Christian scholars were debating whether they should retranslate the Old Testament from the version the Jews were using, and some even suggested using the Samaritan version. Both suggestions were generally dismissed as heretical, as Jesus and the Apostles had quoted from the Septuagint, even though they had access to the Hebrew version then in use.

This argument held in the west until the Middle Ages, when Catholic Bibles switched to the Masoretic texts. In the east, Orthodox Bibles continued to use the Septuagint, as they do today. To the south, the Ethiopian Tewahedo Church continued to use the Septuagint, and across Asia, the Thomas Christians and Nestorians continued to use the Septuagint. Only in Western Europe were the later Masoretic texts adopted, abandoning the more ancient Septuagint, on the assumption that the Jews had copied their texts more faithfully than the Greeks had translated them. This assumption was carried forward into the Protestant Churches that broke off from the Catholic Church, and therefore almost all Protestant Bibles use the Masoretic texts for the basis of the Old Testament.

Unfortunately, this means that the earliest Christian writings are generally confusing and ignored by Protestants and Catholics. The earliest Christians of the first and second centuries quoted books that are no longer in the Bible, and as such, their writings are not always understood. *Septuagint: Exodus* is the second in a series of 21st century translations aimed at correcting this problem.

One of the problems with academic translations of the Septuagint, is the use of unfamiliar names or terms, as the Septuagint was written in Greek, and therefore many names are unrecognizable to modern readers who are used to Hebrew-derived names. This project uses the more commonly understood Hebrew-derived names instead of their Greek translations, such as Canaan instead of Chanaan, and Melchizedek instead of Melchisedec. Common modern names are also used instead of either Greek or Hebrew terms when geographical locations are known, such as the archaeological name Uruk instead of the Greek Orech, or the Hebrew Erech. While this could be argued as not being a correct academic procedure, it does fulfill the goal of making the translation easy to read and understand.

CHAPTER 1

These are the names of the sons of Israel that entered Egypt with Jacob their father. They each entered with their whole family: Reuben, Simeon, Levi, Judah, Issachar, Zebulun, Benjamin, Dan, Naphtali, Gad, Asher, and Joseph was in Egypt. All the lives born from Jacob were seventy-five. Joseph died, and all his brothers, and all from that generation.

The Israelites increased and multiplied, and became numerous and grew powerful, and the land multiplied them. There arose up another king in Egypt, who had not known Joseph. He said to his nation, "Look, the descendants of Israel are a great multitude and are stronger than we have become, so let us deal cunningly with them, in case at any time they increase, and when war comes against us, they ally with our enemies, and once defeating us in war, they will leave out of the land."

He set over them taskmasters, who should punish them in their works, and they built strong cities for Pharaoh,[1] in Pithom,[2] Ramesses,[3] and On[4] (which is now Heliopolis). But as they humbled them, so much they multiplied and grew exceedingly strong, and the Egyptians greatly hated the Israelites. The Egyptians tyrannized the Israelites with force. They antagonized their lives of hard labor, in the clay and in brick-making, and all the works in the plains, according to all the works, in which they caused them to serve with violence.

The king of the Egyptians spoke to the midwives of the Habirus.[5] The name of the one was Shiphrah, and the name of the second, Pua. He said, "When you midwife for the Habiru women deliver a child, if it is a male, kill it. But if a female, save it."

However, the midwives feared the gods[6] and did not do as the king of Egypt ordered them, and they saved the male children. The king of Egypt called the midwives, and asked them, "Why have you have done this, and saved the male children?"

The midwives answered Pharaoh, "The Habiru women are not like the women of Egypt. They deliver before the midwives get to them." So they carried children.

God treated the midwives well, and the people multiplied and grew very strong. As the midwives feared the gods, they established for themselves families. Pharaoh ordered all his people, "Any male child born to the Habirus, throw into the river, and every female, keep it alive."

CHAPTER 1 NOTES

1 Codex Vaticanus: faraō (ⲫⲁⲣⲁⲱ)

- Leningrad Codex: par'ōh (פַּרְעֹה). Translation: Pharaoh

- Peshitta: prȯwn (ܦܪܥܘܢ). Translation: Pharaoh

- Targum Onkelos: malkā' (מַלְכָּא). Translation: king
- Targum Jerusalem: malkā' (מַלְכָּא). Translation: king
- Targum Pseudo-Jonathan: milîk (מְלִיךְ). Translation: ruler
- Sahidic manuscript 2000: Faraō (ⲫⲁⲣⲁⲱ). Translation: Pharaoh

Both the Greek and Hebrew terms were the equivalent of the modern term Pharaoh, a title of the King of Egypt, however, this translation is anachronistic to the era the story it set in. Both the Greek and Hebrew terms are ultimately derived from the Egyptian word pr-åȯ (□), meaning 'big house,' or 'palace.'

During the New Kingdom era, the term became the title of the king of Egypt, which was adopted into Akkadian Cuneiform as pirāú (𒐁𒐁𒌋), Canaanite as prȯh (𐤐𐤓𐤏𐤄), Aramaic as prȯw (פרעו), Greek as Pharaō (Φαραω), and Hebrew as par'ōh (פֶּרְעֹה). The story is set during the Middle Kingdom era, when the king of Egypt's title was nesut (transliterated hieroglyphs: nswt. Spelled variously as †ₒ𓇳, †ₒ𓏏, or †ₒ𓍋 depending on context). As the term "Pharaoh" is found in all copies of Exodus, it likely originated with a reference to the palace, not the king himself.

2 Codex Alexandrinus: Pit̲ōm (ⲡⲓⲑⲱⲙ)
- Codex Ambrosiano A 147: Pit̲ōt̲ (ⲡⲓⲑⲱⲑ)
- Septuagint manuscript 509: Pisōn (ⲡⲓⲥⲱⲛ)
- Septuagint manuscript 15: Fit̲ōm (ⲫⲓⲑⲱⲙ)
- Septuagint manuscript 64: Pit̲ōf (ⲡⲓⲑⲱϥ)
- Septuagint manuscript 135: Fimōt̲ (ⲫⲓⲙⲱⲑ)
- Septuagint manuscript 318: Fitom (ⲫⲓⲑⲟⲙ)
- Septuagint manuscript 55: Pit̲ō (ⲡⲓⲑⲱ)
- Septuagint manuscript 392: Fit̲ōn (ⲫⲓⲑⲱⲛ)
- Septuagint manuscript 730: Pit̲ōm (ⲡϭⲓⲑⲱⲙ)
- Septuagint manuscript 56: Pepit̲ō (ⲡϭⲡϭⲓⲑⲱ)

- Septuagint manuscript 121: Ṭō (Θ∞)
- Septuagint manuscript 75: Piṯōn (Πιθωѻ)
- Septuagint manuscript 78: Piṯōf (Π∂ιθ∞ϸ)
- Septuagint manuscript 82: Piṯōn (Π∂ιθ∞ѻ)
- Septuagint manuscript 458: Plē (Πλѡ)
- Septuagint manuscript 54: Piṯof (Π∂ιθѻϸ)
- Septuagint manuscript 72: Plinṯon (Πλιѡθѻѻ)
- Septuagint manuscript 799: Fiṯōn (Φ∂ιθ∞ѻ)
- Septuagint manuscript 53: Poeṯō (Ποιθ∞)
- Septuagint manuscript 376: Fiṯōm (Φ∂ιθ∞μ)
- Septuagint manuscript 59: Biṯōr (ßιθ∞ℙ)
- Septuagint manuscript 619: Biṯōm (ßιθ∞μ)
- Leningrad Codex: Pitōm (פִּתֹם)
- Dead Sea Scroll 4QExodᶜ: Ptm (פתם)
- Peshitta: Pytwm (ܦܝܬܘܡ)
- Targum Onkelos: Pîtôm (פִּיתוֹם)
- Targum Jerusalem: Ṯānîs (טָנִיס)
- Targum Pseudo-Jonathan: Ṯāʾnês (טָאֲנֵיס)
- Sahidic manuscript 2000: Piṯōm (Πιθωμ)
- Fayyumic manuscripts: Fiṯōṯ (Φιθωθ)
- Bohairic manuscripts: Peṯom (Πεθου)

This is generally accepted as the city of Per-Atum (𓉐 𓇋𓏏𓈖𓇳), later called Heroöpolis by the Greeks. The location of both the Egyptian and Greek cities remains unclear, however, several sites have been located that appear to have been known as Per-Atum at various times in Egyptian history. The difficulty locating the 'city' is likely because the name is actually a reference to a temple, the Temple of Atum, which periodically relocated, and as a result the name of the community it was in changed as well. Excavations at

CHAPTER 1

the Tel El Maskhuta complex, in the western Nile Delta, show a Hyksos era (15th dynasty) settlement that was likely Per-Atum, although the site was later abandoned until the era of Pharaoh Necho II (26th dynasty, circa 600 BCE).

The city of Tanis, included in the Jerusalem and Jonathan Targums, was located in the northeastern Nile Delta. During the 19th dynasty (1200s BCE), the town of Tanis was the capital of the 14th district of Egypt, however, there are no earlier records of the city.

3 Codex Ambrosiano A 147: Ramesē (ⲢⲀⲘⲈⲤⲎ)

- Septuagint manuscript 707: Sēn (Σλͅν)
- Septuagint manuscript 313: Rem (Ρϧμ)
- Septuagint manuscript 72: Ramessē (Ρλμϭϭⲟⲗ)
- Septuagint manuscript 125: Ramesi (Ρλμϭϭι)
- Leningrad Codex: Ra'amses (רַעְמְסֵס)
- Peshitta: Rômsys (ܐ̇ܪܥܡܣܘܣ)
- Targum Onkelos: Ra'amses (רַעְמְסֵס)
- Targum Jerusalem: pilusin (פִּילוּסִין). Translation: Pelusium
- Targum Pseudo-Jonathan: pilusin (פִּילוּסִין). Translation: Pelusium
- Sahidic manuscript 2000: Ramessē (Ⲣⲁⲙⲉⲥⲥⲏ)

The location of Ramesses has been a matter of debate since before the Septuagint was translated, and the translators were not sure which ancient Egyptian city the name Ramesses was referring to. The historic city of Ramesses was built in the era of Pharaoh Shoshenq I (943 to 922 BCE) and was still a major city when the stories found in Numbers were most likely compiled into a book under King Hezekiah (715 to 687 BCE). The Late-Period city of Ramesses was a rebuilding of the New Kingdom era city of Pi-

79

Ramesses, and as the city of Pi-Ramesses was never called Ramesses during the New Kingdom era, it must be assumed that the name was updated when the Torah was updated under Josiah.

The city of Pi-Ramesses, which was founded in 1290 BCE, was itself a rebuilding of Avaris, the Hyksos capital, which had been destroyed when the Hyksos were driven from Egypt in circa 1572 BCE, meaning it is not clear if the name Avaris or Pi-Ramesses was updated to Ramesses. Both Avaris and Pi-Ramesses had served as imperial capital cities when Egypt had ruled Canaan, and so either could be the city in the text, however, if one accepts that Pi-Ramesses was the city called Ramesses, then it dates the events in Exodus to the 1200s BCE, immediately before the Bronze Age Collapse, yet there are already reports from a century earlier of the Shasu (Nomads) of Yhwǎ (𓏤𓈖𓊪𓏭𓄿) in the Seir Region of modern Jordan, which are generally accepted as a reference to the Israelites, meaning the original name was probably Avaris, which had become obscure by Hezekiah's time, and was updated to the contemporary name.

The city of Pelusium, mentioned in the Targum Pseudo-Jonathan and Targum Jerusalem was the easternmost major city in the Nile Delta during the Greco-Roman era. The city had existed since the Old Kingdom era, and therefore it is plausible that it was the original city in the text, however, that is unlikely. The original name of the city was Sin (𓈖𓏌) in the Old Kingdom era, however, it continued to be used alongside later names that were applied to the city, and was the common name of the city in languages using the Akkadian Cuneiform script, commonly spelled as Sin (𒋛𒅔), the Akkadian word for "moon," later spelled as Syân (𐤎𐤉𐤍), Sain (Σαιν), Sîn (סִין), and Sin (Cᴎ) during the Classical era.

During the New Kingdom era, the name of the city was changed to Per-Amen (𓉐𓇋𓏠𓈖), meaning the 'house of Amen,' which also continued to be used, resulting in the Coptic Peremoun (Περεμоγν). During the early Iron Age, the name Per-Sin (סִין‎) developed, which was later transliterated into Greek as Pēlousion (Πηλουσιον), and then adopted into Hebrew and Judean-Aramaic as Pîlûsîn (פִּילוּסִין), meaning the name could not have been in the early Aramaic translation of Exodus. Nevertheless, it is clear that the city was not viewed as being the historic city of Ramesses by the Judeans in the early-Christian era.

4 Codex Vaticanus: Ōn (ⲱⲛ)
- LXX 19: Ōr (ⲱⲣ)
- LXX 53: Om (ⲟⲙ)
- LXX 83: tēn Ōn (ⲧⲏ ⲱⲛ). Translation: the Ōn
- Sahidic manuscript 2000: Ōn (ⲱⲛ)

The Masoretic texts, Peshitta, and Targums do not mention Heliopolis at this point. In the Leningrad Codex's Bereshít, it was called 'Ôn (אֹון). The original Egyptian name Iwnw (𓉺𓏤) means "the pillars," and was one of the ancient holy cities of Egypt since pre-dynastic times. It is currently located in the Ayn Shams district of Greater Cairo. It was the cult-center for several gods, mostly associated with the Sun, which is why the Greeks renamed it Heliopolis. The solar gods worshiped there include the creator-god Atum, the solar-disk Aten, the sun Ra, and the scarab-beetle god Khepri. The major exception was the lunar god Iŏḥw.

As Joseph was given the daughter of a high-priest to wed in Cosmic Genesis, he would become a high-priest as well, although Cosmic Genesis does not clarify which god he was the priest of. Nevertheless, he is never connected to the Sun in any way, and as an interpreter of dreams, the moon makes more sense as Joseph's god, implying he was the priest of Iŏḥw, which is likely the source of the Israelite god Yahweh.

CHAPTER 1

5 Codex Vaticanus: ebraias (ЄΒΡΑΙΑϹ)

* Septuagint manuscript 59: ebraiais (ϵυβαιαιϲ)
* Leningrad Codex: 'Ibriyyôt (עִבְרִיֹּת). Translation: female Eberite
* Peshitta: ôbrytâ (ܥܒܪܝܬܐ). Translation: female crosser
* Targum Onkelos: Yəhûdayātā' (יְהוּדְיָתָא). Translation: Judahite
* Targum Pseudo-Jonathan: Yəhôdayytā' (יְהוֹדִיְּיתָא). Translation: Judahite
* Sahidic manuscript 2000: Hebraia (ϨЄΒΡΑΙΑ)

The Greek term is a translation of Hebrew, using the Second Temple era interpretation of the word, however, the Masoretic spelling is not the correct spelling of Hebrewess, Ôbryt (עברית), but the Aramaic word for a female Eberite, Ôbrywt (ﬠﬧ﬩ﬠ). The Eberites were the descendants of the patriarch Eber, an ancestor of Abraham who lived in Ur, in southern Iraq, according to Genesis. The term ôbr (עבר / ﬠﬧﬠ) means "to cross over" in both Hebrew and Aramaic, indicating that these Eberites were the people otherwise known to the Egyptians as Ôprw (𓂝𓊪𓂋𓅱). The earliest surviving mention of the Ǩabiru (𓂝𓊪𓂋𓅱), was from the time of King Rim-Sin I of Larsa between approximately 1822 and 1763 BCE, who reported they were an Aramean tribe living in southern Iraq.

Over the next 600 years, they were reported in hundreds of surviving documents ranging across the Middle East and Egypt, generally as marauders, although some were reported to be mercenaries, and those in Egypt were generally slaves. They disappeared around the end of the Bronze Age, shortly before the emergence of the Aramean Empire around Damascus and Hama, in the early Iron Age. As this reference is to the Ǩabirus, that name is restored in this text. As there is no common feminine form of the name, the gender neutral form of Habiru is used.

6 Codex Vaticanus: o ṬS (**o͞ec**). Translation: the god

- Leningrad Codex: hā'ĕlōhîm (הָאֱלֹהִים). Translation: the gods (or god)

This verse has not survived intact in any of the fragments found among the Dead Sea Scrolls, however, the word ȃlhym does survive in other verses that have survived among the Dead Sea Scrolls.

- DSS 4QGen-Exodᵃ: ȃlhym (אלהים)
- DSS 4QpaleoGen-Exodˡ: ȃlhym (𐤀𐤋𐤄𐤉𐤌)
- DSS 4QExodᵇ: ȃlwhym (אלוהים)

- DSS 4QExodᶜ: the term is missing in complete text, meaning it was not there. The Masoretic verse is Yǝhwâ ĕlōhîm (יְהוָה אֱלֹהִים), where Dead Sea Scroll 4QExodᶜ has ȃdny yhwh (אדני יהוה) which translates as "lord Yahweh." The Septuagint only has "the god" (o θεος) in this verse, which means that 4QExodᶜ does not correspond to either *Exodus* or *Names*.

- DSS 4QpaleoExodᵐ: ȃlhym (𐤀𐤋𐤄𐤉𐤌)
- Peshitta: ȃlhȃ (ܐܠܗܐ). Translation: God
- Targum Onkelos: yǝyā (??). Translation: Yahweh
- Targum Pseudo-Jonathan: yǝyā (??). Translation: Yahweh
- Sahidic manuscript 2000: pnoute (ⲡⲛⲟⲩⲧⲉ). Translation: the god

The Hebrew translation uses three words for "god:" 'ēl (אֵל), 'ĕlōhē (אֱלֹהֵ), and 'ĕlōhîm (אֱלֹהִים). These words have created a great deal of confusion, as ȃl (𐤋𐤀) was the Phoenician word for "god," ȃlh (𐤀𐤋𐤄) was Canaanite for "goddess," and ȃlhm (𐤌𐤋𐤄𐤀) was Canaanite for "goddesses." This confusion is manifest in various translations, where the gender in the texts shift around elohim, however, the main source texts always agree that 'ĕlōhē is a masculine form in regards to the Israelite god. This is likely because the term ȃl (𐤋𐤀) had become synonymous with El, the patriarch of the Canaanite

CHAPTER 1

pantheon by the beginning of the Iron Age, and the other gods were referred to as ba'al (𐤋𐤏𐤁), meaning "lord." Therefore, Aramaic word ålhå (𐡀𐡋𐡄𐡀), which means "god," was adopted at some point by the Israelites to denote a generic "god."

The term 'ĕlōhē is generally used to connect texts from the time of Moses to older texts, such as the phrase "god of Abraham, god of Isaac, and god of Jacob," suggesting the Aramaic phrases were added circa 710 BCE, when the texts of Bereshít (Cosmic Genesis) and Names (Exodus) were standardized under the rule of King Hezekiah of Judah.

The form 'ĕlōhîm is found in the older sections of text, and is clearly a word used to denote either a singular god in some verses, or a plurality of gods in other verses. The Masoretic texts generally demark the difference between "God" and "gods" by adding "the" to the beginning of the word, rendering the plural form as hā'ĕlōhîm (הָאֱלֹהִים). This is particularly evident in Masoretic Daniel, where "lord of the gods" is rendered as 'ădōnāy hā'ĕlōhîm (אֲדֹנָי הָאֱלֹהִים) in the Aramaic sections. The origin of 'ĕlōhîm as a singular form for the Israelite god, likely dates back the translation of the older sections of text from cuneiform into the Phoenician script early in the Iron Age, plausibly in the Kingdom of Israel.

Unfortunately, the Greek translation doesn't generally distinguish between the singular and plural forms, almost always rendering the term as "the god" (ο θεοσ). In the older uncial (all-caps) manuscripts, this was often abbreviated to ṬS (Θ̄Σ̄). However, this does create some confusing concepts, such as the Egyptians worshiping the God of the Israelites instead of their gods. In order the clarify the text, the distinction of "god" versus "gods" are imported from the Leningrad Codex where the Hebrew reads 'ĕlōhē (אֱלֹהֵי), 'ĕlōhîm (אֱלֹהִים), or hā'ĕlōhîm (הָאֱלֹהִים), when not distinguished in the Septuagint manuscripts.

84

CHAPTER 2

There was a certain man of the tribe of Levi, who took as wife one of the daughters of Levi. She conceived, and carried a male child, and having seen that he was fair, they hid him three months. When they could no longer hide him, his mother took an box for him, and smeared it with vegetable oil, and placed the child into it, and put it in the slime by the river. His sister was watching from a distance, to find out what would happen to him.

The daughter of Pharaoh came down to the river to bathe, and her girls walked by the river's side, and seeing the box in the slime, she sent her girl and picked it up. Having opened it, she saw the baby crying in the box, and the daughter of Pharaoh had compassion on it, and said, "This is one of the Habirus children."

His sister asked the daughter of Pharaoh, "Would you like for me to call a nurse of the Habirus for you, to suckle the child for you?"

The daughter of Pharaoh commanded, "Go!" and the young woman went and called the mother of the child. The daughter of Pharaoh ordered her, "Take care of this child and suckled it for me, and I will pay you," and the woman took the child and suckled it.

CHAPTER 2

When the boy was grown, she brought him to the daughter of Pharaoh, and he became her son, and she called his name, 'Moses,'[1] saying, "I took him out of the water."

It happened in the length of time, that Moses grow up and went out to his brothers the sons of Israel, and saw their distress. He saw an Egyptian striking one of his Habiru brothers, the Israelites, and after looking around and seeing no one watching, and he killed the Egyptian and hid him in the sand. Going out a second day he saw two Habiru men fighting, and he asked the injurer, "Why do you hit your neighbor?"

He answered, "Who made you a ruler and a judge over us? Will you kill me like you killed the Egyptian yesterday?"

Then Moses was concerned, and said, "This matter has become known."

Pharaoh heard this matter and wanted to kill Moses, and Moses departed from the presence of Pharaoh, and traveled to the land of Midian,[2] and having entered the land of Midian, sat by the well. The priest of Midian had seven daughters, feeding the flock of their father Jethro, and they came and drew water until they filled their pitchers, to water the flock of their father Jethro. The shepherds came and were driving them away, and Moses rose up and rescued them, and drew water for them, and watered their sheep. They returned to Jethro their father, and he said to them, "Why have you come so quickly today?"

They answered, "An Egyptian saved us from the shepherds, and drew water for us and watered our sheep."

He said to his daughters, "Where is he? Why have you left the man? Call him, therefore, that he may eat bread."

Moses was established with the man, and he gave Shiphrah his daughter to Moses as a wife. The woman conceived and carried a son, and Moses called his name 'Gershom,' saying, "I am a traveler in a strange land."

In those days after a length of time, the king of Egypt died, and the Israelites groaned because of their tasks and lamented, and their despair because of their tasks went up to the gods. God heard their groaning, and God remembered his covenant made with Abraham and Isaac and Jacob. God looked on the Israelites and was made known to them.

CHAPTER 2 NOTES

1 Codex Vaticanus: Mōusē (ΜѠΥϹΗ)

- Codex Ambrosiano: Mōusēn (ΜѠΥϹΗΝ)

- LXX 53: Mōsēs (Μοσ‌ησ)

- LXX 68: Mōyssēn (Μουσσω)

- LXX 135: Mōsē (Μοσ‌η)

- DSS 4QpaleoGen-Exod[1]: Mšh (𐤀𐤔𐤌)

- Leningrad Codex: Mōšeh (מֹשֶׁה)

- Peshitta: Mwšâ (ܡܘܫܐ)

- Targum Onkelos: Mšeh (מֹשֶׁה)

- Targum Pseudo-Jonathan: Mšeh (מֹשֶׁה)

CHAPTER 2

- Sahidic manuscript 2000: Mōusēs (Mⲱ**ⲩ**ⲥⲏⲥ)

This verse does not survive in most of the fragments found among the Dead Sea Scrolls, however, the name "Moses" does survive in later verses that have survived among the Dead Sea Scrolls.

- DSS 1QExod: Mšh (𐤌𐤔𐤄)
- DSS 2QExodᵃ: Mwšh (𐤌𐤔𐤅𐤄)
- DSS 2QExodᵇ: Mwšh (𐤌𐤔𐤅𐤄)
- DSS 4QGen-Exodᵃ: Mšh (משה)
- DSS 4QExod-Levᶠ: Mšh (משה)
- DSS 4QpaleoExodᵐ: Mšh (𐤌𐤔𐤄)
- DSS 4QExodᶜ: Mwšh (𐤌𐤔𐤅𐤄)
- DSS 4QExodᵇ: Mwšh (𐤌𐤔𐤅𐤄)
- DSS Mur1: Mšh (𐤌𐤔𐤄)
- Targum Jerusalem: Mšeh (מֹשֶׁה)

It is generally accepted that at some point before the Septuagint was translated, half of Moses' name was redacted from the text. This theory is based on the similarity of the Egyptian term msỉ (𓄟𓋴), meaning "give birth to," or "created by," which was a common element of Egyptian names. Many kings of Egypt were known as the "msỉ" of a god, including Ahmose (𓇳𓄟𓋴), Amenmose (𓇋𓏠𓈖𓄟𓋴), Ramses (𓇳𓄟𓋴), Ptahmose (𓁰𓄟𓋴), and Tuthmose (𓅝𓄟𓋴). A theory that has been circulating since at least the time of Josephus in the 1st century CE, is that Moses' original name was Hapymoses, meaning the 'Nile created him.'

If this is the origin of the name, the name of the god that created Moses was likely dropped from the name very early in Israelite history, as there are no known surviving texts with the full name. The latest this is likely to have happened would have been during the Aramaic translation of King Hezekiah, however, it may have happened much earlier. An alternate interpretation is that the name is complete, and is derived from the Egyptian term mw-šảỏ (𓈖𓈗 𓄿𓏤), meaning "beginning on water," which is what the princess state when she names him.

2 Codex Vaticanus: Madiam (ΜΑΔΙΑΜ)

• Leningrad Codex: Midyān (מִדְיָן)

• Peshitta: Mdyn (ܡܕܝܢ)

• Targum Onkelos: Midyān (מִדְיָן)

• Targum Pseudo-Jonathan: Midyān (מִדְיָן)

• Sahidic manuscript 2000: Madiham (ΜΑⲆΙϨΑΜ)

The land of Midiam is generally accepted as being in the Midiyan Mountains in the Hijaz area of Saudi Arabia, east of the Gulf of Aqaba. There is some debate regarding this location, as some scholars in the 1800s preferred the Sinai Peninsula in Egypt, and some preferred regions of Syria. Most of the ruins in the Hijaz date to after 800 BCE, which caused some concern, however, earlier levels of civilization have been found dating back to the 1300s BCE, including pottery described as "Midianite Pottery" or "Qurayyah Painted Ware."

This pottery is widespread, ranging from the Qurayyah region in Hejaz as far north as Israel, Jordan, and the West Bank. The style is similar to the Mycenaean pottery of the era, and there is also older Minoan style pottery found in the region, suggesting the Minoans and later Mycenaean Greeks were using the region as a transshipment center between the Mediterranean and Red Seas for many centuries in the mid to late Bronze Age.

If one accepted the dating for this story in either circa 1300s BCE, or 1500s BCE, then Midian would have been the closest land to the Nile Delta that Moses could have escaped to that was not under the rule of Egypt.

CHAPTER 3

Moses was shepherding the flock of Jethro his father-in-law, the priest of Midian, and he brought the sheep to the edge of the wilderness and came to a mountain in the desert (the mountain of the gods).[1] The messenger of the lord appeared to him in the fire of flame out of the bramble,[2] and he saw that the bramble was burning with fire, but was not consumed. Moses said, "I will approach and see this great sight, and why the bramble is not burned up."

When the Lord saw him approach to watch, the Lord called him out of the bramble, calling, "Moses, Moses!"

He asked, "What is it?"

He answered, "Don't come near here. Remove the sandals from your feet, as this place is holy ground." He continued, "I am the god of your father, the god of Abraham, and the god of Isaac, and the god of Jacob,"[3] and Moses turned away his face, as he was afraid to look at the gods.

The Lord said to Moses, "I have surely seen the suffering of my people that are in Egypt, and I have heard their cry caused by their taskmasters, for I know their suffering. I have come down to deliver them out of the hand of the Egyptians, and to bring them out of that land, and to bring them into a good and wide land, into a land flowing with milk and honey, into the land of the Canaanites, Cypriots,[4] Amorites, Perizzite, Girgashites,[5] Mitanni,[6] and Jebusites. Now see, the cry of the

Israelites has come to me, and I have seen the suffering with which the Egyptians punish them. Now come, I will send you to Pharaoh, king of Egypt, and you will bring out my people the Israelites from the land of Egypt."

Moses asked God, "Who am I, that I should go to Pharaoh king of Egypt, and that I should bring out the Israelites from the land of Egypt?"

He answered Moses,[7] "I will be with you, and this will be the sign to you that I will send you out, when you bring out my people from Egypt, then you will worship the gods on this mountain."

Moses asked God, "Look, I will go to the Israelites, and will say to them, 'the god of our fathers has sent me to you,' and they will ask me, 'What is his name?' How will I answer them?"

God answered Moses, "I am Yahweh,"[8] and he added, "So will you tell the Israelites, 'Yahweh has sent me to you.'"

God continued speaking to Moses, and said, "You will say this to the sons of Israel, the lord of the gods[9] of your fathers appeared to me, the god of Abraham, and the god of Isaac, and the god of Jacob,[10] has sent me to you. This is my name forever, and my memorial to generations and generations.' Go then and gather the elders of the Israelites, and you will say to them, 'Yahweh, the god of your fathers[11] has appeared to me, the god of Abraham, and the god of Isaac, and the god of Jacob, saying, I have surely seen you, and all the things which have happened to you in Egypt.'"

He continued, "'I will bring you up out of the suffering under the Egyptians to the land of the Canaanites and the Cypriots, and Amorites and Perizzite, and Girgashites, and Mitanni, and Jebusites, to a land flowing with milk and honey.' They will listen to your voice, and you and the elders of Israel will go to Pharaoh king of Egypt, and you will say to him, 'the god of the Habirus has called us. We will go on a journey of three days into the wilderness, that we may sacrifice to our god.' But I know that Pharaoh king of Egypt will not let you go, except with a mighty hand, and I will stretch out my hand, and strike the Egyptians with all my wonders, which I will work among them, and after, that he will send you out. I will give these people favor in the sight of the Egyptians, and when you escape, you will not depart empty. But every woman will ask of her neighbor and fellow lodger, articles of gold and silver, and apparel, and you will put them on your sons and your daughters, and plunder the Egyptians."

CHAPTER 3 NOTES

1 Codex Vaticanus: oros Ǩōrēb (ΟΡΟϹΧѠΡΗΒ). Translation: Mount Khoreb

• Codex Ambrosiano: oros tou Ǩōrēb ṬU (ΟΡΟϹΧѠΡΗΒΤΟΥ Θ͞Υ). Translation: Mount of Khoreb God

• LXX 53: oros tō Ǩōrēb (οϱϲ τ∞ χ∞βℓυ). Translation: Mount of the Khoreb

• LXX 72: oros Ǩōrib (οϱϲ χ∞βιυ). Translation: Mount of the Khorib

CHAPTER 3

- LXX 75: oros Ǩorib (ορος Χοβιu). Translation: Mount of the Khorib
- LXX 106: oros Ǩorēb (ορος Χοβλu). Translation: Mount of the Khoreb
- Leningrad Codex: har hā'ĕlōhîm hōrēbâ (הַר הָאֱלֹהִים חֹרֵבָה). Translation: mountain of the gods in desolation (or destruction)
- Peshitta: ṭārā dālhā (ܠܛܘܪܐ ܕܐܠܗܐ). Translation: mountain of God
- Targum Onkelos: lǝṭûrā' dǝ'itgǝlî 'ălôhî yǝqārā' dayyā lǝhôrēb (לְטוּרָא דְאִתְגְלִי עֲלוֹהִי יְקָרָא דַיְיָ לְחוֹרֵב). Translation: the mountain of revelation where commanded by Yahweh in the wastes
- Targum Pseudo-Jonathan: lǝtawwrā' dǝ'itgǝlê 'ălôy yǝqārā' dayyā lǝhôrēb (לְטַוְורָא דְאִתְגְלֵי עֲלוֹי יְקָרָא דַיְיָ לְחוֹרֵב). Translation: the mountain of revelation where the genius commanded by Yahweh in the wastes
- Vetus Latina manuscripts: Choreb montem Dei (ⅽⅮⲞⲢⲉⲃ ⲙⲟⲛⲧⲉⲙ ⲇⲉⅰ). Translation: Choreb mountain of God
- Sahidic manuscript 2000: Ǩōrēb ptōou mpjoeis pnoute (ⲭⲱⲣⲏⲃ ⲡⲧⲟⲟⲩ ⲙ̅ⲡⲭⲟⲉⲓⲥ ⲡⲛⲟⲩⲧⲉ). Translation: Khoreb the mountain of the master the god
- Bohairic manuscripts: Enxrim ptōou pnout (ⲉⲛⲭ̇ⲣⲓⲙ ⲡⲧⲱⲟⲩ ⲡⲛⲟⲩϯ). Translation: Enxrim mountain of God
- Ge'ez manuscripts: Ǩoreb dābǝr 'ămǝlak (ኮሬብ ደብር አምላክ). Translation: Choreb mountain of God

The Greeks, Latins, and others transliterated the Aramaic form of the word ḥwrb (חורב), meaning "destruction" or "desolation," as variations of the name Ǩoreb (Χωρηβ), which indicates that the Old Aramaic translation treated this as a name. However, in Hebrew the -h (ה) sound at the end of a word can be used to indicate a direction (to Horeb), or to indicate the feminine object of a

94

preposition (her Horeb), neither of which fit the sentence. The Greek translation has led to the mountain being confused with the mountain were Moses opened the spring using a k̆ōrēb (חֹרֵב), a translation of the word k̆arbum (𒄯𒅗𒂖𒈨), meaning "heavy plow." As this appears to have been an error, the original meaning is restored. The term "mountain of the gods/God" is also found in some manuscripts, but probably began as a scribal note added circa 710 BCE, when the Phoenician texts of *Names* was standardized during the reign of King Hezekiah of Judah.

2 Codex Vaticanus: aŋgelos K̄Ū en puri flogos ek tou batou (ΑΓΓΕΛΟC K̄Ȳ ΕΝ ΠΥΡΙ ΦΛΟΓΟC ΕΚ ΤΟΥ ΒΑΤΟΥ). Translation: messenger Lord in fire (or lightning) flaming out of the bramble

- Codex Alexandrinus: aŋgelos K̄Ū en flogi puros ek tou batou (ΑΓΓΕΛΟC K̄Ȳ ΕΝ ΦΛΟΓΙ ΠΥΡΟC ΕΚ ΤΟΥ ΒΑΤΟΥ). Translation: messenger Lord in flaming fire (or lightning, wheat) out of the bramble

- LXX 18: aŋgelos kuriou ek tou batou (ΑγℓῨος ℓυℓℓιου ℓℓ τℓ υΛτℓ). Translation: messenger of lord out of the bramble

- LXX 52: aŋgelos o kuriou autō en puri flogos ek tou batou (ΑγℓῨος ο ℓυℓℓιου Λυτℓℓ ℓν ℓℓℓγι πυℓℓc ℓℓ τℓ υΛτℓ). Translation: messenger of the lord in flaming fire (or lightning) out of the bramble

- LXX 58: aŋgelos kuriou autō en puri flogos ek tou batou (ΑγℓῨος ℓυℓℓιου Λυτℓℓ ℓν ℓℓℓγι πυℓℓc ℓℓ τℓ υΛτℓ). Translation: messenger of his lord in flaming fire (or lightning) out of the bramble

- LXX 76: aŋgelos kuriou ek tou baton en flogi puros (ΑγℓῨος ℓυℓℓιου ℓℓ τℓ υΛτℓ ℓν ℓℓℓγι πυℓℓσ). Translation: messenger lord in the bramble in flaming fire (or lightning, wheat)

CHAPTER 3

- LXX 85: kuriou en puri flogos ek tou batou (ⲕⲩⲣⲓⲟⲩ ⲁⲛ ⲫⲗⲟⲅⲓ ⲡⲩⲣⲟⲥ ⲉⲕ ⲧⲟ ⲩⲃⲁⲧⲟ). Translation: lord in flaming fire (or lightning) out of the bramble

- Leningrad Codex: mal'ak Yəhōwâ 'ēlāyw bəlabbat-'ēš mittôk hassənê (מַלְאַ֨ךְ יְהֹוָ֥ה אֵלָ֛יו בְּלַבַּת־אֵ֖שׁ מִתּ֣וֹךְ הַסְּנֶ֑ה). Translation: messenger of Yahweh pillar (or in, towards) of (or in, among, with, at) in flames (or confusing bewildering) fire from inside the bramble (or bramble)

- Peshitta: mlåkh dmryå mn gw lhå dnwrå båsqå mn ḥr snyå (ܡܠܐܟܗ ܕܡܪܝܐ ܡܢ ܓܘ ܠܗܐ ܕܢܘܪܐ ܒܣܩܐ ܡܢ ܚܪ ܣܢܝܐ). Translation: messenger of master (or lord) from (or out of, through) inside flame of fire in the transformation in the bramble (or shrub)

- Targum Onkelos: 'itgəlî mal'ākā' dayyā lēh bəšalhôbît 'ešātā' migô 'asānā' (אִתְגְּלִי מַלְאֲכָא דַייָ לֵהּ בְּשַׁלְהוֹבִית אֶשָׁתָא מְגוֹ אַסָנָא). Translation: revealed messenger of the Yahweh she was in flames (or inflamed) of fire from inside thorn-bramble (or bramble)

- Targum Pseudo-Jonathan: 'itgəlê zagnûgā'ēl mal'ākā' dayyā lêh bəlahăbê 'ēšātā' migô sanyā' (אִתְגְּלֵי זַגְנוּגָאֵל מַלְאֲכָא דַייָ לֵיהּ בְּלַהֲבֵי אֵישָׁתָא מְגוֹ סָנְיָא). Translation: revealed clearness of god (or Zagzagel) messenger of the Yahweh to him in flames of fire from inside thorn-bramble (or shrub)

- Sahidic manuscript 2000: aŋgelos mpjoeis hn oušah nsate ebol hn oubatos (ⲁⲅⲅⲉⲗⲟⲥ ⲙ̅ⲡⲭⲟⲉⲓⲥ ⲏ̅ⲛ ⲟⲩϣⲁϩ ⲛ̅ⲥⲁⲧⲉ ⲉⲃⲟⲗ ⲏ̅ⲛ ⲟⲩⲃⲁⲧⲟⲥ). Translation: angel of the master in (or by) a flame of fire out of a thorn-bush

This sentence is essentially the same in all ancient sources, although some do shorten it. It appears to be another rendering of the "column of fire" (עמוד אש) that later guided the Israelites after they left Egypt, however, in this verse, the pillar was inside a bramble. The difference in the Hebrew phrases, suggests they were derived from different languages. The later Hebrew ômwd

CHAPTER 3

(עמוד) is essentially the same as the Aramaic ŏmwdå (עמודא) and the Arabic 'amūd (مُود). Conversely, the word ålyw (אליו) is of unclear origin and is of ambiguous meaning, however, it was used to denote a round shape under an arch in the Masoretic texts, which is generally translated as a column. This fiery plant messenger of god is likely a misunderstanding of what Moses wrote in his Egyptian text, as none of the Israelites were with him at this point. It is later established that he wrote the Ten Commandments in hieroglyphs, and therefore his writing was probably generally written in hieratic. It is also established that he did not speak Canaanite well, as Aaron spoke to the Israelites on his behalf.

There is a direct parallel to this fiery messenger of god found in Egyptian religion: wåḏt (𓇅𓏏𓆟), generally rendered as wadjet, also called "the green one." The term wadjet referred to a messenger of god, who specifically served several goddesses associated with the sky, dawn, dusk, or the afterlife. Wadjets were generally depicted as a flying serpents in Egyptian art, sometimes with hands and legs. A very similar creature was depicted in Old Sumerian art, the muškigĩr (𒈲𒆕), which translates as "snake with dagger." The Akkadians later interpreted this as muškuššu (𒈲𒄕𒂞), meaning "snake with fire." This serpent with a dagger or a fire was depicted as a scaly animal with arms and legs like a lion's legs, talons like an eagle, a long neck and tail, two bovine horns on its head, and a serpentine tongue. Most of these attributes were also used in the later Israelite texts to describe cherubs, suggesting a common origin.

The wadjets were also represented iconographically with the wadjet eyes (𓂀 𓂁). There were two wåḏt eyes, the Eye of Horus (𓂁), and the Eye of Ra (𓂀), one represented Venus as the morning star, and the other as Venus as the evening star. Additionally, a wadjet eye reprinted Sirius during the heliacal rising, which announced the beginning of the flood season. As such,

97

the wadjets were representatives of several goddesses, including the sky cow Hathor, and the goddess of medicine Sekhmet. In Iwnw, a wadjet was the messenger with the goddess Iusaaset, the wife of the creator god Atum. Wadjet's voice was described as being fire, however, she was also reported to be eternally green, described as the "intact one," and her name included the hieroglyph wåḏ (Ỉ) meaning "papyrus plant," which would explain where the interpretation of "bramble" came from.

The iconography of the wadjet continued within by the Israelites for almost a thousand years, as statues of the seraphs were placed inside King Solomon's temple in Jerusalem. Śārāp (שָׂרָף), the word used in the Masoretic texts, means "burning serpent" and the prophet Isaiah described the statues of the seraphs in the temple as having wings shortly before they were destroyed. When they were destroyed, the bronze statue of a serpent on a pole that Moses carved was also destroyed. It had reportedly been moved into the temple at the same time as the box of the covenant, and other artifacts from the time of Moses. This indicates that Moses statue was viewed as a seraph by the time King Solomon had the seraph statues made.

3 Codex Vaticanus: T̄S tou patros sou T̄S Abraam kai T̄S Isaak kai T̄S Iakōb (ΘC ΤΟΥ ΠΑΤΡΟC CΟΥ ΘC ΑΒΡΑΑΜ ΚΑΙ ΘC ΙCΑΑΚ ΚΑΙ ΘCΙΑΚѠΒ). Translation: god of your father, god of Abraham and god of Isaac and god of Jacob

• Codex Alexandrinus: T̄S tou patros sou o T̄S Abraam kai T̄S Isaak kai T̄S Iakōb (ΘC ΤΟΥ ΠΑΤΡΟC CΟΥ Ο ΘC ΑΒΡΑΑΜ ΚΑΙ ΘC ΙCΑΑΚΚΑΙΘCΙΑΚѠΒ). Translation: god of your father, the god of Abraham and god of Isaac and god of Jacob

• LXX 53: ṯeos tou patros sou Abraam kai ṯeos Isaak kai ṯeos Iakōb kai eipe mōisēs tis ei su (θϭoc τω πατρος σου Αυραδμ ha/ θϭoc ιℭαλι ⲕⲁⲓ ⲑⲉⲟⲥ ⲓⲁⲕⲱⲟⲩ ⲕⲁⲓ ϥⲡϭ ⲙⲱⲓⲥⲏⲥ ϫⲓⲥ ϥ ⲥⲟⲩ). Translation: god of your father Abraham and god of Isaac and god of Jacob, and Moses said "It is you"

- LXX 54: ṯeos tou patros sou Abraam kai ṯeos Isaak kai ṯeos Iakōb (ⲑⲉⲟⲥ ⲧⲱ ⲡⲁⲧⲣⲟⲥ ⲥⲟⲩ Ⲁⲩⲣⲁⲁⲙ ⲕⲁⲓ ⲑⲉⲟⲥ ⲓⲥⲁⲕ ⲕⲁⲓ ⲑⲉⲟⲥ ⲓⲁⲕⲟⲟⲩ). Translation: god of your father Abraham and god of Isaac and god of Jacob

- LXX 56: ṯeos Abraam kai ṯeos Isaak kai ṯeos Iakōb (ⲑⲉⲟⲥ Ⲁⲩⲣⲁⲁⲙ ⲕⲁⲓ ⲑⲉⲟⲥ ⲓⲥⲁⲕ ⲕⲁⲓ ⲑⲉⲟⲥ ⲓⲁⲕⲟⲟⲩ). Translation: god of Abraham and god of Isaac and god of Jacob

- LXX 58: ṯeos tōn prōn sou ṯeos Abraam kai ṯeos Isaak kai ṯeos Iakōb (ⲑⲉⲟⲥ ⲧⲱⲥ ⲱⲣⲥ ⲥⲟⲩ ⲑⲉⲟⲥ Ⲁⲩⲣⲁⲁⲙ ⲕⲁⲓ ⲑⲉⲟⲥ ⲓⲥⲁⲕ ⲕⲁⲓ ⲑⲉⲟⲥ ⲓⲁⲕⲟⲟⲩ). Translation: god before you, god of Abraham and god of Isaac and god of Jacob

- LXX 72: ṯeos tou patros sou ṯeos Abraam kai Isaak kai Iakōb (ⲑⲉⲟⲥ ⲧⲱ ⲡⲁⲧⲣⲟⲥ ⲥⲟⲩ ⲑⲉⲟⲥ Ⲁⲩⲣⲁⲁⲙ ⲕⲁⲓ ⲓⲥⲁⲕ ⲕⲁⲓ ⲓⲁⲕⲟⲟⲩ). Translation: god of your father, god of Abraham and Isaac and Jacob

- LXX 85: ṯeos tou patros sou ṯeos Abraam tou pros sou kai ṯeos Isaak kai ṯeos Iakōb (ⲑⲉⲟⲥ ⲧⲱ ⲡⲁⲧⲣⲟⲥ ⲥⲟⲩ ⲑⲉⲟⲥ Ⲁⲩⲣⲁⲁⲙ ⲧⲟⲩ ⲱⲣⲥ ⲥⲟⲩ ⲕⲁⲓ ⲑⲉⲟⲥ ⲓⲥⲁⲕ ⲕⲁⲓ ⲑⲉⲟⲥ ⲓⲁⲕⲟⲟⲩ). Translation: god of your father, god of Abraham before you and god of Isaac and god of Jacob

- LXX 135: ṯeos tou patros Abraam kai ṯeos Isaak kai ṯeos Iakōb (ⲑⲉⲟⲥ ⲧⲱ ⲡⲁⲧⲣⲟⲥ Ⲁⲩⲣⲁⲁⲙ ⲕⲁⲓ ⲑⲉⲟⲥ ⲓⲥⲁⲕ ⲕⲁⲓ ⲑⲉⲟⲥ ⲓⲁⲕⲟⲟⲩ). Translation: god of father Abraham and god of Isaac and god of Jacob

- Leningrad Codex: 'ĕlōhē 'ābîkā 'ĕlōhē 'Abrāhām 'ĕlōhē Yiṣḥāq wē'lōhē Ya'ăqōb (אֱלֹהֵי אָבִיךָ אֱלֹהֵי אַבְרָהָם אֱלֹהֵי יִצְחָק וֵאלֹהֵי יַעֲקֹב). Translation: god of you father, god of Abraham, god of Isaac, and god of Jacob

- Peshitta: ålhå dbbwk, ålhå dAbrhm, ålhå dAyshq wålhå dYoqwb (ܐܠܗܐ ܕܒܒܘܟ، ܐܠܗܐ ܕܐܒܪܗܡ، ܐܠܗܐ ܕܐܝܣܚܩ ܘܐܠܗܐ ܕܝܥܩܘܒ

CHAPTER 3

ܓܝܣܘܒ ܐܠܗܐ). Translation: god of you father, god of Abraham, god of Isaac, and god of Jacob

• Targum Onkelos: 'ĕlāhā' də'ābûk 'ĕlāhā' də'Abrāhām 'ĕlāhā' dəYishāq wē'lāhā' dəYa'ăqōb (אֱלָהָא דְאָבוּךְ אֱלָהָא דְאַבְרָהָם אֱלָהָא דְיִצְחָק וֵאלָהָא דְיַעֲקֹב). Translation: god of you father, god of Abraham, god of Isaac, and god of Jacob

• Targum Pseudo-Jonathan: 'ĕlāhêh də'ābûk 'ĕlāhêh də'Abrāhām 'ĕlāhêh dəYishāq wē'lāhêh dəYa'ăqb (אֱלָהֵיהּ דְאָבוּךְ אֱלָהֵיהּ דְאַבְרָהָם אֱלָהֵיהּ דְיִצְחָק וֵאלָהֵיהּ דְיַעֲקֹב). Translation: god of you father, god of Abraham, god of Isaac, and god of Jacob

• Sahidic manuscript 2000: anok pe pnoute mpekeiōt Abraham pnoute nIsak pnoute nIakōb (ⲀⲚⲞⲔ ⲡⲉ ⲡⲚⲞⲨⲦⲉ Ⲙ̄ⲡⲈⲔⲈⲒⲰⲦ ⲀⲂⲢⲀϨⲀⲘ ⲡⲚⲞⲨⲦⲉ Ⲛ̄Ⲓ̈ⲤⲀⲔ ⲡⲚⲞⲨⲦⲉ Ⲛ̄Ⲓ̈ⲀⲔⲰⲂ). Translation: I am the god of your fathers Abraham the god of Issac the god of Jacob

4 Codex Vaticanus: Ǩettaiōn (ΧΕΤΤΑΙⲰΝ)
• LXX 58: Ǩetgaiōn (Χⲟⲧⲅⲁⲓⲟⲟⲛ)
• Leningrad Codex: Hittî (חִתִּי). Translation: Cypriots
• Peshitta: Htyå (ܚܬܝܐ)
• Targum Onkelos: Hittā'ê (חִתָּאֵי)
• Targum Pseudo-Jonathan: Hîttā'ê (חִיתָּאֵי)
• Sahidic manuscript 2000: Ǩettaios (ΧⲈⲦⲦⲀⲒⲞⲤ)

This term has created a great deal of confusion since the misidentification of the ruins of the Neshites as being 'Hittite' in the 1800s. The modern archaeological name 'Hittite,' is not derived from an ancient name for the culture applied by themselves, or anyone else, but rather adopted from the biblical reference to a then-unknown civilization somewhere in the region. There was an ancient culture in the region called the Hattians, however, they

100

were conquered by the Neshites before 1700 BCE, and subsequently disappeared from the historic records.

The name was applied to culture today referred to as "Hittites," before the "Hittite" language had been translated, and is incorrect. Since 1906, excavations at Boğazköy, the ancient 'Hittite' capital Hattusa have uncovered more than 10,000 'Hittite' texts, including the royal achieve. The actual name of the 'Hittite' language and people was Nešili (𒉈𒅆𒇷), which is now rendered in some academic literate as Nesite or Neshite. As early as the mid-1800s some scholars disputed the identification of the Neshites as the Biblical Hittites, including the Orientalist Max Müller, who was one of many claiming the Biblical Hittites were ancient Greeks or some other Mediterranean people. Later in the Septuagint's translation of the Maccabees, the similar term Ǩettiim (Χεττιιμ) as a reference to all Greek-speaking lands, and therefore the Biblical Hittites were likely the Minoans or the Achaean Greeks.

In the 1st century CE, the Jewish historian Josephus reported that Ketima was the name of Cyrus in Aramaic, and the Ǩettim were the descendants of Noah's grandson Ǩetimus, who had settled on Cyprus. Josephus reported that the name was preserved in the Greek name of the town Kition (Κίτιον). Most historians view it as more likely that the Aramaic name was derived from the city-state of Cition, which was known as Kåtjây (𓈖 𓃾𓏤 𓅓) in Egyptian records from the New Kingdom Era in the late Bronze Age, and Kt (𐤊𐤕) or Kty (𐤊𐤕𐤉) in Phoenician records from the early Iron Age. While this may be the origin of the term, by the era of the Neo-Assyrian era, the term must have also referred to other Greek islands, as both the prophets Isaiah and Ezekiel used the term "Islands of Kittim." As the term referred to the entire island of Cyprus in Aramaic, the translations of "Cyprus" and "Cypriots" are used here.

5 Codex Vaticanus: Gergesaiōn (ⲅⲉⲣⲅⲉⲥⲁⲓⲱⲛ)

- Septuagint manuscript 58: Gergessaiōn (Γόβϛσσαγοον)
- Septuagint manuscript 135: Gersaiōn (Γόβσαγοον)
- Septuagint manuscript 246: Gerseōn (Γόβσόοον)
- Peshitta: Gergesayón (ܓܪܓܣܝܘܢ)
- Codex Lugdunensis: Gergesseorum (Çercesseoruϣ)
- Sahidic manuscript 2000: Gergesaios (ⲅⲉⲣⲅⲉⲥⲁⲓⲟⲥ)
- Ge'ez manuscripts: Gerəgesa'wan (�)

This term is missing from the list in the Leningrad Codex and Targums, but is included in every other ancient translation. The term is used in the Leningrad Codex's *Bereshít* (*Cosmic Genesis*), *Words* (*Deuteronomy*), *Joshua*, *Ezra-Nehemiah*, and *Dibrê hayyāmîm* (*1st Paralipomenon*) where it is spelled as Girgāšî (גִּרְגָּשִׁי). This group was mentioned in the bn Grgš (𒀭 𒈨𒄀) in the Bronze Age Ugaritic Texts, meaning "sons of Girgish." In the 5th century BCE, Herodotus reported a land called Gergis (Γεργισ) on the Aegean coast of Anatolia, which is likely where these people originated. In the 4th century BCE, Xenophon of Athens reported that the Gergites (Γεργιτες) lived in the northern Anatolian coast of the Aegean, near the ruins of Troy. In the 3rd century CE, Athenaeus reported that the indigenous people of the southern Anatolian coastal region around Miletus were the Gergites.

As the name was removed from this Hebrew translation and Targums, but not the other translations, it suggests that the Hebrew translation of Names was between 169 and 166 BCE, when the Maccabean Revolt broke out against the Governor of Judea, Philip the Phrygian. Phrygia was a land in western Anatolia, whose national god Sabazios was interpreted as another version of the Judean god Sabaoth under Greek rule.

CHAPTER 3

6 Codex Vaticanus: Euaiōn (ⲈⲨⲀⲒⲰⲚ)

- Septuagint manuscript 44: Ebaeōn (Ⲉⲩⲁⲓⲟⲟⲛ)
- Leningrad Codex: Ḥiûî (חִוִּי)
- Peshitta: Hwyå (ܚܘܝܐ)
- Targum Onkelos: Ḥiwā'ê (חִוָּאֵי)
- Targum Pseudo-Jonathan: Ḥîwāw'ê (חִיוָואֵי)
- Sahidic manuscript 2000: Euaios (ⲈⲨⲀⲒⲟⲥ)

The term is believed to have been derived from the name of the Hurrians, however, is derived separately from the other term Ḥōrî (חֹרִי). Ḥōrî is accepted as referring to the Hurrians, which the Egyptians called Ǩårw (𓂝𓏏 𓈎), and the Babylonians called Ǩuurri (𒆳𒌷). The Hurrians were one of the oldest cultures in the Middle East, however, became largely a slave culture within the Akkadian and Old Babylonian empires. Under the Mitanni empire, they rose to a position of wealth, and formed the noble caste. The Greek transliteration of this term was variations of Ǩorrąious (Χορραιους), which, like the Hebrew term, was used interchangeably in the texts with Euaîon (Ευαῖον) / Ḥiûî (חִוִּי), although that term generally applied to the rules and priests.

The ultimate origin of the terms Euaîon (Ευαῖον) and Ḥiûî (חִוִּי), both appear to be the cuneiform word Éān (𒂍𒀭), meaning temple or sacred. In the Amarna Letters, which date to the 1330s BCE, the term Éān (𒂍𒀭) was the name of a people, who appear to be the Mitanni, or the Mitanni-Aryan priesthood within the Mitanni. A similar correlation between the terms is found in the Septuagint's 1st Paralipomenon and Masoretic *Dibrê-hayyāmîm*, where the Greek translation uses Baithani (Βαιθανι), however, the Hebrew uses the term Mitnî (מִתְנִי). This term also refers to a group of people, meaning the underlying Edomite text the Greeks translated would have been "people of the House of Ån" (𐤉𐤕+𐤕𐤍), a direct Canaanite translation of É Ān (𒂍𒀭).

103

CHAPTER 3

While Mitnî was the transliteration used in the Edomite text that formed the basis of the Hebrew translation of *Dibrê-hayyāmîm*, it was replaced with Hiûî (חִיּוִי) in the Judahite texts, which served as the basis of most of the Masoretic texts. This likely originated in a Judahite copy of the text, after the Aramaic translation had been made, where an N (𐤍) was replaced with a W (𐤅). The Aramaic translation would have already been made in the time of King Manasseh, were the term was transliterated as Hyån (𐡄𐡉𐡍), itself a transliteration of the early Canaanite Hyån (𐤄𐤉𐤍).

The term Ebaiōn (Εβαιων), which is found as a substitute for Euaîon (Εὐαῖον) in some copies of the Septuagint for term, must have originated in an intentional alteration to the text, as there are no similar letters for B (𐤁, 𐤁, 𐤁) and Y (𐤉, 𐤉, 𐤉) in the Semitic alphabets the text was previously in. This probable origin was an Ebionite translation in the 1st century CE. The Ebionites were an early Judeo-Christian sect based in Judea before the First Jewish-Roman war. Many fled east to Mesopotamia with the Mandeans and other smaller Judahite religious groups, while others fled south into Arabia. The Arabian Ebionites are generally viewed as shaping the Islamic view of the prophet Jesus (عِيسَى).

---

7 Codex Vaticanus: eipen de o T̄S̄ Mōusei legōn oti (ЄΙΠЄΝΔЄΟ ΘСΜШΥϹЄΙΛЄΓШΝΟΤΙ). Translation: spoke and said the god to Moses

• Codex Alexandrinus: eipen de o T̄S̄ Mōusei oti (ЄΙΠЄΝΔЄΟΘС ΜШΥϹЄΙΟΤΙ). Translation: spoke yet the god to Moses

• LXX 19: apekrithē de o teos Mōusei légōn oti (ἀπόϗρίθϩ ϪϬ ο θϬος Μοουσϥ λϟγοον οϫ). Translation: replied and said the god to Moses

• LXX 53: eipen de Mōusei légōn oti (ϥπϭΝ ϪϬ Μοουσϥ λϟγοον οϫ). Translation: spoke and said to Moses

104

- LXX 106: de o ṯeos Mōusei légōn oti (Ⲇⲉ̄ ο ⲑⲉ̄ⲟⲥ Ⲙⲟⲟⲩⲥⲉ̄ ⲗⲁ̄ⲅⲅⲟⲟⲛ ⲟ]ⲓ). Translation: but said the god to Moses
- LXX 108: eipen de K̄S̄ o ṯeos Mōusei légōn oti (ⲇⲡⲉ̄ⲛ Ⲇⲉ̄ K̄Σ̄ ο ⲑⲉ̄ⲟⲥ Ⲙⲟⲟⲩⲥⲉ̄ ⲗⲁ̄ⲅⲅⲟⲟⲛ ⲟ]ⲓ). Translation: spoke and Lord the god said to Moses
- LXX 121: autō o T̄S̄ Mōusei légōn oti (Ⲁⲩⲧⲟⲟ ο Θ̄Σ̄ Ⲙⲟⲟⲩⲥⲉ̄ ⲗⲁ̄ⲅⲅⲟⲟⲛ ⲟ]ⲓ). Translation: he the god said the god to Moses
- LXX 130: eipen de K̄S̄ o ṯeos Mōusei légōn oti (ⲇⲡⲉ̄ⲛ Ⲇⲉ̄ K̄Σ̄ ο ⲑⲉ̄ⲟⲥ Ⲙⲟⲟⲩⲥⲉ̄ ⲗⲁ̄ⲅⲅⲟⲟⲛ ⲟ]ⲓ). Translation: spoke and Lord the god said to Moses
- Leningrad Codex: wayyō'mer (וַיֹּ֤אמֶר). Translation: and will say
- Peshitta: åqyrh ålhå (ܐܠܗܐ ܦܩܕܗ). Translation: commanded god
- Targum Onkelos: wa'ămar (וַאֲמַר). Translation: and say (or command)
- Targum Pseudo-Jonathan: wa'ămar (וַאֲמַר). Translation: and say (or command)
- Sahidic manuscript 2000: pejaf nae nhi pnoute mMōusēs (ⲡⲉϫⲁϥ ⲛ̄ⲁⲉ ⲛ̄ϭⲓ ⲡⲛⲟⲩⲧⲉ ⲙ̄ⲙⲱⲩ̈ⲥⲏⲥ). Translation: said in particular namely the master to Moses
- Sahidic manuscript 2002: pejaf ae nhi pnoute mMōusēs (ⲡⲉϫⲁϥ ⲁⲉ ⲛ̄ϭⲓ ⲡⲛⲟⲩⲧⲉ ⲙ̄ⲙⲱⲩ̈ⲥⲏⲥ). Translation: said in even namely the master to Moses

7 Codex Vaticanus: legōn egō eimi o Ōn (ⲗⲉⲅⲱⲛ ⲉⲅⲱ ⲉⲓⲙⲓ ⲟ ⲱⲛ). Translation: say I am the Ōn

- Codex Alexandrinus: egō eimi o Ōn (ⲉⲅⲱ ⲉⲓⲙⲓ ⲟ ⲱⲛ). Translation: I am the Ōn

CHAPTER 3

• Dead Sea Scroll 4QGen-Exoda: -hyh åšr åhyh (היהא אשר היהא-). This is a damaged version of the text found in the Leningrad Codex.

• Leningrad Codex: 'ehyeh 'ăšer 'ehəyeh (אֶהְיֶה אֲשֶׁר אֶהְיֶה). Translation: I will exist (or happen to be, own) that (or which, who, whom) I will exist (or happen to be, own)

• Peshitta: åhyh åšrhyh (ܐܗܝܗ ܐܗܝܗܪܫܐ). Translation: I will be Asrhyh

• Targum Onkelos: 'ehyeh 'ăšer 'ehəyeh (אֶהְיֶה אֲשֶׁר אֶהְיֶה). This is a direct copy of the phrase found in the Leningrad Codex.

• Targum Jerusalem: dên də'āmar lə'almā' hĕwê wahăwâ wə'ātîd ləmêmar lêh hĕwê wahăwâ (דֵין דְּאָמַר לְעָלְמָא הֱוֵי וַהֲוָה וְעָתִיד לְמֵימַר לֵיה הֱוֵי וַהֲוָה). Translation: he who said to the word 'be,' and it was, and he who he will saw to the world 'be,' and it will be. The Targum Jerusalem also includes the phrase "Tell the sons of Israel 'Ehyeh sent me to you'" (כְּדֵין תֵּימַר לִבְנֵי יִשְׂרָאֵל אֶהְיֶה שְׁלָחַנִי לְפָנֵיכֶם) at the end of the verse, repeating the Masoretic and Onkelos versions. In this Targum, Ehyê is used as a proper name, although does not appear to be one.

• Targum Pseudo-Jonathan: dên də'āmar wahăwâ 'almā' 'āmar wahăwâ kûlā' (דֵין דְּאָמַר וַהֲוָה עָלְמָא אָמַר וַהֲוָה כּוּלָא). Translation: he who spoke and the world existed, who spoke all things existed. The Targum Pseudo-Jonathan also includes "Tell the sons of Israel 'Ana, he in proper conduct and in good standing sent me to you'" (כְּדְנָא תֵּימַר לִבְנֵי יִשְׂרָאֵל אֲנָא הוּא דַּהֲוֵינָא וְעָתִיד לְמֶהֱוֵי שַׁדְרַנִי לְוַותְכוֹן), at the end of the verse. This Targum seems to mirror the Septuagint's use of Ōn as a name, however, that could also be interpreted as something like "Behold..."

• Sahidic manuscript 2000: anok pe petšoop tai te ṮE (ⲀⲚⲞⲔ ⲠⲈ ⲠⲈⲦϢⲞⲞⲠ ⲦⲀⲪ ⲦⲈ ⲐⲈ). Translation: I will exist mountain the God (assuming ⲐⲈ is a transliteration of the Greek ⲐⲈ)

CHAPTER 3

• Old Armenian manuscripts: Es em Astowats or ēn (Ես եմ Աստուած որ էս). Translation: I am God (or the sun) that is

The various Septuagint manuscripts, Leningrad Codex, Peshitta, targums, and other translations show a great deal of confusion in this verse. Some Septuagint manuscripts use the name Ōn (Ὤν), which is mirrored in the longer verse of the Targum Jerusalem with 'Ănā' (אֲנָא) being used as a name. It is also mirrored in chapter 6 of the Peshitta where Ånå (ܐܢܐ) is used as a name. Many Septuagint manuscripts omit the name Ōn, both here and later in the verse. Some manuscripts combine the sentences around the missing word, while others skip the entire sentence.

The Targum Pseudo-Jonathan's longer verse appears to be merging two older versions, because the beginning of the verse is very similar to the Septuagint's version, except the name is 'Ehyeh (אֶהְיֶה). The word 'ehyeh is also beginning of the parallel verse in the Leningrad Codex, the somewhat whimsical phrase 'ehyeh 'ăšer 'ehəyeh (אֶהְיֶה אֲשֶׁר אֶהְיֶה), meaning "I will be what I will be."

These variations of Ōm, 'Ănā', Ånå, and 'Ehyeh, as well as the singular interpretation of the word 'ĕlōhîm can all be explained if the original phrase in the late Bronze Age texts used the name ^{deity}Éa (𒀭𒂍𒀀). Elum (𒀭) was the Babylonian word for "god," which was descended from the Old Sumerian Am (𒀭), and pronounced in Neo-Sumerian as ^{deity}Anu (𒀭𒀭). ^{deity}Éa (𒀭𒂍𒀀) was the Babylonian pronunciation of the old Akkadian name Ia (𒂊𒀀), the god of life and fresh water. The Canaanite version of Ia was Ym (ים), the god of the sea, therefore transliterating ^{deity}Éa (𒀭𒂍𒀀) into the Phoenician script by Israelites at the beginning of the Iron Age would have rendered it as Ålhym (𐤀𐤋𐤄𐤉𐤌), the exact word found in Dead Sea Scroll 4QpaleoGen-Exodl, which was later transliterated into Hebrew as ålhym (אלהים). This god was certainly not Ba'al Yam, the Canaanite "lord of the sea," and so the generic word âlh (𐤀𐤋𐤄) would have been used, even if it rendered a word very similar to the Phoenician word âlhm (𐤄𐤌𐤋𐤀) meaning "goddesses."

In chapter 6, it is established that Abraham's god was named El Shaddai, which would have been spelled as ^{deity}Šadi (✳𐏐𐏓) in Old Babylonian Cuneiform, meaning that ^{deity}Éa (✳𐎹𐎹𐎹) could not have been in the pre-Mosaic texts regarding Abraham. This suggests it was added by the Levites when the lost Egyptian language *Book of Moses* was translated into Canaanite after the Israelites settled in Samaria. ^{deity}Éa (✳𐎹𐎹𐎹) could have been used as a translation of Îôhw (𓇋𓏭𓎛𓅱), the lunar calf god which was likely the deity represented by Aaron's golden calf. This would have been even more likely if the original god of Abraham was interpreted as being Ia, who had simply identified himself as Shaddai because Abraham was living in the land of the Amorites, who worshiped Shaddai.

In most verses where Exodus used the name "Ōn," Names reads Shaddai (שַׁדַּי), however, in this case contains a completely different phrase. This appears to be part of the redaction of the name Shaddai from the era of the Judahite king Manasseh. The term El Shaddai was only used 48 times in the Masoretic text, including 31 times in *Job*, 6 times in *Bereshít* (Masoretic *Cosmic Genesis*), and once in *Names*. Both the *Cosmic Genesis* and *Names* appear to have been redacted in regards to the identity of El Shaddai, as there is no reference to El Shaddai in *Cosmic Genesis*, and there is no reference to Ōn in *Names*.

The Septuagint and Masoretic translations often differ in regards to the name or title Shaddai, suggesting that the Aramaic and Canaanite source texts they worked from differed in regards to this word. The cause of the confusion over the term Shaddai, is likely due to the difference between the meaning of the word in Canaanite versus Aramaic. In Akkadian cuneiform, which was adopted as the written script by many cultures, the term was ^{deity}šēdu (𒀭𒆘), however, it referred to a "protective spirit" or "lesser god."

In the later Aramaic language, the word became šydå (𐡔𐡉𐡃𐡀), meaning "demon" in the classical sense, as a type of muse or nymph. Whereas in Canaanite, šdy (𐤔𐤃𐤉) took on different meaning, generally interpreted as "powerful" by the Early Classical Era, which is likely where the Greeks ultimately derived the term "omnipotent" (παντοκράτορος), which was used later in the Septuagint where the Masoretic text generally uses the term šdy.

This alternate interpretation of the šdy (𐤔𐤃𐤉) in Canaanite is likely due to the Egyptian New Kingdom era rule over Canaan, when Shed (𓈙𓂧𓀭, transliteration: šd), was worshiped in the region. Shed, who was often referred to as "the savior," was virtually identical to the earlier Canaanite god Resheph who was largely suppressed after the fall of the Hyksos dynasty. During the Hyksos Dynasty, Resheph was generally associated with the Egyptians gods of war, Set and Montu, however, one cult in Íwnw (Heliopolis), viewed him as the Amorite version of Atum. This belief abruptly disappeared from Egypt with the fall of the Hyksos dynasty, suggesting that Moses was a member of that cult.

In the Masoretic version of Job, Eliphaz referred to humanity as the "sons of Resheph" (בני-רשף) instead of the "sons of Adam," and then uses Shaddai as the name of a god. This god Shaddai was explicitly listed alongside the god El in Masoretic Job, whereas in the Septuagint's Job they are not explicitly listed as two separate gods. The Greek translation of Shaddai (שַׁדָּי) in Job is consistent with most of the Septuagint, using a term that translates as "omnipotent" (παντοκράτορος), however, the name El (אל) is generally translated as a word meaning "strong" (ἰσχυρὸς). It is likely because the Masoretic text lists them side by side, as "god El

CHAPTER 3

and god Shaddai," (אל-אל ואל-שדי), which the Greek translators did not do, instead routinely dropping the second reference to a god when they were listed together.

The terms "god Shaddai" (אל-שדי) and "god El" (אל-אל) are repeatedly found in Masoretic Job, and are themselves direct translations of the same terms in Akkadian Cuneiform: [deity]šēdu (✳𒁁) and [deity]Ān (✳✳). Unfortunately, the Akkadian meaning of the word šēdu was "demonic," which is likely the cause of it's redaction. Based on the linguistics of Masoretic Job, the text book existed in a Hieratic or Proto-Canaanite form during the Hyksos Dynasty, and therefore the name Resheph is not out of place, as Resheph was one of the main gods of the Hyksos rulers.

During subsequent the New Kingdom era, Resheph worship was suppressed due to his associated with the earlier Hyksos dynasty. During the early New Kingdom era, holy texts about Resheph would have been updated to Shed (𓋴𓂧𓇋), which would have been transliterated into Canaanite using the Akkadian Cuneiform script in the late New Kingdom era as [deity]šēdu (✳𒁁), before being translated into Canaanite using the Phoenician script in the early iron age as šdy (𐤔𐤃𐤉), resulting in the confusing "demonic" god in Aramaic.

The Coptic translation of this verse replaced the term with "Mountain of ṬE." Assuming that ṬE (ⲐⲈ) is a transliteration of the Greek ṬE (ΘΕ), it would have been a nomen sacrum form of ṭee (θεε), the vocative form of "god." This suggests that the word "mountain" (ⲧⲁⲓ) was originally a name, and likely a translation of Shaddai, indicating the text the Greek translators worked from read "I will be god Shaddai" (𐤔𐤃𐤉 𐤀𐤋 𐤀𐤄𐤉𐤄); however, this Greek translation does not appear to have survived to the present.

The earliest Aramaic terms within the Masoretic text is found in *Bereshít* (Masoretic *Cosmic Genesis*), in the genealogy of nations,

110

which is internally dated to between 713 and 708 BCE, meaning it would have been composed during the life of King Hezekiah. According to the Tractate Sanhedrin (103a) in the Talmud, Hezekiah's heir King Manasseh removed "the name" from the Torah, and while this is generally assumed to be the name Yahweh, the archaeological record shows that Yahwism continued to grow throughout the era, indicating it was a different name he removed. As these changes to the text appear to have been more prevalent in the Aramaic text, it is likely that it was the name Shaddai that he removed, likely substituting the Neo-Assyrian word Ān (⊬), meaning "god," which later resulted in the strange Greek translation.

As there was originally a name in the text, yet Ōn (Ων), 'Ănā' (אֲנָא), and Ånå (ܐܢܐ) would have originated with the word Ān (⊬), meaning "god," while 'Ehyeh (אָהְיָה) likely originated with Ia (𐎛), the name Yahweh is used in this translation.

8 Codex Vaticanus: KS o TS (K̄C̄ O Θ̄C̄). Translation: Lord the god

• DSS 4QGen-Exodª: -ălhy (-אלֹהי). Translation: - god. The name is missing due to damage to the text

• DSS 4QExodᵇ: Yhwh ål- (-אל יהוה). Translation: Yahweh god-. The word god is damaged, however, the text does appear to be the same as the Leningrad Codex

• Leningrad Codex: Yəhōwâ 'ĕlōhê (יְהֹוָה אֱלֹהֵי). Translation: Yahweh god

• Peshitta: mryå ålhå (ܡܪܝܐ ܐܠܗܐ). Translation: master (or lord) god (or gods)

• Targum Onkelos: Yəyā 'ĕlāhā' (יְיָ אֱלָהָא). Translation: Yahweh god

111

CHAPTER 3

• Targum Pseudo-Jonathan: Yəyā 'ēlāhā' (אֱלָהָא יְיָ). Translation: Yahweh god

• Sahidic manuscript 2000: pjoeis pnoute (ⲡϪⲟⲉⲓⲥ ⲡⲚⲟⲨⲦⲈ). Translation: the master the god

The name Yahweh was transliterated into Greek as Iaō (Ιαω) and Latin as Iaw from the Egypto-Aramaic form of Yåw (יאו). The more common form in Aramaic-speaking countries was Yhw (יהו), however, fewer examples of the name have survived in Aramaic than in Egypto-Aramaic due to the dryness of Egyptian garbage dumps. The correlation of these two names is proven by the Elephantine papyri, which include letters that were sent between Zerrubabel's Temple in Jerusalem and the Israelite Temple in Elephantine. In later translations of Hebrew texts into Greek, the name was rendered as Ieuō (Ιευω). However, none of the surviving Septuagint manuscripts include the name, indicating the Aramaic texts they were translated from used the term "lord of the gods." This phrase survives as 'ădōnāy hā'ĕlōhîm (הָאֱלֹהִים אֲדֹנָי) in the Aramaic sections of Masoretic Daniel that were not translated into Hebrew.

9 Codex Vaticanus: T̄S̄ Abraam kai T̄S̄ Isaak kai T̄S̄ Iakōb (ⲞⲤ ⲀⲂⲢⲀⲀⲘ ⲔⲀⲒ ⲞⲤ ⲒⲤⲀⲀⲔ ⲔⲀⲒ ⲞⲤ ⲒⲀⲔⲰⲂ). Translation: god of Abraham and god of Isaac and god of Jacob

• LXX 54: teos Abraam kai teos Iakōb kai teos I'saaak (ⲑⲉⲟⲥ Ⲁⲩⲣⲁⲁⲙ ⲕⲁⲓ ⲑⲉⲟⲥ Ⲓⲁⲕⲟⲟⲩ ⲕⲁⲓ ⲑⲉⲟⲥ ⲒⲤⲁⲁⲗⲓ). Translation: god of Abraham and god of Jacob and god of Isaaac

• LXX 57: teos Abraam kai teos Iakōb kai teos Isaak et' Iaka (ⲑⲉⲟⲥ Ⲁⲩⲣⲁⲁⲙ ⲕⲁⲓ ⲑⲉⲟⲥ Ⲓⲁⲕⲟⲟⲩ ⲕⲁⲓ ⲑⲉⲟⲥ ⲒⲤⲁⲁⲗⲓ ⲟⲧ' ⲒⲀⲕⲁ). Translation: god of Abraham and god of Jacob and god of Isaac also Iaka

CHAPTER 3

• LXX 707: ṭeos Abraam kai ṭeos Iakōb kai ṭeos Isaak (θ϶ος Ⲁⲩⲣⲁ̅ⲙ ⲕⲁⲩ θ϶ος ⲓⲇ̅ⲕⲟⲟⲩ ⲕⲁⲩ θ϶ος ⲓⲤⲁⲕ). Translation: god of Abraham and god of Jacob and god of Isaac

• DSS 4QExod[b]: âlwhy Âbrhm wâlwhy Yš- -y Yåqwb (אלוהי אבדחם ואלוהי ישׁ- -י ויעקוב). The text is damaged, however, likely read "god of Abraham and god of Is(aac and god) of Jacob" or "god of Abraham and god of Is(rael and god) of Jacob".

• Leningrad Codex: 'ĕlōhē 'Abrāhām Yiṣḥāq wəYa'ăqōb (אֱלֹהֵי אַבְרָהָם יִצְחָק וְיַעֲקֹב). Translation: god of Abraham Isaac and Jacob

• Peshitta: ålhå dÅbrhm, dÅyśḥq, wdYôqwb (ܐܠܗܐ ܕܐܒܪܗܡ, ܕܐܝܣܚܩ, ܘܕܝܥܩܘܒ). Translation: god of Abraham, of Isaac, and of Jacob

• Targum Onkelos: 'ĕlāhêh də'Abrāhām Yiṣḥāq wəYa'ăqōb (אֱלָהֵהּ דְּאַבְרָהָם יִצְחָק וְיַעֲקֹב). Translation: god of Abraham, Isaac, and Jacob

• Targum Pseudo-Jonathan: 'ĕlāhêh də'Abrāhām Yiṣḥāq wəYa'äqb (אֱלָהֵיהּ דְּאַבְרָהָם יִצְחָק וְיַעֲקֹב). Translation: god of Abraham Isaac and Jacob

• Sahidic manuscript 2000: pjoeis pnoute nnetneiote (ⲡϪⲟⲉⲓⲥ ⲡⲛⲟⲩⲧⲉ ⲛ̄ⲛⲉⲧⲛ̄ⲉⲓⲟⲧⲉ). Translation: the master the god of of your fathers

The various sources all generally agree on the this being the god of Abraham, Isaac, and Jacob, however, the Septuagint manuscripts often reverse the order of Isaac and Jacob. Septuagint manuscript 57 adds someone called Iaka to the list, however, this manuscript dates to the 11th century and so this is likely a later addition. The verse has survived in one Dead Sea Scroll: 4QExod[b], which includes the slightly longer text found in the Septuagint manuscripts: "god of Abraham, god of Isaac, and god of Jacob," instead of the shorter "god of Abraham, Isaac, and Jacob" found in the Leningrad Codex, Peshitta and targums. The phrase is damaged in the 4QExod[b], and

CHAPTER 3

either Isaac is spelled in an unusual way, or he was referred to as Israel in the scroll.

10 Codex Vaticanus: Kurios o ṯeos tōn paterōn umōn (ΚΥΡΙΟϹ Ο ΘΕΟϹ ΤѠΝ ΠΑΤΕΡѠΝ ΥΜѠΝ). Translation: Lord the god of the fathers of y'all

• LXX 19: Kurios o ṯeos tōn paterōn ēmōn (Κυβιος ο θϭος τῶ πλτϛοον ʰμων). Translation: Lord the god of the fathers of ours

• Leningrad Codex: Yəhōwâ 'ĕlōhē 'ăbōtêkem (יְהֹוָה אֱלֹהֵי אֲבֹתֵיכֶם). Translation: Yahweh god of your fathers

• Peshitta: mryẚ, ȧlhẚ dbbwtwywn (ܡܳܪܝܳܐ, ܐܰܠܳܗܳܐ ܕܰܒܒܘܬܘܝܘܢ). Translation: master god of your ancestors

• Targum Onkelos: Yəyā 'ĕlāhā' də'abhatkôn (יְיָ אֱלָהָא דְאֲבָהַתְכוֹן). Translation: Yahweh god of your ancestors

• Targum Pseudo-Jonathan: Yəyā 'ĕlāhā' də'abhatkôn (יְיָ אֱלָהָא דְאֲבָהַתְכוֹן). Translation: Yahweh god of your ancestors

• Sahidic manuscript 2000: pjoeis pnoute nnetneiote (ⲡϫⲟⲉⲓⲥ ⲡⲛⲟⲩⲧⲉ ⲛ̄ⲛⲉⲧⲛⲉⲓⲟⲧⲉ). Translation: the master the god of of your fathers

114

CHAPTER 4

Moses asked, "If they don't believe me and don't listen to my voice, and they say, 'God has not appeared to you,' what will I say to them?"

The Lord asked him, "What is it that is in your hand?"

He answered, "A wand."

He ordered, "Throw it on the ground."

When he threw it on the ground, it became a serpent, and Moses fled from it. The Lord ordered Moses, "Stretch out your hand, and grab its tail." So he stretched out his hand and grabbed the tail, and it became a wand in his hand. "So they will believe you, that the god of your fathers has appeared to you, the god of Abraham, and the god of Isaac, and the god of Jacob."

The Lord continued speaking to him, "Touch your hand to your chest," and touched his hand to his chest, and brought his hand away from his chest, and his hand had become like snow. He said again, "Put your hand to your chest," and he put his hand to his chest, and brought his hand away from his chest, and it was again restored to the color of his other skin. "If they will not believe you, or listen to your voice after the first sign, they will believe your voice after the second sign. If they will not believe you after these two signs, and will not listen to your voice, then you will take water from the river and pour it on the dry land, and the water which you will take from the river will become blood on the dry land."

Moses said to the Lord, "I beg Lord, I have not been sufficient in the past, that you have begun to speak to your servant. I am weak in speech, and slow-tongued."

The Lord said to Moses, "Who has given a mouth to man, and who has made the very hard of hearing, and the deaf, the seeing and the blind? Haven't I, God? Now go and I will open your mouth, and will instruct you in what you will say."

Moses said, "I beg you, Lord, appoint an able person who you will send."

The Lord was enraged by Moses, and said, "Look! Is not Aaron the Levite your brother? I know that he will surely speak to you. Look, he will come out to meet you, and seeing you he will celebrate within himself. You will speak to him, and you will put my words into his mouth, and I will open your mouth and his mouth, and I will instruct you in what you will do. He will speak for you to the people, and he will be your mouth, and you will be for him like the gods.[1] This wand that was turned into a serpent you will take in your hand, where you will work miracles."

Moses went and returned to Jethro his father-in-law, and said, "I must leave and return to my brothers in Egypt, and will see if they are still alive."

Jethro replied to Moses, "Go in health."

CHAPTER 4

In those days after some time, the king of Egypt died, and the Lord told Moses in Midian, "Go, leave for Egypt, for all that wanted your life are dead."

Moses took his wife and his children, and mounted them on the animals, and returned to Egypt, and Moses took the wand of the gods[2] in his hand. The Lord said to Moses, "When you go and return to Egypt, see all the miracles I have put into your hands, you will work before Pharaoh. I will harden his heart, and he will certainly not send away the people. You will say to Pharaoh, 'The Lord said, Israel is my firstborn, and I say to you, "Send my people away, that they may serve me. If you will not send them away, know, I will kill your firstborn son."'"

It happened that the messenger of the lord met him along the road at an inn, and wanted to kill him. Shiphrah took a stone and cut off the foreskin of her son, and fell at his feet saying, "The blood of the circumcision of my son has stopped," and he departed from them because she had said, "The blood of the circumcision of my son has stopped."

The Lord told Aaron, "Go into the wilderness to meet Moses," and he went and met him in the mountain of the gods, and they kissed each other. Moses reported to Aaron all the words of the Lord, which he sent, and all the things which he ordered him.

Moses and Aaron went and gathered the elders of the Israelites. Aaron spoke all these words, which God had said to Moses, and worked the miracles before the people. The

117

people believed and rejoiced, because God had visited the Israelites and because he saw their suffering, and the people bowed and worshiped.

CHAPTER 4 NOTES

1 Codex Vaticanus: su de autō esē ta pros ton T̄N̄ (ϹΥ ΔΕ ΑΥΤⲰ ΕϹΗ ΤΑ ΠΡΟϹ ΤΟΝ Θ̄Ν̄). Translation: but you are to him that which is before the god

• Codex Ambrosiano: su de autō esē ta pros ṯeon (ϹΥ ΔΕ ΑΥΤⲰ ΕϹΗΤΑΠΡΟϹΘΕΟΝ). Translation: but you are to him that which is before god

• LXX 18: su de autos esē ta pros ton ṯeon (συ Δϭ Δυτοσ ϭσⲑ τΔ πϱϲ τⲷ θϭⲷ). Translation: but you are to him that which is before the god

• LXX 53: su de esē autō ta pros ton ṯeon (συ Δϭ ϭσⲑ Δυτοο τΔ πϱϲ τⲷ θϭⲷ). Translation: but you for him are that which is before the god

• LXX 75: su de esei auton ta pros ton ṯeon (συ Δϭ ϭσᑫ Δυτⲷ τΔ πϱϲ τⲷ θϭⲷ). Translation: but y'all for him are that which is before the god

• LXX 344: soi de autō esē ta pros ton ṯeon (σⲷ Δϭ Δυτοο ϭσⲑ τΔ πϱϲ τⲷ θϭⲷ). Translation: but you are to him that which is before the god

• Leningrad Codex: wə'attâ tihyê-lô lē'lōhîm (וְאַתָּ֗ה תִּֽהְיֶה־לּ֖וֹ לֵֽאלֹהִֽים). Translation: and you will be like the gods

• Peshitta: wảnt bt hwyt ảlh lảlhả (ܘܐܢܬ ܗܘܝܬ ܠܗ ܠܐܠܗܐ). Translation: and you will be god the god

CHAPTER 4

- Targum Onkelos: wə'att təhê lêh lərāb (וְאַתְּ תְּהֵי לֵהּ לְרָב).
Translation: and you will consider yourself her rabbi

- Targum Jerusalem: wə'att tehĕwê lêh kitba' 'ûləpan min qŏdām
Yəyā (וְאַתְּ תְּהֱוֵי לֵיהּ כְּתְבַע אוּלְפָן מִן קֳדָם יְ׳). Translation: and you for
him to inquire instruction from before Yahweh

- Targum Pseudo-Jonathan: wə'ant tehĕwê lêh lərab təbôa'
'ûləpan min qŏdām Yəyā (וְאַנְתְּ תְּהֱוֵי לֵיהּ לְרַב תְּבוֹעַ אוּלְפָן מִן קֳדָם יְ׳).
Translation: and you for him the rabbi to inquire instruction from
before Yahweh

- Sahidic manuscript 2000: nae knašŏpe naf nnahrm pnoute (ⲛ̄ⲁⲉ
ⲕⲛⲁϣⲱⲡⲉ ⲛⲁϥ ⲛ̄ⲛⲁϩⲣ̄ⲙ ⲡⲛⲟⲩⲧⲉ). Translation: and you will
become like him before the god

- Sahidic manuscript 2148: ae knašŏpe naf nnahrm pnoute (ⲁⲉ
ⲕⲛⲁϣⲱⲡⲉ ⲛⲁϥ ⲛ̄ⲛⲁϩⲣ̄ⲙ ⲡⲛⲟⲩⲧⲉ). Translation: and you will
become like him before the god

2 Codex Vaticanus: rabdon tēn para tou T̄N̄ (ⲢⲀⲂⲆⲞⲚⲦⲎⲚⲦⲀⲢⲀ
ⲦⲞⲨⲐⲚ̄). Translation: wand (or stick, scepter, staff) that from the
god

- LXX 52: rabdon tēn apó tou teon (ⲣⲁⲩⲆⲱ ⲧ̂ⲏ ⲁⲡ̄ⲩ ⲧⲟ ⲑⲉⲱ).
Translation: wand (or stick, scepter, staff) from the god

- LXX 53: tēn rabdon para tou teon (ⲧ̂ⲏ ⲣⲁⲩⲆⲱ ⲡⲁⲣⲁ ⲧⲟ ⲑⲉⲱ).
Translation: that wand (or stick, scepter, staff) from the god

- LXX 77: tēn rabdon (ⲧ̂ⲏ ⲣⲁⲩⲆⲱ). Translation: that wand (or stick,
scepter, staff)

- Leningrad Codex: 'et-mattê hā'ĕlōhîm (אֶת־מַטֵּה הָאֱלֹהִים).
Translation: a wand (or stick, scepter, staff) of the gods

- Peshitta: lhwrâ dâlhâ (ܚܘܛܪܐ ܕܐܠܗܐ). Translation: the wand
(or stick, scepter, staff) of god

119

CHAPTER 4

• Targum Onkelos: yāt ḥûṭərā' də'it'ăbîdû bēh nisîn min qŏdām Yəyā (יָת חוּטְרָא דְּאִתְעֲבִידוּ בֵּהּ נִסִין מִן קֳדָם יְיָ). Translation: the wand (or stick, scepter, staff) with which he would abdominally smite carried away from Yahweh

• Targum Pseudo-Jonathan: wə'ant tehĕwê lêh lərab təbôa' 'ûləpan min qŏdām Yəyā (וְאַנְתְּ תֶּהֱוֵי לֵיהּ לְרַב תְּבוֹעַ אוּלְפָן מִן קֳדָם יְיָ). Translation: and you for him the rabbi to inquire instruction from before Yahweh

• Sahidic manuscript 2000: nae ji mpherōb pebol hitootf mpnoute (ⲚⲀⲈ ϪⲒ ⲘⲠϬⲈⲢⲰⲂ ⲠⲈⲂⲞⲖ ϨⲒⲦⲞⲞⲦϤ ⲘⲠⲚⲞⲨⲦⲈ). Translation: and take the rod in his hand of the god

CHAPTER 5

After this Moses and Aaron went to Pharaoh and said to him, "The lord of the god of Israel has said the following, 'Send my people away, that they may have a feast to me in the wilderness.'"

Pharaoh asked, "Who is he that I should listen to his voice and that I should send away the Israelites? I do not know the Lord, and I will not let Israel go!"

They said to him, "The god of the Habirus has called us to him. We will go on a three days' journey into the wilderness so we can sacrifice to our god, in case at any time death or slaughter happens to us."

The king of Egypt asked them, "Why do you, Moses and Aaron, turn the people from their work? Return each of you to your work!" Pharaoh said, "Now look, the people are very numerous. Let's not give them rest from their work." The Pharaoh gave orders to the taskmasters of the people and the accountants, "You will no longer give straw to the people for brick-making as before, but let them go themselves, and collect straw for themselves. You will impose on them daily the quota of brick-making which they perform. You will not abate anything, for they are lazy. Therefore have they cried, saying, 'Let us go and make sacrifices to our god.' Let the works of these men be made grievous, and let them care for these things, and not care for vain words."

CHAPTER 5

The taskmasters and the accountants hurried them, and they said to the people, "So says Pharaoh, 'I will give you straw no longer.' Go you, yourselves, get for yourselves straw whenever you can find it, for nothing is diminished from your quota."

So the people were dispersed in all the land of Egypt, to gather stubble for straw, and the taskmasters hurried them, saying, "Fulfill your regular daily tasks, even as when straw was given you."

The accountants of the race of the Israelites, who were set over them by the masters of Pharaoh, were scourged, men saying, "Why have you not fulfilled your quotas of brick-making as previously, today also?" The accountants of the Israelites went in and cried to Pharaoh, saying, "Why do you act so to your servants? Straw is not given to your servants, and they tell us to make bricks, and see your servants have been whipped. You will, therefore, injure your people."

He said to them, "You are lazy, you are idlers! Therefore you say, 'Let us go and sacrifice to our god.' Now then go and work, for straw will not be given to you, yet you will return the quota of bricks."

The accountants of the Israelites saw themselves in a terrible plight, men saying, "You will not fail from the brick-making to deliver that which belongs to each day."

They met Moses and Aaron coming out to meet them as they returned from Pharaoh, and they said to them, "The Lord will look on you and judge you, for you have made our savior abominable before Pharaoh, and before his servants, to put a sword into his hands to kill us."

Moses turned to the Lord, and said, "I beg, Lord, why have you afflicted these people? And also why have you sent me? From the time that I went to Pharaoh to speak in your name, he has punished these people, and you have not delivered your people."

CHAPTER 6

The Lord said to Moses, "Now you will see what I will do to Pharaoh. He will send them away with a mighty hand, and with a high arm will he throw them out of his land."

The gods seized Moses,[1] and said, "I'm Yahweh,[2] and I appeared to Abraham, Isaac, and Jacob, as their god Shaddai,[3] and I did not tell them my name was Yahweh. I established my covenant with them, to give them the land of the Canaanites, the land in which they stayed, in which previously they lived as strangers. I listened to the groaning of the Israelites the affliction with which the Egyptians enslave them and I remembered your covenant. Go, speak to the Israelites, and say, 'I am the Lord, and I will lead you out from the tyranny of the Egyptians, and I will deliver you from slavery, and I will ransom you with a high arm, and great judgment. I will take you to be a people for myself, and be your god, and you will know that I am the lord of the gods, who brought you out from the tyranny of the Egyptians. I will bring you into the land concerning which I stretched out my hand to give it to Abraham and Isaac and Jacob, and I will give it to you for an inheritance. I am the Lord.'"

Moses spoke so to the sons of Israel, and they did not listen to Moses for fearfulness and their hard tasks.

CHAPTER 6

The Lord said Moses, "Go speak to Pharaoh, king of Egypt, tell him that he must send out the Israelites from his land."

Moses replied to the Lord, "Look, the Israelites did not listen to me, so why will Pharaoh listen to me? I am not eloquent."

The Lord spoke to Moses and Aaron and gave them an order for Pharaoh king of Egypt, that he should send out the Israelites out of the land of Egypt.

These are the heads of the houses of their families: the sons of Reuben the firstborn of Israel; Enoch and Phallu, Hezron, and Carmi, this is the families of Reuben.

The sons of Simeon: Jemuel and Jimna, and Ohad, and Jachin and Zohar, and Saul the son of a Phoenician woman, these are the families of the sons of Simeon.

These are the names of the sons of Levi according to their families, Gershon, Kohath, and Merari, and the years of the life of Levi were a hundred and thirty-seven. These are the sons of Gershon: Libni, and Shimei, the houses of their family. The sons of Kohath: Amram and Izhar, Hebron, and Uzziel, and the years of the life of Kohath were a hundred and thirty-three years.

The sons of Merari: Mahali, and Mushi, these are the houses of the families of Levi, according to their families. Amram took as wife Jochebed the daughter of his father's brother, and she carried for him both Aaron and Moses, and Mariam their sister: and the years of the life of Amram were a hundred and thirty-two[4] years.

CHAPTER 6

The sons of Izhar: Korah, and Nepheg, and Zichri.

The sons of Uzziel: Mishael, and Elizaphan, and Zithri.

Aaron took for himself as wife Elisabeth, the daughter of Amminadab's sister Nahshon, and she carried for him Nadab, Abihu, Eleazar, and Ithamar.

The sons of Korah: Assir, and Elkanah, and Abiasaph, these are the generations of Korah.

Eleazar the son of Aaron took to himself for a wife one of the daughters of Phutiel, and she carried fot him Phinehas. These are the heads of the family of the Levites, according to their generations.

This is Aaron and Moses, who God told to bring the Israelites out of the land of Egypt with their forces. These are those who spoke with Pharaoh, king of Egypt, and Aaron himself and Moses brought out the Israelites from the land of Egypt, in the day in which the Law spoke to Moses in the land of Egypt. Then the Lord said to Moses, "I am the Lord. Tell Pharaoh, king of Egypt whatever I tell you."

Moses replied to the Lord, "Look, I am not good at speech, and why will Pharaoh listen to me?"

CHAPTER 6 NOTES

1 Codex Vaticanus: eipen kurios pros Mōusēn (ειπεν κγριοc προcμωγchν). Translation: said lord to Moses

- LXX 44: eipen de kurios pros Mōusēn (ϥπαν Δϭ ⲕⲩⲣⲓⲟⲥ ⲡⲣⲟⲥ Ⲙⲟⲟⲩⲥⲓⲱ). Translation: said yet lord to Moses

- Leningrad Codex: wayədabbēr 'ĕlōhîm 'el-mōšê wayyō'mer 'ēlāyw (וַיְדַבֵּר אֱלֹהִים אֶל־מֹשֶׁה וַיֹּאמֶר אֵלָיו). Translation: and seized gods into Moses, and said to him

- Peshitta: åmyrh qryh lMwšå (ܐܡܝܪܗ ܩܪܝܗ ܠܡܘܫܐ). Translation: recite (or say) reading to Moses

- Targum Onkelos: ûmallîl Yəyā 'im Mšê (וּמַלִּיל יְיָ עִם מֹשֶׁה). Translation: and at night Yahweh near Moses

- Targum Pseudo-Jonathan: wa'ămar Yəyā ləMšê (וְאָמַר יְיָ לְמֹשֶׁה). Translation: and said Yahweh to Moses

- Sahidic manuscript 2000: apnoute šaje mn Mōusēs (ⲁⲡⲛⲟⲩⲧⲉ ϣⲁϫⲉ ⲙⲛ ⲙⲱⲩ̄ⲥⲏⲥ). Translation: and the god speak to Moses

The version of the verse found in *Names* is longer, and most likely preserves the original meaning of the verse, in which Moses experienced seizures, which was considered a sign of a prophets. The Peshitta verse claims this took place at night, implying it was a dream, however, this way likely part of the astrological edits found in the Peshitta's version of *Exodus*.

2 Codex Vaticanus: egō K̄S̄ (ⲉⲅⲱⲕ̄ⲥ̄). Translation: I'm Lord

- LXX 19: egō kúrios o ţeos (ⲉⲅⲱ̄ ⲕⲁⲃⲣⲓⲟⲥ ⲟ ⲑ́ⲉⲟⲥ). Translation: I'm lord the god

- Leningrad Codex: 'ănî Yəhōwâ (אֲנִי יְהֹוָה). Translation: I'm Yahweh

- Peshitta: ånå ånå mryå (ܐܢܐ ܐܢܐ ܡܪܝܐ). Translation: I'm Ana master (or lord)

- Targum Onkelos: 'ănā' yəyā (אֲנָא יְיָ). Translation: I'm Yahweh

- Targum Pseudo-Jonathan: 'ănā' yəyā (אֲנָא יְיָ). Translation: I'm Yahweh

• Sahidic manuscript 2000: anok pe pjoeis (ⲁⲛⲟⲕ ⲡⲉ ⲡϫⲟⲉⲓⲥ). Translation: I am the master

• Old Armenian manuscripts: Yes Yes yem ter (Ես Ես եմ տէր). Translation: I I be master (or owner)

• Ge'ez manuscripts: inē gētawi nenyi (እነ ጌታዊ ነኒ). Translation: I'm the lord I am.

The standard reading of the Septuagint's verse is incomplete, either showing that the name Yahweh was redacted, or that "of the gods" was redacted. Both readings are supported, either in the Masoretic version or the minority Septuagint manuscripts that add "the god" (ο θεοσ). The Peshitta, Ge'ez, Old Armenian manuscripts, and Justin Martyr's quote from the 2nd century suggest a third possibility, that an older version of the text once included the term that was translated as Ōm (Ωμ) and 'Ănā' (אֲנָא) in chapter 3, and later in this chapter. Martyr's quote was "I I'm lord" (εγω ειμι Κυριος), which is paralleled in the Old Armenian and Ge'ez manuscripts, indicating they were translated from a verse that read like the Peshitta. If the second ånå (ܐܢܐ) in the Peshitta is ultimately derived from the dinger (✳) in the cuneiform precursor to the text, then it would probably have originally been Ia (𒅀) before being redacted, and so the name Yahweh is imported from the Leningrad Codex.

3 Codex Vaticanus: T̄S̄ Ōn (ⲐⲤ ⲰⲚ). Translation: god On

• Septuagint manuscript 318: teos ōn (θεος ων). Translation: god real

• Leningrad Codex: 'ēl šadday (אֵל שַׁדָּי). Translation: god Shaddai (or powerful)

• Peshitta: åylšdy (ܐܝܠܫܕܝ)

CHAPTER 6

- Targum Onkelos: 'ēl šaddāy (אֵל שַׁדָּי). Translation: god Shaddai (or demonic, ghoulish)

- Targum Jerusalem: 'ĕlāhā' šəmayā' (אֱלָהָא שְׁמַיָּא). Translation: god sky

- Targum Pseudo-Jonathan: 'ēl šadāy (אֵל שַׁדָּי). Translation: god Shaddai (or demonic, ghoulish)

- Sahidic manuscript 2000: eeišoop nau nnoute (ⲉⲉⲓϣⲟⲟⲡ ⲛⲁⲩ ⲛ̄ⲛⲟⲩⲧⲉ). Translation: I am existing as a vision of the god

The Masoretic verse confirms that the name Shaddai was viewed as being in the pre-Mosaic texts by the author. The term El Shaddai was used 48 times in the Masoretic texts, including 31 times in the book of Job, and 6 times in *Bereshít* (*Cosmic Genesis*), but only once in *Names* (*Exodus*). El Shaddai was the supreme god of the Amorites, who they called Bel Šadi (𒂗𒂄𒁀), and who as known as [ilu]Šadi (𒀭𒂄𒁀) by the Babylonians at the time, although the name [ilu]Amurru (𒀭𒈥𒌅) was more common, meaning "western god" as the Amorites lived to the west of the Babylonians.

Both the *Cosmic Genesis* / *Bereshít* and *Exodus* / *Names* appear to have been redacted in regards to the names El Shaddai, Ōn / 'Ănā', and 'Ehyeh, as there is no reference to El Shaddai in *Cosmic Genesis*, no reference to Ōn / 'Ănā' in *Names*, and no a reference of 'Ehyeh in *Exodus*. Ōn is used as a Greek translation for both Shaddai and 'Ehyeh in *Exodus*, while in *Cosmic Genesis* the translation of Masoretic Shaddai is "Omnipotent" (παντοκράτορος). The redaction of El Shaddai from the Aramaic version of *Cosmic Genesis* likely took place under the rule of King Manasseh of Judah, who was reported to have removed the name of god from the Torah circa 700 BCE, as the name continued to be used in Samaritan texts. The substitution of Ān (𒀭) for [ilu]Šadi (𒀭𒂄𒁀) in the Aramaic version of *Exodus* likely happened around the same time in Samaria. As the original term must have been ^{ilu}Šadi (✳🝔❮⟠), the term "god Shaddai" is imported from the Leningrad Codex.

4 Codex Vaticanus: ekaton triakonta dyo (ЄΚΑΤΟΝ ΤΡΙΑΚΟΝΤΑΔΥΟ). Translation hundred thirty two (132)

• Codex Alexandrinus: ekaton triakonta ex (ЄΚΑΤΟΝ ΤΡΙΑΚΟΝΤΑЄΖ). Translation hundred thirty six (136)

• Leningrad Codex: šeba' ûšəlšîm ûmə'at (שֶׁבַע וּשְׁלֹשִׁים וּמְאַת). Translation: seven and thirty and hundred (137)

• Peshitta: måå wtltyn wšbò (ܡܐܐ ܘܬܠܬܝܢ ܘܫܒܥ). Translation: hundred and thirty and seven (137)

• Targum Onkelos: mə'â ûtəlātîn ûšəba' (מְאָה וּתְלָתִין וּשְׁבַע). Translation: hundred and thirty and seven (137)

• Targum Pseudo-Jonathan: mə'â ûtəlātîn ûšəba' (מְאָה וּתְלָתִין וּשְׁבַע). Translation: hundred and thirty and seven (137)

• Sahidic manuscript 2000: še mabcašfe (ϣЄ ΜΑΒϹΑϢϥЄ). Translation: hundred thirty-seven (137)

CHAPTER 7

The Lord told Moses, "I have given you the words of the gods for Pharaoh, and Aaron your brother will be your spokesman. You will say to him all things that I order you, and Aaron your brother will tell Pharaoh, that he should send the Israelites out of his land. I will harden the heart of Pharaoh, and I will multiply my signs and wonders in the land of Egypt. Pharaoh will not listen to you, and I will lay my hand on Egypt and will bring out my people the Israelites with my power out of the land of Egypt with great vengeance. All the Egyptians will know that I am the Lord, stretching out my hand on Egypt, and I will bring out the Israelites out of the middle of them."

Moses and Aaron did as the Lord commanded them. Moses was eighty years old, and Aaron his brother was eighty-three years old when they spoke to Pharaoh. The Lord spoke to Moses and Aaron, saying, "Now if Pharaoh should speak to you, saying, 'Give us a sign or a wonder,' then will you say to your brother Aaron, 'Take your wand and throw it on the ground before Pharaoh,' and before his servants, and it will become a serpent."

Moses and Aaron went in before Pharaoh, and before his servants, and they did so, as the Lord commanded them, and Aaron threw down his wand before Pharaoh, and before his servants, and it became a serpent. But Pharaoh called together the wise men of Egypt, and the sorcerers and the charmers also of the Egyptians did likewise with their sorcery. They each threw down their wands, and they became serpents, but the wand of Aaron swallowed up their wands. And the heart of Pharaoh was hardened, and he did not listen to them, as the Lord had commanded.

The Lord said to Moses, "The heart of Pharaoh is made hard so that he would not let the people go. Go to Pharaoh early in the morning. Look, he goes out to the water, and you will meet him on the bank of the river, and you will take in your hand the wand that was turned into a serpent. You will say to him, 'Yahweh the god of the Habirus has sent me to you, saying, "Send my people away, that they may serve me in the wilderness," and, see, until now you have not listened.' The Lord says, 'So will you know that I am the Lord, look, I strike with the wand that is in my hand on the water which is in the river, and it will change it into blood. The fish that are in the river will die, and the river will stink afterward, and the Egyptians will not be able to drink water from the river.'"

The Lord said to Moses, "Say to your brother Aaron, 'Take your wand in your hand and stretch out your hand over the waters of Egypt, and their rivers, and their canals, and their ponds, and all their standing water,' and it will become blood. There was blood in all the land of Egypt, both in vessels of wood and of stone."

Moses and Aaron did as the Lord commanded them, and Aaron having lifted his hand with his wand, struck the water in the river before Pharaoh, and before his servants, and changed all the water in the river into blood. The fish in the river died, and the river stank thereupon, and the Egyptians could not drink water from the river, and the blood was in all the land of Egypt. The charmers also of the Egyptians did so with their sorcery, and the heart of Pharaoh was hardened, and he did not listen to them, even as the Lord said. Pharaoh turned and entered into his house, and he did not pay attention even to this. All the Egyptians dug round about the river, to drink water, as they could not drink water from the river, and seven days passed after the Lord has struck the river.

CHAPTER 8

The Lord said to Moses, "Go to Pharaoh, and say to him, 'the Lord says, send out my people, that they may serve me. If you will not send them away, I punish all your coasts with frogs, and the river will swarm with frogs, and they will go up and enter into your houses, and into your bedrooms, and on your beds, and on the houses of your servants, and of your people and on your dough, and on your ovens. On you, and on your servants, and on your people, will the frogs come up.'"

The Lord said to Moses, "Tell Aaron your brother, 'Stretch out your hand and wand over the rivers, and the canals, and the pools, and bring up the frogs.'"

Aaron stretched out his hand over the waters of Egypt and brought up the frogs, and the frogs were brought up and covered the land of Egypt. The charmers of the Egyptians also did likewise with their sorcery and brought up the frogs on the land of Egypt. Pharaoh called Moses and Aaron, and said, "Pray for me to the Lord, and let him take away the frogs from me and my people, and I will send them away, and they will sacrifice to the Lord."

Moses said to Pharaoh, "Pick a time for me, when I will pray for you and your servants, and your people, to make the frogs disappear from you, and your people, and your houses, only in the river will they be left behind."

CHAPTER 8

He replied, "Tomorrow!"

He said, therefore, "As you have said. That you may know, that there is no other god like the lord of the gods. The frogs will be removed away from you, and from your houses and villages, and your servants, and your people, they will only be left in the river. Moses and Aaron left Pharaoh, and Moses cried to the Lord concerning the restriction of the frogs, as Pharaoh appointed him. The Lord did as Moses said, and the frogs died out of the houses, and out of the villages, and out of the fields. They gathered them together in heaps, and the land stank.

When Pharaoh saw that there was relief, his heart was hardened, and he did not listen to them, as the Lord had said. The Lord said to Moses, "Tell Aaron, 'Stretch out your wand in your hand and strike the dust of the land, and there will be lice both on man, and on quadrupeds, and in all the land of Egypt.'"

So Aaron stretched out his wand with his hand and struck the dust of the land, and the lice were on men and quadrupeds, and there were lice in all the dust of the land. The charmers also did so with their sorcery, to bring up the lice, and they could not. The lice were both on the men and the quadrupeds. So the charmers said to Pharaoh, "This is the finger of the god."

But the heart of Pharaoh was hardened, and he did not listen to them, as the Lord had said. The Lord said to Moses, "Rise early in the morning, and stand before Pharaoh, and

CHAPTER 8

Look, he will go out to the water, and you will say to him, 'The Lord says, "Send away my people, that they may serve me in the wilderness. If you will not let my people go, I send to you, and your servants, and your people, and your houses, the dog-fly, and the houses of the Egyptians will be filled with the dog-fly, all throughout the land.[1] I will distinguish marvelously in that day the land of Goshen, on which my people dwell, in which the dog-fly will not be, that you may know that I am the lord of the gods in all the land. I will put a difference between my people and your people, and tomorrow will this be on the land."'"

The Lord did so, and the dog-fly came in abundance into the houses of Pharaoh, and the houses of his servants, and across all the land of Egypt, and the land was destroyed by the dog-fly. Pharaoh called Moses and Aaron, saying, "Go and sacrifice to your gods in the land."

Moses said, "It can't be so, for we will sacrifice to the lord of the gods before the abominations of the Egyptians, as if we sacrifice before the abominations of the Egyptians, we will be stoned. We will go on a journey of three days into the wilderness, and we will sacrifice to our the lord of the gods, exactly as we were told."

Pharaoh said, "I will let you go, and you sacrifice to your gods in the wilderness, but do not go very far away. Pray then for me to the Lord."

Moses said, "I will go out from you and pray to God, and the dog-fly will depart both from your servants, and from your people tomorrow. Do not, Pharaoh, deceive again, and not send the people away to do sacrifice to the Lord."

Moses went out from Pharaoh and prayed to God. The Lord did as Moses asked, and removed the dog-fly from Pharaoh, and his servants, and his people, and there were none left. Pharaoh hardened his heart, even on this occasion, and he would not send the people away.

CHAPTER 8 NOTES

1 This plague seems to be related to the Ugaritic text's story of Ba'al's ability to control flies. This Canaanite story likely gave rise to the Zeus Apomyios cult in Greece, in which Zeus was believed to protect people from flies. The Canaanite term likely also gave rise to the Baalzebub (Βααλζεβουβ) and Baal Muian (Βααλ Μυιαν) of the Septuagint's *2nd Kingdoms*, and Ba'al Zəbûb (בַּעַל זְבוּב) from the Masoretic *Kings*.

CHAPTER 9

The Lord said to Moses, "Go to Pharaoh and say to him, "Yahweh the god of the Habirus says, 'Send my people away so they may serve me. If however, you will not send my people away, but yet detain them, the hand of the Lord will be on your livestock in the fields, the horses, donkeys, camels, oxen, and sheep, a very great death. I will make a marvelous distinction in that time between the livestock of the Egyptians, and the livestock of the Israelites, nothing will die of all that is of the children of Israel. God fixed a limit, saying, tomorrow the Lord will do this thing on the land.'"

The Lord did this the next day, and all the livestock of the Egyptians died, but none of the livestock of the Israelites died. When Pharaoh saw that none of all the livestock of the Israelites had died, the heart of Pharaoh was hardened, and he did not let the people go.

The Lord said to Moses and Aaron, "Take handfuls of ashes from a furnace and let Moses throw it towards the sky in front of Pharaoh his servants. Let it become dust over all the land of Egypt, and there will be inflamed sores breaking out both on men and animals across all the land of Egypt."

So he took of the ashes from a furnace before Pharaoh, and Moses scattered it towards the sky, and it became inflamed sore breaking out both on men and animals. The sorcerers could not stand before Moses because of the sores, for the sores were on the sorcerers, and in all the land of Egypt. The Lord hardened Pharaoh's heart, and he did not listen to them, as the Lord appointed.

The Lord said to Moses, "Rise early in the morning and stand before Pharaoh, and say to him, 'Yahweh the gods of the Habirus, says, 'Send away my people so they may worship me. Until now I sent out all my plagues into your heart and the heart of your servants and your people, so you may know that there is not another like me in all the land. Now, I will stretch out my hand and strike you and kill your people, and you will be consumed from off the land. For this purpose have you been preserved, that I might display in you my strength and that my name might be published in all the land. Do you then yet work to hinder my people, and not to let them go? Look, tomorrow at this hour I will rain intense hail, such as has not been in Egypt from the time it was created until this day. Now then hurry to gather your livestock, and all that you have in the fields, for all the men and livestock as many as will be found in the fields, and will not enter into a house, will die.'"

Those of the servants of Pharaoh that feared the words of the Lord gathered his livestock into his houses. Those that did not listen in his mind to the word of the Lord, left the livestock in the fields. The Lord said to Moses, "Stretch out your hand to the sky, and there will be hail through all the land of Egypt, both on the men and the livestock, and all the plants in the land. Moses stretched out his hand to the sky, and the Lord sent thunder and hail, and the fire ran along on the ground, and the Lord rained hail on all the land of Egypt. There was hail and flaming fire mingled with the hail, and the hail was more intense than before in Egypt or from then onward.[1] The hail struck in all the land of Egypt both man and animal, and the hail struck all the grass in the field, and the hail broke in pieces all the trees in the field. Only in the land of Goshen where the Israelites were, it did not hail.

Pharaoh sent and called Moses and Aaron, and said to them, "I have sinned this time. The Lord is righteous, and I and my people are wicked. Pray then for me to the Lord, and let him cause the thunder of God to stop, and the hail and the fire, and I will send you out and you will no longer be here."

Moses said to him, "When I will have departed from the city, I will stretch out my hands to the Lord, and the thunder will stop and the hail and the rain will stop, that you may know that the land is the Lord's, but as for you and your servants, I know that you still do not fear the Lord."

The flax and the barley were struck, for the barley was in the ear, and the flax was seeding. But the wheat and the rye were not struck, for they were late. Moses went out from the city of Pharaoh and stretched out his hands to the Lord, and the thunders ceased and the hail and the rain did not fall on the land. When Pharaoh saw that the rain and the hail and the thunders stopped, he continued to sin, and he hardened his heart and the hearts of his servants. The heart of Pharaoh was hardened, and he did not send away the Israelites, as the Lord had told Moses.

CHAPTER 9 NOTES

1 This plague of hail and fiery hail, along with the preceding plague of ash, and the subsequent plague of darkness, all seem to indicate a massive volcanic eruption in the northern hemisphere, such as the Minoan eruption of the island of Thera (Santorini), which took place during the rule of King Apepi of Northern Egypt, circa 1583 BCE. The Tempest Stele of Ahmose I, from 1582 BCE, described a time of storms like the ones depicted in Exodus, and likely weakened the Hyksos enough that Ahmose, the king of Southern Egypt, could conquer the north. The Minoan eruption was one of the largest in recorded history, with over 100 km³ of debris thrown into the sky. Ahmose I was the founder of the 18th Dynasty that reunited Egypt after the previous Hyksos dynasty had been driven out of Lower Egypt.

The 1st century Jewish General and Historian Josephus claimed the ancestors of the Israelites were the Hyksos, and the Torah's history had become corrupted, and therefore, if one accepted his claims, the king in Exodus would have been Ahmoses I, and Moses would have likely been Khamudi, the last of the Hyksos kings in northern Egypt. This claim has been rejected by almost all scholars, and it is not clear why Josephus would have believed this.

An alternate theory would be that the king in Exodus was Apepi, who died during the fallout of the Minoan eruption at the Sea of Papyrus incident. His own son, Prince Apepi, seems to have died immediately before this during the eruption, supporting the idea that the "firstborn" of the king died. Kamose, the southern king, died a few months later in a failed invasion of northern Egypt; however, his heir Ahmose I sailed up the Nile a few months later and surveyed the damage of the storms. He does not appear to have experienced much resistance south of the Nile Delta. Iwnw

(Heliopolis) fell without resistance, supporting the idea that the authorities in the town had fled. Ahmoses then fought a decade-long war to capture the Hyksos capital of Avaris, circa 1572 BCE, and then a war to capture the Hyksos fortified city of Sharuhen in southern Canaan, circa 1567 BCE. In 1560 BCE, he sent a campaign into Djahy, the Bronze Age precursor to the Iron Age Kingdom of Judah. The years for these events are debated, and these years are based on the radiocarbon dating of Ahmose's corpse to circa 1557 BCE.

This would explain some of the strange events described during the exodus, but would mean that the era of the Exodus was significantly earlier than the estimated life of Moses between 1391 and 1271 BCE by Rabbinical Jews. Nevertheless, it does correspond with the estimated life of Moses circa 1592 BCE, calculated by Jerome, and circa 1571 BCE, calculated by James Ussher.

CHAPTER 10

The Lord said to Moses, "Go to Pharaoh, for I have hardened his heart and the hearts of his servants, that these signs may come on them, in order that you may tell your children, and your children's children, in how many ways I have insulted the Egyptians, and my wonders which I worked among them, and you will know that I am the Lord."

Moses and Aaron went in before Pharaoh, and they said to him, "Yahweh the gods of the Habirus said, 'How long do you refuse to obey me? Send my people away, that they may serve me. But if you will not send my people away, Look, at this hour tomorrow, I will bring an abundance of locusts on all your lands. They will cover the face of the land, and you will not be able to see the land, and they will devour all that is left of the abundance of the land, which the hail has left you, and will devour every tree that grows for you on the land. Your houses will be filled, and the houses of your servants, and all the houses in all the land of the Egyptians, things which your fathers have never seen, nor their forefathers, from the day that they were on the land until this day.'"

Moses turned away and departed from Pharaoh, and the servants of Pharaoh said to him, "How long will this be a snare to us? Send away the men, so they may serve their god. Will you have Egypt be destroyed?"

CHAPTER 10

They brought back both Moses and Aaron to Pharaoh, and he said to them, "Go and serve your god. But, who are those that are going with you?"

Moses answered, "We will go with the young and the old, with our sons and daughters, and sheep and oxen, for it is a feast of the lord."

He replied to them, "So let the Lord go with you. I'll send you away, but must I send away your property also? I see that evil has attached itself to you. No, just let the men go and serve your god, as that is what you are seeking," and they threw them out from the presence of Pharaoh.

The Lord said to Moses, "Stretch out your hand over the land of Egypt, and let locusts come across the land, and they will devour every plant in the land, and all the fruit of the trees, which the hail left."

Moses lifted his wand towards the sky, and the Lord brought a south wind on the land, all that day and all that night. The morning dawned, and the south wind brought up the locusts and deposited them all over the land of Egypt. They landed in large numbers over all the territory of Egypt. Before then there were never so many locusts, and neither will there be again. They covered the face of the land, and the land was wasted, and they devoured all the plants of the land, and all the fruit of the trees, which was left by the hail, there was nothing green left on the trees, nor all the shrubs of the field, in all the land of Egypt.

CHAPTER 10

Pharaoh rushed to call Moses and Aaron, saying, "I have sinned before the lord of the gods, and against you. Accept therefore my sin again this time, and pray to the lord of the gods, and let him take away from me this death."

Moses went out from Pharaoh and prayed to God, and the Lord brought in the opposite direction a strong wind from the sea, and took up the locusts and threw them into the Papyrus Sea, and there were no locusts left along all the coasts of Egypt. The Lord hardened the heart of Pharaoh again, and he did not send away the Israelites.

The Lord said to Moses, "Stretch out your hands to the sky, and let there be darkness across the land of Egypt, a darkness that may be felt."

Moses stretched out his hand to the sky, and there was darkness, including a storm over all the land of Egypt for three days. For three days no man saw his brother, and no man rose up from his bed for three days, but all the Israelites had light in all the places where they were.

Pharaoh called Moses and Aaron, saying, "Go, serve the lord of the gods, only leave behind your sheep and your oxen, and let your other property go with you."

Moses replied, "Not unless you will give us whole burnt offerings and sacrifices, which we will sacrifice to the lord of the gods. Our livestock will go with us, and we will not leave a hoof behind, as from them we will sacrifice to the lord of the gods. We won't know in what manner we will serve the lord of the gods until we arrive there."

CHAPTER 10

But the Lord hardened the heart of Pharaoh, and he would not let them go, and Pharaoh said, "Leave me, beware of seeing me again because on that day you will die."

Moses replied, "As you have said, I will not come before you again."

CHAPTER 11

The Lord said to Moses, "I will bring one more plague on Pharaoh and Egypt, and after that, he will send you away, and when he sends you out with everything, he will indeed drive you out. Speak therefore secretly in the ears of the people, and let everyone borrow from his neighbor jewels, silver, gold, and clothing."

The Lord gave his people favor in the sight of the Egyptians, and they lent to them as the man Moses was very important before the Egyptians, and before Pharaoh and his servants.

Moses said, "The Lord said, 'About midnight I go out into the middle of Egypt, and every firstborn in the land of Egypt will die, from the firstborn of Pharaoh who sits on the throne, to the firstborn of the slave-woman that is by the mill, and to the firstborn of all livestock. There will be a great cry through all the land of Egypt, such as has not been, and such will not be repeated again. But among all the Israelites will not a dog snarl with his tongue, either at man or animal, that you may know how wide a distinction the Lord will make between the Egyptians and Israel. All these your servants will come down to me, and do me reverence, saying, 'Go out, you and all the people over whom you preside, and afterward I will go out.'"

CHAPTER 11

Moses left Pharaoh in anger, and the Lord told Moses, "Pharaoh will not listen to you, and I will greatly increase my signs and wonders in the land of Egypt."

Moses and Aaron worked all these signs and wonders in the land of Egypt before Pharaoh, and the Lord hardened the heart of Pharaoh, and he did not listen to send out the Israelites out of the land of Egypt.

CHAPTER 12

The Lord said to Moses and Aaron in the land of Egypt, "This month will be the beginning of the year for you. It is the first for you among the months of the year. Tell all the congregation of the Israelites, "On the tenth day of this month let them take each man a sheep according to the houses of their families, every man a lamb for his household. If they are few in a household so that there are not enough for the lamb, he will invite a neighbor that lives near to him, as to the number of minds, every one according to that which suffices him will make a reckoning for the lamb. It will be an unblemished lamb, a year old male. You will take it from the lambs and the kids.'"

"'It will be kept by you until the fourteenth of this month and all the multitude of the congregation of the Israelites will kill it towards evening. They will take some of the blood and will put it on the two doorposts, and on the lintel, in the houses where they will eat them. They will eat the flesh this night roasted with fire, and they will eat unleavened bread with bitter plants. You will not eat it raw or boiled in water but only roasted with fire, the head with the feet, and the rest. Nothing will be left of it in the morning, and you will not break a bone of it. That which is left of it until the morning you will burn with fire. You will eat it with your loins clothed, and your sandals on your feet, and your wands in your hands. You will eat it quickly. It is a Passover to the Lord.'"

"'I will go throughout the land of Egypt in that night, and will strike every firstborn in the land of Egypt both man and animal, and on all the gods of Egypt[1] will I execute vengeance. I am the Lord. The blood will be for a sign to you on the houses in which you are, and I will see the blood and will protect you, and there will not be on you the plague of destruction when I strike the land.'"

"'This day will be to you a memorial, and you will keep it a feast to the Lord through all your generations, and you will keep it a feast for a perpetual ordinance. Seven days you will eat unleavened bread, and from the first day, you will utterly remove leaven from your houses. Whoever will eat leaven, that mind will be utterly destroyed from Israel, from the first day until the seventh day. The first day will be called holy, and the seventh day will be called holy to you. You will do no servile work on them, only the things as are necessary for everyone, will you do. You will keep this commandment, for on this day will I bring your forces out of the land of Egypt, and you will make this day a perpetual ordinance for you throughout your generations. Beginning the fourteenth day of the first month, you will eat unleavened bread from the evening, until the twenty-first day of the month, until evening. Seven days leaven will not be found in your houses, but whoever will eat anything leavened, that mind will be cut off from the congregation of Israel, both among the occupiers of the land and the original inhabitants. You will eat nothing leavened, but in every habitation of yours you will eat unleavened bread.'"

Moses called all the elders of the Israelites, and said to them, "Go away and take to yourselves a lamb according to your families and kill the Passover lamb. You will take a bunch of hyssops, and having dipped it into some of the blood that is by the door, you will touch the lintel, and will put it on both doorposts, including of the blood which is by the door. You will not go out, everyone from the door of his house until the morning. The Lord will pass by to strike the Egyptians, and will see the blood on the lintel, and on both the doorposts, and the Lord will pass by the door, and will not allow the destroyer to enter into your houses to strike you. Follow this as an ordinance for yourself and your children forever. If you should enter into the land, which the Lord will give you, as he has spoken, keep this service. It will happen, if your sons say to you, 'What is this service?' Then you will answer them, 'This Passover is a sacrifice to the Lord, who defended the houses of the Israelites in Egypt when they struck the Egyptians but delivered our houses.'"

The people bowed and worshiped, and the Israelites departed and did as the Lord had commanded Moses and Aaron. It happened at midnight that the Lord struck all the firstborn in the land of Egypt, from the firstborn of Pharaoh[2] who sat on the throne, to the firstborn of the slave-woman in the dungeon, and the firstborn of all livestock. Pharaoh rose up at night, and his servants, and all the Egyptians, and there was a great cry in all the land of Egypt, for there was not a house in which there was not someone dead. Pharaoh called Moses and Aaron that night, and said to them, "Rise and depart from my people, both you and the Israelites. Go and serve the lord of the gods, even as you said. Take with you, your sheep and your oxen. Bless me also, I beg you."

The Egyptians grabbed the people, and they threw them out of the land quickly, as they said, "We all will die."

The people took their dough before their lumps of meal were leavened, bound up as it were in their garments, on their shoulders. The Israelites did as Moses commanded them, and they asked of the Egyptians articles of silver and gold and apparel. The Lord gave his people favor in the sight of the Egyptians, and they had loaned to them, and they plundered the Egyptians. The Israelites departed from Ramesses and went to the corrals, six hundred thousand infantry, counting the men, besides the slaves. A great mixed company went up with them, and sheep and oxen, and a large amount of livestock. They baked the dough which they brought out of Egypt, unleavened cakes, for it had not been leavened, as the Egyptians threw them out, and they could not remain, and they did not prepare provisions for the journey.

The time of the Israelites, which they stayed in the land of Egypt and the land of Canaan, was 430 years. It happened after the four hundred and thirty years, all the forces of the Lord came out of the land of Egypt by night. It is a watch kept to the Lord, so that he should bring them out of the land of Egypt, and that very night a watch was kept to the Lord so that it should be for all the Israelites to their generations.

CHAPTER 12

The Lord said to Moses and Aaron, "This is the law of the Passover, and no stranger will eat of it. Every slave or servant bought with silver, you will circumcise, and then he may eat of it. A traveler or employee will not eat of it. In one house will it be eaten, and you will not carry the flesh out from the house, and a bone of it you will not break. All the congregation of the Israelites will keep it. If any convert will join you to keep the Passover of the Lord, you will circumcise every male of him, and then will he approach and sacrifice it, and he will be even as the original inhabitant of the land. No uncircumcised person will eat of it. There will be one law to the native, and the convert coming among you."

The Israelites did as the Lord commanded Moses and Aaron for them to do. It happened on that day that the Lord brought the Israelites out from the land of Egypt with their forces.

CHAPTER 12 NOTES

1 Codex Vaticanus: ṭeois tōn Aiguptiōn (ΘΕΟΙC ΤⲱΝ ΑΙⲄΥΠΤΙⲱΝ). Translation: gods of Egypt

• Leningrad Codex: 'ĕlōhê Miṣrayim (אֱלֹהֵי מִצְרַיִם). Translation: god of Egypt

• Peshitta: âlhâ dMṣrym (ܐܠܗܐ ܕܡܨܪܝܢ). Translation: god of Egypt

• Targum Onkelos: ta'ăwat Miṣrayim (טַעֲוַת מִצְרָיִם). Translation: mistakes of Egypt

CHAPTER 12

• Targum Pseudo-Jonathan: ta'āwawt Misrā'ê (טָעֲווֹת מִצְרָאֵי).
Translation: mistakes of Egypt

• Sahidic manuscript 2000: nnoute tērou nrrmnkēme (ⲚⲚⲞⲨⲦⲈ
ⲦⲎⲢⲞⲨ ⲚⲢ̄ⲢⲘⲚ̄ⲔⲎⲘⲈ). Translation: the god all of them of us Egyptians

• Sahidic manuscript 16L: hnnoute tērou nkēme (ϨⲚⲚⲞⲨⲦⲈ ⲦⲎⲢⲞⲨ
Ⲛ̄ⲔⲎⲘⲈ). Translation: to the god all of them of Egypt

2 The firstborn son of King Apepi died sometime before he did,
although the details are not clear. He is referred to Prince Apepi by
Egyptologists, as he had the same name as his father. King
Khamudi, who followed King Apepi, was not a close relative, and
there appears to have been significant confusion about who was the
legitimate heir. Very little was recorded of him, although his name
has been found on relics from the ruins of Avaris and Canaan as far
north as Lebanon. Some believe he was the "Phoenician king"
Cadmus, who founded the city of Thebes in the late Bronze Age.

CHAPTER 13

The Lord said to Moses, "Sacrifice to me every firstborn, first produced, opening every womb among the Israelites, both from man and animal. It is mine."

Moses said to the people, "Remember this day, in which you came out of the land of Egypt, out of the house of slavery, for with a strong hand the Lord brought you out of there, and leaven will not be eaten. For on this day you go out in the month of new grain. It will happen when the lord of the gods will have brought you into the land of the Canaanites, Cypriots, Amorites, Mitanni, Jebusites, Girgashites, and Perizzites, which he swore to your fathers to give you, a land flowing with milk and honey, that you will perform this service in this month. Six days you will eat unleavened bread, and on the seventh day is a feast to the Lord. Seven days will you eat unleavened bread; nothing leavened will be seen with you, neither will you have leaven in all your lands."

"You will tell your son in that day, saying, 'The Lord did this to me, as I was going out of Egypt.' It will be to you a sign on your hand and a memorial before your eyes, that the law of the Lord may be in your mouth, for with a strong hand the lord of the gods brought you out of Egypt. Keep this law according to the times of the seasons, from days to days. It will happen when the lord of the gods will bring you into the land of the Canaanites, as he swore to your fathers, and will give it to you, that you will dedicate every offspring opening the womb, the males to the Lord, every one that opens the womb out of the herds or among your livestock, as many as you will have, you will dedicate the males to the Lord. Every offspring opening the womb of the donkeys you will exchange for a sheep, and if you will not exchange it, you will redeem it. Every firstborn male of your sons will you redeem."

"If your son should ask you from now on, saying, 'What is this?' Then you will say to him, 'With a strong hand the Lord brought us out of Egypt, out of the house of slavery. When Pharaoh hardened his heart so as not to send us away, he killed every firstborn in the land of Egypt, both the firstborn of men and the firstborn of animals, and therefore I sacrifice every offspring that opens the womb, the males to the Lord, and every firstborn of my sons I will redeem. It will be for a sign on your hand, and immovable before your eyes, for with a strong hand the Lord brought you out of Egypt."

(When Pharaoh sent out the people, God did not lead them on the road to the land of the Pelesets,[1] which was near, as God thought, 'In case at any time the people repent when they see war and return to Egypt.')

God led the people along the road through the wilderness, to the Papyrus Sea. In the fifth generation, the Israelites left the land of Egypt. Moses took the bones of Joseph with him, for he had solemnly adjured the Israelites, saying, "God will surely visit you, and you will carry up my bones here with you."

CHAPTER 13

The Israelites departed from the corrals[2] and camped in Etham[3] by the wilderness. God led them, in the day by a column of cloud,[4] to show them the way, and in the night by a column of fire.[5] The column of cloud did not fail by day, or the column of fire at night, before all the people.

CHAPTER 13 NOTES

1 Codex Vaticanus: gēs Fulistiim (ΓΗϹ ΦΥΛΙϹΤΙΙΜ). Translation: land of Philistines (or Palestinians, Pelesets)

• LXX 19: gēs Filistieim (γʰϲ Φιλιϛιϕμ). Translation: land of Philistines (or Palestinians, Pelesets)

• LXX 120: gēn Fulistiim (γʷ Φυλιϛιιμ). Translation: land of Palestinians (or Pelesets)

• Leningrad Codex: 'eres pəlištîm (אֶרֶץ פְּלִשְׁתִּים). Translation: land of Pelesets (or Palestinians)

• Peshitta: ároa dplštyå (ܐܪܥܐ ܕܦܠܫܬܝܐ). Translation: land of the Pelesets (or Palestinians)

• Targum Onkelos: 'ar'ā' Pəlištā'ê (אַרְעָא פְּלִשְׁתָּאֵי). Translation: land of Pelesets

• Targum Pseudo-Jonathan: 'ăra' Pəlîšətā'ê (אֲרַע פְּלִישְׁתָּאֵי). Translation: land of Pelesets

• Sahidic manuscript 2000: jimoeit hētou etehiē mfulisteim (ϫΙΜΟΕΙΤ ϨΗΤΟΥ ΕΤΕϨΙΗ ̄ΜΦΥΛΙϹΤΙΕΙΜ). Translation: the followed the path to the north namely the road of the Philistines (or Palestinians, Pelesets)

The Pelesets were an ancient people based in the region of the modern Gaza Strip of the Palestinian Territories. The earliest surviving mention of them is from the reliefs of the Temple of

Ramses III at Medinet Habu in Egypt that dates back to some time between 1186 and 1155 BCE, in which they were called Pwlåsåtî (𓂋𓏤𓐍𓀂𓀀𓏥). They were also known in Middle Babylonian as the ᵏᵘʳPalastu (𒆳𒉿𒆷𒀸𒌈). It is unclear where they came from, however, one theory is that they were the Pala, a Luwian people from the Black Sea coast of Anatolia. The region was an independent country called Palaa (𒉺𒆷𒀀) in the Neshite (Hittite) records from the 1600s BCE, however, have become part of the Neshite Empire by the 1500s BCE. Around the time the Pelesets invaded Canaan, the Pala were driven from their homeland by the neighboring Kaskians from northeast Anatolia, which supports the connection between the groups, however, it has yet to be proven conclusively. The presence of the Pelesets in Southern Canaan during the time of Moses is anachronistic, and therefore this section of text found in both the Septuagint and the Masoretic texts likely dates to the original Phoenician translation in the early Iron Age.

The presence of the Pelesets in Southern Canaan during the time of Moses and Aaron is anachronistic, and therefore this section of text, found in both the Septuagint and the Masoretic texts, was likely an addition made in the Iron Age when the text of Names / Exodus was complied in the Phoenician script. It is an unusual text, as it purports to explain the thoughts of God, and reads like a note to explain why the Israelites did not encounter the Pelesets by a scribe who did not know the Pelesets arrived in the region much later.

The Targum Jerusalem includes a unique paragraph that claims the Israelites were afraid to go into Peleset lands was the tribe of Ephraim had sent an expedition from Egypt 30 years before the time of the exodus to attack Gath, and 200,000 Ephraimites were killed. This seems contradictory to the concept of the Israelites being enslaved in Egypt, as it would have happened while Moses was in Midian. If it was a real event, it would have been an attack on the old Canaanite city of Gath, today identified as the ruins at Tell es-Safi. There was a settlement at the site since at least the 5th millennium BCE. Gath was mentioned as a Canaanite city in the El Amarna letters over a century before the Pelesets invaded the region. Archaeological evidence from the site indicates the population was Egyptianized Canaanites at the time.

During the Hyksos dynasty, there was a major fortification at Gath, and the city appears to have been important to King Khyan. The era of Khayn's reign is debated, and there may have been two Khyans, one in the early 15th dynasty, and another late in the 15th dynasty. The name is accepted as an Egyptian form of the Amorite name Ǩaiaan (𓎡𓇌𓈖𓈖𓏏) and is documented beyond the one or two Hyksos kings that bore it. The king who died around 1550 BCE during the Minoan eruption, and according to the book of Exodus / Names, at the Papyrus Sea, was King Apepi, also transliterated as King Apophis. Apepi ruled for 40 years, so any attack launched by Egyptian Israelites against Gath early in his reign would have been viewed as an insurrection. This incident, if it happened would have been after Moses left Egypt for Midian, and therefore, it seems strange it would have ever been mentioned in a book about Moses. If it is a report of something that happened, it was likely recorded in some other ancient Israelite book, possibly a Book of Ephraim.

In *1st Paralipomena* (Masoretic *Dibrê-hayāmîm*), the patriarch Ephraim had sons who were killed while cattle-rustling in Gath. This may have been the actual origin of the Ephraimite fear of traveling to Gath, which was expanded upon in some now-lost book.

2 Codex Vaticanus: Sokǩōṯ (ⲥⲟⲕⲭⲱⲑ)
- LXX 19: Saǩōṯ (Σλχ∞θ)
- LXX 72: Koǩōṯ (Κοχ∞θ)

- LXX 82: Sok̆ōṭa (Σοχ∞θλ)
- LXX 426: Sak̆k̆ōṯ (Σλχχ∞θ)
- LXX 509: Ok̆ōṯ (Οχ∞θ)
- Leningrad Codex: Sukkōt (סֻכֹּת). Translation: corral (or hut)
- Peshitta: Skwt (ܣܟܘܬ)
- Targum Onkelos: sukkôt (סֻכּוֹת). Translation: corral (or hut)
- Targum Pseudo-Jonathan: sukkôt (סֻכּוֹת). Translation: corral (or hut)
- Sahidic manuscript 2000: Sok̆k̆ōṯ (Coxxⲱⲉ)
- Bohairic manuscripts: Suk̆oṯ (Ⲋⲧxoⲉ)

As the Hebrew and Aramaic word simply means "corral," and the Israelites were later described as having livestock, the term is translated directly from the Leningrad Codex.

3 Codex Vaticanus: Oṯom (Οⲑ OⲘ)
- LXX 15: Iōṯam (Ιⲟⲟθλμ)
- LXX 18: Enaṯōm (Ⲉⲛⲗθ∞μ)
- LXX 25: Enamṯom (Ⲉⲛλμθoμ)
- LXX 52: Anaṯom (ⲗⲛλθoμ)
- LXX 53: Aṯōṯ (ⲗθ∞θ)
- LXX 54: Anṯōm (ⲗⲛθ∞μ)
- LXX 57: Anaṯōm (ⲗⲛλθ∞μ)
- LXX 72: Oṯōm (Ο θ∞μ)
- LXX 75: Naṯom (Ⲛλθoμ)
- LXX 76: Aṯom (ⲗθoμ)
- Leningrad Codex: 'Ētām (אֵתָם)
- Peshitta: Åtm (ܐܬܡ)
- Targum Onkelos: 'Ētām (אֵתָם)

- Targum Pseudo-Jonathan: 'êtām (אֵיתָם). Translation: orphan (or completed)
  - Vetus Latina manuscripts: Othon (OTꜧON)
  - Sahidic manuscript 2000: Oṭom (Oⲑoⲙ)
  - Bohairic manuscripts: Eṭom (Ⲉⲑoⲙ)

This is believed to represent "Khetam," one of the Egyptian fortresses that sat east of the Nile Delta.

4 Codex Vaticanus: en stulō nefelēs (ⲉⲛ ⲥⲧⲩⲗⲱ ⲛⲉⲫⲉⲗⲏⲥ). Translation: in (or on, at, among) column (or pillar, wooden pole) of cloud

- Leningrad Codex: bǝ'ammûd 'ānān (בְּעַמּוּד עָנָן). Translation: in (or at, with) column (or pillar, page) of cloud
- Peshitta: gw stwnå dǒnnå (ܟܘܢ̇ܐ ܟܠܘܬܐ ܓܘ). Translation: in (or among) storm of cloud
- Targum Onkelos: bǝ'amûdā' da'ănānā' (בְּעַמּוּדָא דַעֲנָנָא). Translation: in (or among) a pillar (or column) of cloud
- Targum Pseudo-Jonathan: bǝ'ammûdā' da'ănānā' (בְּעַמּוּדָא דַעֲנָנָא). Translation: in (or among) a pillar (or column) of cloud
- Sahidic manuscript 2000: noustulos nkloole (ⲛⲟⲩⲥⲧⲩⲗⲟⲥ ⲛ̄ⲕⲗⲟⲟⲗⲉ). Translation: in a column of cloud

5 Codex Vaticanus: en stulō puros (ⲉⲛ ⲥⲧⲩⲗⲱ ⲡⲩⲣⲟⲥ). Translation: in (or on, at, among) column (or pillar, wooden pole) of fire (or wheat, lightning)

- LXX 15: en stúlǭ purós tou faínein autois odenein ēméras kaí nuktós (ⲉ̀ⲛ ⲥⲧⲁⲃⲗⲱ ⲡⲩⲣⲟ̀ⲥ ⲧⲟⲩ ⲫⲁⲑⲛⲟ̀ⲓⲛ ⲁⲩⲧⲟⲓⲥ ⲟⲗⲟ̀ⲛⲟ̀ⲓⲛ ⲭⲙⲟ̀ⲣⲁⲥ ⲕⲁⲑ ⲛⲩⲕⲧⲟ̀ⲥ). Translation: in (or on, at, among) column (or pillar, wooden pole) of fire (or wheat, lightning) the shining itself being revealed day and night

CHAPTER 13

• LXX 58: en stúlǭ purós tou faínein autois ēméras kaí nuktós (ἐν στύλῳ πυρὸς του φαφνϭιν ἀυτοις ℏμᾳρβἀς ℏἀφ νυῑτ℞c). Translation: in (or on, at, among) column (or pillar, wooden pole) of fire (or wheat, lightning) the shining itself day and night

• Leningrad Codex: bə'ammûd 'ēš (בְּעַמּוּד אֵשׁ). Translation: in (or at, with) column (or pillar, page) of fire

• Peshitta: gw stwnå dywnå (ܓܘ ܣܬܘܢܐ ܕܝܘܢܐ). Translation: in (or among) storm of fire (or mirror)

• Targum Onkelos: bə'amûdā' də'ešātā' (בְּעַמּוּדָא דְּאֶשָׁתָא). Translation: in (or among) pillar (or column) of fire

• Targum Pseudo-Jonathan: 'ammûdā' də'êšātā' (עַמּוּדָא דְּאֵישָׁתָא). Translation: pillar (or column) of fire

• Sahidic manuscript 2000: noustulos nsate (ⲚⲞⲨⲤⲦⲨⲖⲞⲤ ⲚⲤⲀⲦⲈ). Translation: in a column of fire

CHAPTER 14

The Lord said to Moses, "Speak to the Israelites, and let them stop and camp at the village, between Migdol[1] and the sea, near Ba'al Zephon.[2] Between them, you will camp by the sea. Pharaoh will say to his people, 'As for these Israelites, they are wandering in the land, as the wilderness has trapped them.' I will harden the heart of Pharaoh, and he will pursue them, and I will be glorified in Pharaoh, and all his armies and all the Egyptians will know that I am the Lord," and they did so.

It was reported to the king of the Egyptians that the people had fled, and the heart of Pharaoh was turned, and that of his servants against the people, and they said, "What have we done, letting the Israelites go, so that they no longer serve us?"

So Pharaoh harnessed his chariots, and led off all his people with himself, and took six hundred chosen chariots, and all the cavalry of the Egyptians, and rulers over all. The Lord hardened the heart of Pharaoh, king of Egypt and his servants, and he pursued after the Israelites, and the Israelites went out with a strong arm. The Egyptians chased after them and found them camped by the sea, and all the horse of the chariots of Pharaoh, and the cavalry, and his army were near the settlement of Ba'al Zephon.

CHAPTER 14

Pharaoh approached, and the Israelites looked up and saw, and the Egyptians camped behind them, and they were terrified. The Israelites cried to the Lord, and asked Moses, "Have you brought us out to kill us in the wilderness because there were no graves in the land of Egypt? What is this that you have done to us, having brought us out of Egypt? Is not this the words which we said to you in Egypt, saying, 'Leave us alone that we may serve the Egyptians.' It was better for us to serve the Egyptians than to die in this wilderness!"

Moses said to the people, "Be courageous! Stand and see salvation from the Lord, which he will work for us this day. As you have seen the Egyptians today, you will never see them again forever. The Lord will fight for you, and you will hold your peace."

The Lord asked Moses, "Why do you call me? Speak to the Israelites, and let them harness the horses again. Lift your hand with your wand, and stretch out your hand over the sea, and divide it, and let the Israelites enter into the middle of the sea on the dry land. I will harden the heart of Pharaoh and all the Egyptians, and they will go after them, and I will be glorified before Pharaoh, and on all his armies, and his chariots and his horses. All the Egyptians will know that I am the Lord when I am glorified before Pharaoh and his chariots and his horses."

The messenger of God that went before the camp of the Israelites moved and went behind, and the column of the cloud also moved from before them and stood behind them. It went between the camp of the Egyptians and the camp of

Israel and stood, and there was darkness and blackness, and the night passed, and they did not come near to one another during the whole night. Moses stretched out his hand over the sea, and the Lord carried back the sea with a strong south wind all night and made the sea dry, and the water was divided. The Israelites went into the middle of the sea on the dry land, and the water of it was a wall on the right hand and a wall on the left. The Egyptians pursued them and went in after them, and every horse of Pharaoh, and his chariots, and his horsemen, into the middle of the sea.

It happened in the morning watch that the Lord looked out on the camp of the Egyptians through the column of fire and cloud, and troubled the camp of the Egyptians, and caught the axles of their chariots, and caused them to travel with difficulty, and the Egyptians said, "Let us flee from the face of Israel, for the Lord fights for them against the Egyptians."

The Lord told Moses, "Stretch out your hand over the sea and let the water return to its place and let it cover the Egyptians, covering both the chariots and the riders. Moses stretched out his hand over the sea, and the water returned to its place of the day, and the Egyptians fled from the water, and the Lord shook off the Egyptians in the middle of the sea. The water returned and covered the chariots and the riders, and all the forces of Pharaoh, who entered after them into the sea. There was none left of them, not even one, but the Israelites went along dry land in the middle of the sea, and the water was to them a wall on the right hand and a wall on the left.

CHAPTER 14

So the Lord delivered Israel that day from the hands of the Egyptians, and Israel saw the Egyptians dead by the shore of the sea. Israel saw the mighty hand, the things which the Lord did to the Egyptians, and the people feared the Lord, and they believed in God and Moses, his servant.

CHAPTER 14 NOTES

1 Codex Vaticanus: Magdōlou (ⲘⲀⲄⲆⲰⲖⲞⲨ)

- LXX 14: Madōlou (ⲘⲀⲆⲰⲗⲟⲩ)
- LXX 18: Bagdolou (ⲂⲀⲅⲆⲟⲗⲟⲩ)
- LXX 53: Megdolōn (ⲘⲈⲅⲆⲟⲗⲱⲛ)
- LXX 56: Magdōlōn (ⲘⲀⲅⲆⲱⲗⲱⲛ)
- LXX 59: Magdala (ⲘⲀⲅⲆⲁⲗⲁ)
- LXX 72: Magdalōn (ⲘⲀⲅⲆⲁⲗⲱⲛ)
- LXX 76: Gadōlou (ⲅⲀⲆⲱⲗⲟⲩ)
- Leningrad Codex: Migdōl (מִגְדֹּל). Translation: tower, fortification, platform
  - Peshitta: Mgdwl (ܡܓܕܘܠ)
  - Targum Onkelos: Migdôl (מִגְדּוֹל)
  - Targum Jerusalem: Migdôl (מִגְדּוֹל)
  - Targum Pseudo-Jonathan: Migdôl (מִגְדּוֹל)
  - Sahidic manuscript 2000: Meḥtōl (ⲘⲈⳓⲦⲰⲗ)
  - Bohairic manuscripts: Meštōl (Ⲙⲉϣⲧⲱⲗ)

A Ptolemaic-era geographical text housed at the Cairo Museum lists four border fortresses along the Greek-era Arsinoe Canal, including Migdol and Ba'al Zephon. It seems likely these later fortresses were named after the fortresses in the Torah, which the

CHAPTER 14

Ptolemys had paid to have translated at the Library of Alexandria. Most scholars associate the Migdol with El Qantara, a city that today lays along the Suez Canal, between the Mediterranean Port Said and the Bitter Lakes. This location is possible, however, the term is generic enough to refer to any fortified tower.

In the Middle Kingdom era Tale of Sinuhe, the protagonist Sinuhe sneaked past a major fortification in the region under cover of night. He then proceeded to the Bitter Lakes, which show up later in the Exodus' route of Egypt.

2 Codex Vaticanus: Beelsepfōn (ΒΕΕΛϹΕΠⳐⲰΝ)

- Codex Alexandrinus: Beelsefōn (ΒΕΕΛϹΕⳐⲰΝ)
- LXX 53: Belsepfōn (Βελσεπφων)
- LXX 56: Belsefōn (Βελσεφων)
- LXX 72: Beelsepfō (Βεελσεπφω)
- LXX 82: Beṭlepfōn (Βεϑλεπφων)
- LXX 426: Beelseffōn (Βεελσεφφων)
- Leningrad Codex: Ba'al Səpōn (בַּעַל צְפֹן)
- Vetus Latina manuscripts: Belsephon (Belsephon)
- Peshitta: Bōlspwn (ܒܥܠܨܦܘܢ)
- Targum Onkelos: Bə'êl Səpôn (בְּעֵיל צְפוֹן). Translation: Lord Zephon
- Targum Jerusalem: ṭa'ăwawt Səpôn (טַעֲוות צְפוֹן). Translation: mistakes (or errors) of Zephon
- Targum Pseudo-Jonathan: ṭa'ăwat Səpôn dəmištayyêr mikkol ṭa'ăwāwn dəmisrāyim bəgîn dəyēmərûn miṣrā'ê bāhîr hû' Ba'al Səpôn mikkol ṭa'ăwāwtā' də'ištayyêr wəlā' lāqā' dəyêtûn ləmisgôd lÊh (טַעֲות צְפוֹן דְּמִשְׁתַּיֵּיר מִכָּל טַעֲוון דְּמִצְרַיִם בְּגִין דְּיֵימְרוּן מִצְרָאֵי בָחִיר הוּא בַּעַל צְפוֹן מִכָּל טַעֲוותָא דְּאִשְׁתַּיֵּיר וְלָא לְקָא דְּיֵיתוּן לְמִסְגּוֹד לֵיהּ). Translation: mistakes of Zephon, the last place of all the mistakes of

171

the Egyptians, for protection of the rebels of Egypt. Chosen was Baal Zephon from all mistakes because it remained and was not destroyed, the final place of worship of Êh.

- Sahidic manuscript 2000: Belsefōn (Ⲃⲉⲗⲥⲉϥⲱⲛ)
- Bohairic manuscripts: Belsepfōn (Ⲃⲉⲗⲥⲉⲡϥⲱⲛ)

Ba'al Zephon was a Canaanite god mentioned in the Ugaritic Texts from the 1300 BCE. The origin of the name appears to have been Mount Zephon in on the modern Syrian-Turkish border at the northern-most frontier of Canaan. Its usage in Egypt appears to be based on a group of Canaanites settling in the area of Lake Bardawil on the north coast of the Sinai Peninsula, a shallow saline lake with a surface area of 147,000 acres (59,500 hectares). Ba'al Zephon continued to be worshiped in the region well into the Greek era.

The story of the sea being blown away so the Israelites could walk across it, only to return and drown the Egyptian army is reminiscent of the Greek story of the Serbonian Bog, also called Lake Serbonis, which had a deceptive appearance of looking solid, but was a bog that swallowed people that tried to pass through it. The Serbonian Bog myth has been identified with Lake Bardawil since the Greeks ruled Egypt. In ancient Egyptian records, Lake Bardawil was described as a quagmire that whole armies had been swallowed up by. Given that Ba'al Zephon is identified in this chapter, and is known to refer to Lake Bardawil, it is clear that this unusual event took place in Lake Bardawil, and not in the Red Sea, as later writers assumed.

It isn't clear where the longer verse found in the Targum Jerusalem came from, however the author is believed to have copied his longer verses from a variety of older copies of the Torah. Unlike the much shorter Jerusalem Targum, it does not appear to have originated with a specific sect of Israelites. There do not

CHAPTER 14

appear to have ever been any Greek translations that incorporated this longer verse.

CHAPTER 15

Then Moses and the Israelites sang this song to God, "Sing of the Lord who has gloriously thrown the horse and rider into the sea! My assistant and protector in my salvation. This is my God and I will glorify him, my father's God, and I will praise him. Yahweh, man is food for him. Yahweh is his name.[1] He has thrown the chariots of Pharaoh and his army into the sea, the chosen mounted captains! They were swallowed up in the Papyrus Sea.[2] He covered them with the sea. They sank to the depth like a stone."

"Your right hand, God! Has been glorified in strength. Your right hand, God! Has broken the enemies. In the abundance of your glory, you have broken the adversaries to pieces. You sent out your anger, it devoured them like stubble. By the breath of your anger the water parted asunder, the waters were congealed like a wall, the waves were congealed in the middle of the sea. The enemy said, 'I will pursue, I will overtake, I will divide the plunder. I will satisfy my mind! I will destroy with my sword, and my hand will have dominion!' You sent out your wind, and the sea covered them. They sank like lead in the mighty water."

"Who is like you among the gods, Lord? Who is like you? Glorified in holiness, marvelous in glories, doing wonders. You stretched out your right hand, and Eretz[3] swallowed them up. You have guided in your righteousness this your people whom you have redeemed, by your strength you have called them into your holy resting-place. The nations heard and were angry, pangs have seized on those under obligation to the Pelesets.[4] Then the princes of Edom and the chiefs of the Moabites ran as trembling took hold on them, and all the inhabitants of Canaan melted away."

"Let trembling and fear fall on them. By the greatness of your arm, let them become like a stone until your people pass over, Lord! Until these, your people pass over, who you purchased. Bring them in and plant them in the mountain of their inheritance, in your prepared habitation, which you, Lord, have prepared, the sanctuary of the Lord, which your hands have prepared. Lord, reigning forever and ever and ever. For the horse of Pharaoh went in with the chariots and cavalry into the sea, and the Lord brought on them the water of the sea, but the Israelites walked through dry land in the middle of the sea."

Then Mariam the prophetess, the sister of Aaron, took a timbrel in her hand, and danced with all the women, each with timbrels. Mariam led them, saying, "Sing of the Lord who has gloriously thrown the horse and rider into the sea!"

Then Moses brought up the Israelites from the Papyrus Sea and brought them into the Wilderness of Shur,[5] and they went three days in the wilderness and found no water to drink. They came to Marah,[6] and could not drink at Marah, for it was bitter, therefore he named the name of that place, Bitterness.[7] The people murmured against Moses, saying, "What will we drink?"

176

CHAPTER 15

Moses cried to the Lord, and the Lord showed him a tree, and he threw it into the water, and the water was sweetened. There he established for him ordinances and judgments, and there he tested him, and said, "If you will indeed listen to the voice of the lord of the gods, and do things pleasing before him, and will listen to his commands, and keep all his ordinances, no disease which I have brought on the Egyptians will I bring on you, for I am the lord of the gods who heals you."

They came to Elim,[8] and there were there twelve fountains of water, and seventy stems of palm-trees and they camped there by the waters.

CHAPTER 15 NOTES

1 Codex Vaticanus: $\overline{KS}$ suntribōn polemous $\overline{KS}$ onoma autō ($\overline{KC}$ ϹΥΝΤΡΙΒⲰΝ ΠⲞⲗⲈⲘⲞΥϹ $\overline{KC}$ ⲞⲚⲞⲘⲀ ⲀΥΤⲰ). Translation: lord (or main, chief, dominant, master) of catastrophes (or destructions, demolitions) battles (or wars) lord name of him

- Leningrad Codex: Yəhōwâ 'îš milḥāmâ Yəhōwâ šəmô (יְהוָה אִישׁ מִלְחָמָה יְהוָה שְׁמוֹ) Translation: Yahweh man (or husband) of war (or battle). Yəhwa is his name.

- Peshitta: mryå gnbrå wqrbtnå mryå šmyh (ܡܪܝܐ ܓܢܒܪܐ ܘܩܪܒܬܢܐ ܡܪܝܐ ܫܡܗ). Translation: master (or lord) Orion (or giant, hero, strongman) and Ursa Minor (or the 'bed,' the four stars: Kochab, Pherkad, Anwar al Farkadain, and Akhfa al Farkadain), master of the sky

177

CHAPTER 15

• Targum Onkelos: yəyā mārê nişhān qərābayā' yəyā šəmēh (יְיָ
מָרֵי נִצְחָן קְרָבַיָּא יְיָ שְׁמֵהּ). Translation: Yahweh master of splendors
(or eternities, perfections) to be near (or to fight, to make war).
Yahweh of desolation (or 'is his name.')

• Targum Jerusalem: yəyā bîqar šəkînətêh hû' da'ăbêd ləkôn
nişhānê qərābêkôn bəkāl dar wādar môda' gəbûrətêh lə'amā' bêt
yišrā'ēl yəyā šəmô kî kišmêh kēn gəbûrətêh yəhē' šəmêh
məšabbaḥ lə'almê 'almîn (יְיָ בִּיקַר שְׁכִינְתֵּיהּ הוּא דַּעֲבֵיד לְכוֹן נִצְחָנֵי
קְרָבֵיכוֹן בְּכָל דַּר וְדַר מוֹדַע גְּבוּרָתֵּיהּ לְעַמָּא בֵּית יִשְׂרָאֵל יְיָ שְׁמוֹ כִּי כִשְׁמֵיהּ כֵּן
גְּבוּרָתֵּיהּ יְהֵא שְׁמֵיהּ מְשַׁבַּח לְעָלְמֵי עָלְמִין). Translation: Yahweh
honored in (or heavy is, visiting) his dwelling that was made (or
served, slaved, done) to direct victories in wars (or battles), to
generally dwell in, and to exist as a notice (or advertisement) for
the people of the house of Israel. Yahweh is his name, because like
his name is the power (or force). Let sky gusts from the virgin (or
unmarried girl, Virgo) forever.

• Targum Pseudo-Jonathan: 'āmərîn bənê yišrā'ēl yəyā gabrā'
'ābêd qərābênān bəkāl dar wādar minda' gəbûrətêh lə'ammêh bêt
yišrā'ēl yəyā šəmêh kišmêh kēn gəbûrətêh yəhê šəmêh məbārak
lə'āləmê 'almîn (אָמְרִין בְּנֵי יִשְׂרָאֵל יְיָ גַּבְרָא עָבֵיד קְרָבֵינָן בְּכָל דַּר וְדַר מִנְדָּע
גְּבוּרָתֵּיהּ לְעַמֵּיהּ בֵּית יִשְׂרָאֵל יְיָ שְׁמֵיהּ כִּשְׁמֵיהּ כֵּן גְּבוּרָתֵּיהּ יְהֵי שְׁמֵיהּ מְבָרַךְ
לְעָלְמֵי עָלְמִין). Translation: It has been said by the children of Israel,
"Yahweh man (or husband) makes prosperous (or labors in,
produces) all who circle (or orbit, go around), and to dwell in
knowledge (or intelligence) as a notice (or advertisement) for the
people of the house of Israel. Yahweh towards name, because like
his name is the power (or force). Let exist sky blessings from the
virgin (or unmarried girl, Virgo) forever.

• Sahidic manuscript 2000: nnetouēh hm Fulistieim (ⲚⲚⲈⲦⲞⲨⲎϨ
ϨⲘ ϥⲩⲗⲓⲥⲧⲓⲉⲓⲙ). Translation: the abode of the Philistines (of
Palestinians)

CHAPTER 15

The verse has clears caused a great deal of confusion based on the difference in the Hebrew and Aramaic texts. Nevertheless, the Septuagint, Vetus Latina, Bohairic, Ge'ez, and Old Armenian texts all read virtually identically. The Peshitta's verse seems to be a relic of the Judeo-astrological religion of the Neo-Babylonian era. Given the uniformity of the non-Hebrew and non-Aramaic verses, the Egypto-Aramaic version of the verse must have been fairly standardized before the Greek and Old Latin translations were made.

Assuming the Hebrew form was once written in the Canaanite script, it would have read "Yahweh, man is food for him. Yahweh is his name" (ץ ﬡﬡ ﬡ ﬡ). While this is macabre, it would parallel the cannibalism of the Greek Titan Cronos and the Hurrian god Kumarbi, both of with were viewed as the "father of the gods." The Bronze Age Phoenician historian Sanchuniathon equated Cronus with El, and claimed he ate his father Epigeius, which supports the idea that El was viewed as cannibalistic in the Bronze Age. It would also explain the requirement for the sacrifice of the first born, including human first born.

If this was the Old Samaritan or Judahite version of the text, it could not have been translated into Aramaic, as none of the translations are particularly close. The Septuagint's version likely represents the original Aramaic translation, as it is the most similar to the Hebrew text, however, interpreting mlhmh (ﬡ) as the word "wars," instead of " is food for him." The root term of both words is lhm (ﬡ), specifically meaning "bread" in old Canaanite, however, expanded to means "meat" in Aramaic, Arabic, and Hebrew, and by extension, "butchery," "bloody battle," and "warfare." As Yahweh does appear to have been in the early form of *Exodus / Names*, it is imported in this verse from the Leningrad Codex.

CHAPTER 15

2 Codex Vaticanus: Erutra talassē (ⲉⲣⲩⲑⲣⲁ ⲑⲁⲗⲁⲥⲥⲏ). Translation: Erythraean Sea (the Red Sea, Gulf of Aden, Persian Gulf, and Indian Ocean)

- Leningrad Codex: yam-sûp (יַם־סוּף). Translation: sea of papyrus (or reeds)
- Peshitta: ymå dswp (ܝܡܐ ܕܣܘܦ). Translation: sea of papyrus (or reeds)
- Targum Onkelos: yamā' dəsûp (יַמָא דְסוּף). Translation: sea of papyrus (or reeds)
- Targum Jerusalem: yamā' dəsûp (יַמָא דְסוּף). Translation: sea of papyrus (or reeds)
- Targum Pseudo-Jonathan: yamā' dəsûp (יַמָא דְסוּף). Translation: sea of papyrus (or reeds)
- Sahidic manuscript 2000: tErutra talassa (ⲧⲉⲣⲩⲑⲣⲁ ⲑⲁⲗⲁⲥⲥⲁ). Translation: the Erythraean Sea

The Greek term is not geographically specific, allowing for the Israelites to have passed from Egypt to the wilderness at any point in the Red Sea or even the Gulf of Aden. The Greek name appears to be a translation of the Persian term Erostras, which referred to the entire Persian Gulf, Red Sea, and the Indian Ocean. The Greeks were likely referring to the Gulf of Suez, however, this was known to the ancient Egyptians as the 'Sea of Calm,' which is what the Israelites would have called it if that was where they were.

The Greeks transliterated the name as the Sea of Sif (Θαλάσσης Σιφ) in the Codex Vaticanus' translation of Judges, confirming that the name Swf was in the Aramaic text they worked from. The Aramaic term swf (סוף) and Phoenician term swf (𐤎𐤅𐤐), both meaning papyrus plants were adopted from the Egyptian term twfi (𓏏𓅱𓆑𓇇), which referred to papyrus, papyrus plants, and papyrus marshes. The Egyptian term continued to be used into the Classical era as the Coptic words joouf (ϫⲟⲟⲩϥ), honf (ϭⲟⲛϥ), and

180

homf (ϭoмϥ), all meaning papyrus. Conversely, the Egyptian name of the Red Sea was the Sea of Heh (𓈗), meaning 'very large sea' from the Middle Kingdom era onward, however, it is believed to have originally been named after the ancient Egyptian frog god Heh (𓎛𓇳). As the Greek translation of Erythraean Sea is anachronistic, the translation of Papyrus Sea is imported from the Masoretic texts.

The Hebrew term "Sea of papyrus" is not geographically specific either, however, does match the description of the shallow Lake Bardawil which has been a major source for papyrus reeds throughout Egyptian history. This lake was called the "Rope Sea" (חֶבֶל הַיָּם) in Masoretic *Zephaniah* and Dead Sea Scroll MurXII's *Zephaniah*, the "Reed Sea" (Σχοινισμα της θαλασσης) in the Septuagint's *Zephaniah*, and the "Scroll Sea" (בְּסְפַר יְמָא) in the Targum Jerusalem's *Zephaniah*. The sea in *Zephaniah* is described as a being south along the Mediterranean coast past the Peleset lands of the modern Gaza Strip, which can only be Lake Bardawil.

3 Codex Vaticanus: Gē (ΓΗ). Translation: Ge (or land, earth, country)

• Codex Alexandrinus: ē gē (ΗΓΗ). Translation: the land (or earth, country)

• Leningrad Codex: 'Āres (אָרֶץ). Translation: Eretz (or land, earth, country, soil)

• Peshitta: årȯå (ܐܪܥܐ). Translation: land

• Targum Onkelos: 'ar'ā' (אַרְעָא). Translation: land

• Targum Jerusalem: 'ar'ā' (אַרְעָא). Translation: land

• Targum Pseudo-Jonathan: 'ar'ā' (אַרְעָא). Translation: land

• Sahidic manuscript 2000: mmoou (ⲙⲟⲟⲩ). Translation: water

CHAPTER 15

The Earth (Eretz / Ge) is depicted as the same type of primordial deity in the Septuagint as it was in the Greek myths and called on to witness blessings and curses, implying consciousness. She is described as opening her mouth to swallow things more than once in the Torah and in other ancient Israelite texts. She also spoke and had free will, meaning she continued to be seen as a type of goddess by some Israelites until the Classical era. In both the Targums Jerusalem and Jonathan, this verse is preceded by a debate between Ara (land) and Yama (sea) about which of them should consume the Egyptians, ultimately resulting in Ara opening her mouth and consuming them. Strangely, all versions of the story agree that it was the sea that consumed them, and all versions of the song agree that it was the land.

4 Codex Vaticanus: katoikountas fulistiim (ΚΑΤΟΙΚΟΥΝΤΑϹ ΦΥΛΙϹΤΙΙΜ). Translation: under-obligation to the Philistines (or Palestinians)

• LXX 19: katoikountas Filistieim (κατ⊕κρωτὰϲ Φιλιϛιέμ). Translation: under-obligation to the Philistines (or Palestinians)

• LXX 44: pantes oi katoikountes Filistieim (πᾶντόϲ ⊕ κατ⊕κρωτόϲ Φιλιϛιέμ). Translation: all those under-obligation to the Philistines (or Palestinians)

• LXX 59: katoikounta Filistieim (κατ⊕κρωτα Φιλιϛιειμ). Translation: under-obligation to the Philistines (or Palestinians)

• LXX 72: katoikountas Fulieim (κατ⊕κρωτὰϲ Φυλιέμ). Translation: under-obligation to the Phulieim

• LXX 108: katoikountes Fulistiim (κατ⊕κρωτόϲ Φυλιϛιιμ). Translation: under-obligation to the Philistines (or Palestinians)

• LXX 314: katoikountas en Fulistieim (κατ⊕κρωτὰϲ εν Φυλιϛιέμ). Translation: under-obligation within the Philistines (or Palestinians)

CHAPTER 15

• Leningrad Codex: yōšəbê Pəlāšet (יֹשְׁבֵי פְּלָשֶׁת). Translation: inhabitants of Palestine (or Philistia, Peleset)

• Peshitta: lytbh dPlšt (ܕܦܠܫܬ ܡܟܬܒ ܠܝܬܒ). Translation: settlement of Pelesets (or Palestinians)

• Targum Onkelos: lədahawô yātəbîn biPlāšet (לְדַהֲווֹ יָתְבִין בִּפְלָשֶׁת). Translation: those who inhabited Plashet (or Palestine, Philistia, Peleset)

• Targum Pseudo-Jonathan: dayyrê 'ar'ăhôn dippəlištā'ê (דְיְירֵי אַרְעֲהוֹן דִּפְלִשְׁתָּאֵי). Translation: the fires ruling (or pasturing in) the Pelisht (or Palestinian) land

• Sahidic manuscript 2000: nnetouēh hm fulistieim (ⲚⲚⲈⲦⲞⲨⲎϨ ϨⲘ ⲪⲨⲖⲒⲤⲦⲒⲈⲒⲘ). Translation: the abode of the Philistines (of Palestinians)

• Ge'ez manuscripts: kananakorum (ከናንኮሩም). This appears to be a Ge'ez transliteration of kəna'ănî 'eqrôn (כְּנַעֲנִי עֶקְרוֹן), probably via the Coptic Ǩanan Akarōm (ⲬⲀⲚⲀⲚ ⲀⲔⲀⲣⲱⲚ). Ekron was a major city in southern Canaan during the era of the exodus. The city had undergone major rebuilding and expansion circa 1600 BCE and was a major Canaanite city until the Pelesets destroyed it during their invasion of Canaan circa 1200 BCE. The Pelesets later rebuilt the city, and it was one of the five major Peleset cities during the early Iron Age. The term found in the Ge'ez manuscript is not proper Ge'ez for "Canaanite Ekron," and must have been transliterated from a now lost Greek or Coptic manuscript.

The text refers to the Moabites, Edomites, and other Canaanites as being under obligation to the Pelesets (or Philistines, Palestinians) which is anachronistic as the Pelesets did not arrive in the region for another 300 years. This suggests that the word replaced another older term when the Phoenician translation was made. The Targum Onkelos includes the curious deviation of "those who lived in Philistia," indicating that Onkelos knew that they were not the Pelesets.

183

CHAPTER 15

At the time, the region was under the rule of the Hyksos (𓁶),
whose regional capital was at Sharuhen, in the modern Palestinian
Gaza Strip. The Hyksos were driven from the region within a
decade of the Septuagint's dating of the exodus, and therefore their
name would have meant nothing 400 years later when the
Phoenician translation was made. The Targum Jerusalem includes
the strange reference to the "fires" who "ruled Philistia," which
appears to be a mistranslation of a Middle Egyptian version of the
verse. Most Egyptologists currently view the Hyksos nobility as
being Amorites, who the Egyptians called the Åmw (𓄿𓅓𓏲), a
homonym of åmw (𓄿𓅓𓏲𓏏), meaning "fires."

The Ge'ez manuscripts have a strange term that appears to be a
transliteration via Greek or Coptic of "Canaanite Ekron." As Ekron
was a major Canaanite city at the time, it is possible that this was
the regional capital north of Sharuhen, which is believed to have
been in the Gaza Strip. As Sharuhen wasn't destroyed until three
years after Avaris, and Avaris wasn't destroyed until the reign of
King Kamose, the heir of King Apepi, the king likely killed in the
Papyrus Sea incident, it is more likely Sharuhen was the original
term in the text.

5 Codex Vaticanus: erēmon Sour (ΕΡΗΜΟΝ ϹΟΥΡ). Translation:
desert of Sour

• Leningrad Codex: midbar-šûr (מִדְבַּר־שׁוּר). Translation: desert (or
pastureland) or Shur

• Peshitta: mdbrå dšwr (ܡܕܒܪܐ ܕܫܘܪ). Translation: desert (or
wilderness) of Shur

• Targum Onkelos: madbərā' dəhagrā' (מַדְבְּרָא דְחַגְרָא). Translation:
desert (or wilderness, steppe, leader, guide) of limping

CHAPTER 15

- Targum Jerusalem: 'ôrəhā' dəhālûṣā' (אוֹרְחָא דְחָלוּצָא).
Translation: road of Chalutza (possibly meaning 'purification' from
the Arabic kalaṣa – خلص)
- Targum Pseudo-Jonathan: madbərā' dəhālûṣā' (מַדְבְּרָא דְחָלוּצָא).
Translation: desert (or wilderness, steppe, leader, guide) of Chalutza
(possibly meaning "purification" from the Arabic kalaṣa - خلص)
- Sahidic manuscript 16L: eterēmos nSiour (ⲉⲧⲉⲣⲏⲙⲟⲥ ⲛ̄ⲥⲓⲟⲩⲣ).
Translation: the wilderness (or desert) of Siour

The location of the "Wilderness of Shur" is debated, however, the
location of "Shur" is known. Shur is the Canaanite pronunciation of
the Egyptian name šă-ḥr (𓈙𓄿), meaning the "plains of Horus," a
region on the Mediterranean coast between the Nile Delta and
Lake Bardawil. This indicates the Wilderness of Shur was the
Northern Sinai Peninsula, which seems to be supported in the
following paragraphs which discuss the "Bitter Waters." This
means the Israelites headed south from Lake Bardawil, away from
the "Pelesets" in Sharuhen.

6 Codex Vaticanus: Merṛa (ⲘⲉⲢⲢⲀ)

- Codex Alexandrinus: Merṛan (ⲘⲉⲢⲢⲀⲚ)
- Codex Ambrosiano: Marṛan (ⲘⲀⲢⲢⲀⲚ)
- LXX 30: Mera (Μέϱα)
- LXX 53: Meran (Μέϱαν)
- Leningrad Codex: mārâ (מָרָה). Translation: bitter
- Peshitta: mwrt (ܡܘܪܬ)
- Targum Onkelos: mārâ (מְרָה). Translation: bitter
- Targum Pseudo-Jonathan: mārâ (מָרָה). Translation: bitter
- Sahidic manuscript 16L: Murra (ⲘⲩⲢⲢⲀ)

The Greek translation deviates from the Hebrew and Aramaic
versions in that both transliterates and translates the Hebrew and

Aramaic word for "bitter," treating it as the toponym Merra (Μερρα), but then switching to the translation of pikria (πικρια), meaning "bitter" in Greek.

The location of this bitter water has been debated, and is largely dependent on where the events involving the Papyrus Sea and Mount Sinai took place. Based on the Papyrus Sea being Lake Bardawil, the bitter waters would be the Bitter Lakes, half-way between the Mediterranean coast and the Gulf of Suez. The larger of the two Bitter Lakes, the Great Bitter Lake had dried out completely by the time the Suez Canal was constructed in the late 1800s, which now connects these two lakes, as well as linking them to the Mediterranean and Gulf of Suez. The Pyramid Texts, which date back to the Old Kingdom era, mention the Great Bitter Lake, implying the existence of one or more Small Bitter Lake(s), and therefore the name is very ancient, long preceding the era of Moses. It seems unlikely that there would have been another area of bitter waters in the region that the Egyptians somehow never noticed through thousands of years of occupation, and therefore, the Bitter Lakes are almost certainly the place being described in this chapter. If this interpretation is correct, it would mean the Israelites started moving east along the coastal road to Canaan, and then turned back and headed south into the Sinai Peninsula after the events at the Papyrus Sea.

7 Codex Vaticanus: pikria (ⲡⲓⲕⲣⲓⲁ). Translation: bitter
- Leningrad Codex: mārâ (מָרֹה). Translation: bitter
- Peshitta: mwrt (ܡܘܪܬܐ)
- Targum Onkelos: mārâ (מָרָה). Translation: bitter
- Targum Pseudo-Jonathan: mārâ (מְרָה). Translation: bitter
- Sahidic manuscript 16L: Siše (ⲥⲓϣⲉ). Translation: bitterness
See the previous note for more information.

8 Codex Vaticanus: Ailim (ΑΙΛΙΜ)

- Codex Ambrosiano: Eleim (ЄΛЄΙΜ)
- LXX 15: Elēm (Ελημ)
- LXX 82: Elim (Ελιμ)
- LXX 84: Salēm (Σαλλημ)
- Leningrad Codex: 'Êlimā (אֵילִ֔מָה)
- Peshitta: ålym (ܐܠܝܡ)
- Targum Onkelos: 'Êlim (אֵילִם)
- Targum Pseudo-Jonathan: 'Êlîm (אֵלִים)
- Sahidic manuscript 16L: Eleim (Єλειм)
- Bohairic manuscripts: Elim (Єλιμ)
- Old Armenian manuscripts: Alim (Ալիմ)

The word is Semitic for "stags" or "rams," written in ayyalum (𒀀𒈗) in Akkadian, åylm (𐎀𐎊𐎍𐎎) in Ugaritic, åylm (𐤀𐤉𐤋𐤌) in Phoenician, åylm (𐩱𐩺𐩡𐩣) in Sabean, åylåm (𐡀𐡉𐡋𐡌) in Aramaic, åylym (אילים) in Hebrew, and åylām (ܐܝܠܡ) in Syriac. While the word is phonetically the same as the word for stags, neither the Greek nor Hebrew translations translate the term directly, treating it as a toponym.

The location of Elim is debated, like the other stations along the route the Israelites took out of Egypt. Its location is largely based on the assumptions about the events of the Papyrus Sea, the location of the Bitter Waters, and ultimately the location of the Wilderness of Sin and Mount Sinai. It is traditionally identified by Muslims as the Oyun Musa (عيون موسى), meaning "Spring of Moses" in the western Sinai, where there are twelve ancient wells. It is not clear when the location was named, and it is plausible that this location was named after Moses by Emperor Constantine's mother, Helena Augusta, when she named Mount Sinai and the Sinai Peninsula in the 330s CE. As the Greek translators did not identify the town, it

187

could not have been widely known as the "Moses" Spring' circa 250 BCE. Another theory is the Elim may have referred to the Wadi Gharandel in the Sinai peninsula, again this is based on the theory that Exodus' Mount Sinai was the large mountain range named Sinai by Helena Augusta in the 330s CE.

If the Israelites were trying to leave Egypt, and one would assume Moses was leading them towards Midian, where he first encountered the wdjat, then the logical direction was east following the southern road across the Sinai Peninsula, which runs east from the Bitter Lakes to the modern town of An-Nekhel in central Sinai, before continuing on to mountains of Hashem El Tarif in eastern Sinai. An-Nekhel is known to have been used as a watering hole along the southern road since Pharaonic times. It is postulated to have been a Canaanite town, founded during the Hyksos era, named after the Canaanite goddess Nikkal, meaning "Great lady of the Fruitful," who was the goddess of orchards.

If this theory is correct, then there must have been a settlement with orchards in the region, matching to some degree the Exodus' description of a place of wells and trees. Nikkal was the wife of the Canaanite moon god Yarikh, which supports the town being somewhere in, or near, the Wilderness of Sin if the name Sîn (סִין) is accepted as being an indirect transliteration of the cuneiform word Sîn (𒀭𒌍), meaning "moon."

CHAPTER 16

They departed from Elim, and all the congregation of the Israelites came to the Wilderness of Sin,[1] which is between Elim and Sinai,[2] and on the fifteenth day, in the second month, after they left the land of Egypt, all the congregation of the Israelites murmured against Moses and Aaron. The Israelites said to them, "If only we had died, struck down by the Lord in the land of Egypt, when we sat by the fleshpots, and ate bread to satisfaction! You have brought us out into this wilderness, to starve us all to death!"

The Lord said to Moses, "Look, I will rain bread on you out of the sky, and the people will go out, and they will gather their daily portion each day, so I may test them, whether they follow my commandments or not. It will happen on the sixth day that they will prepare whatever they have brought in, and it will be double of what they will have gathered for the day, in previous days."

Moses and Aaron said to all the congregation of the Israelites, "So you will know that the Lord has brought you out of the land of Egypt, in the morning you will see the glory of the Lord, as he has heard your murmuring against God. Who are we, that you continue to murmur against us?"

Moses said, "This is the day when the Lord gives you flesh to eat in the evening, and bread in the morning until you are full because the Lord has heard your murmuring, which you murmur against us. Who are we? Your murmuring is not against us, but God!"

Moses said to Aaron, "Tell all the congregation of the Israelites, 'Come before God because he has heard your murmuring.'"

When Aaron spoke to all the congregation of the Israelites, and they turned towards the wilderness, then the glory of the Lord appeared in a cloud. The Lord said to Moses, "I have heard the murmuring of the Israelites. Tell them, 'Towards evening you will eat flesh, and in the morning you will be satisfied with bread, and you will know that I am the lord of the gods.'"

It was evening, and quails came up and covered the camp, in the morning it happened as the dew ceased around the camp, that they saw the face of the wilderness was covered in a small thing like white coriander seed, like frost on the land. When the Israelites saw it, they said one to another, "What is this?" As they did not know what it was.

Moses told them, "This is the bread which the Lord has given you to eat. This is that which the Lord has said, 'Gather of it each man for his family, a measure for each person, by the head according to the number of your minds, gather each of you with his neighbors."

The Israelites did so, and gathered, some more and some less. Having measured the measure full, he who gathered more had nothing left over, and he who had gathered less had no shortage. Each gathered just sufficient for the need of those who belonged to him.

Moses told them, "Let no man leave any of it until the morning." But they did not listen to Moses, and some left it until the morning, and it bred worms and stank, and Moses was irritated with them. They gathered it every morning, each man what he needed, and when the sun grew hot it melted. It happened on the sixth day, they gathered double what was needed, two measures for one man, and all the chiefs of the congregation went in and reported it to Moses.

Moses said to them, "Is this not the word that the Lord said? Tomorrow is the sabbath, a holy rest to for the Lord. Bake, you who bake, and see what you will see. All that is left over leave is to be stored for tomorrow."

They left it until the morning as Moses commanded them, and it did not stink and there were no worms in it.

Moses commanded, "Eat that today, for today is a sabbath to the Lord. It will not be found in the plain. Six days you will gather it, and on the seventh day is a sabbath, as there will be none on that day."

It happened on the seventh day that some of the people went out to gather, and found none. The Lord said to Moses, "How long are you unwilling to listen to my commands and my law? See, the Lord has given you this day, the sabbath, therefore he has given you on the sixth day the bread of two days. You will sit each of you in your houses, let no one go out from his place on the seventh day."

CHAPTER 16

The people kept sabbath on the seventh day. The Israelites called the name of it manna,[3] and it was as white coriander seed, and the taste of it was like a wafer with honey.

Moses said, "The Lord has commanded, 'Fill a measure with manna, to be stored up for your generations, that they may see the bread which you ate in the wilderness when the Lord led you out of the land of Egypt."

Moses said to Aaron, "Take a golden pot and gather into it one full measure of manna, and you will store it near God, to be kept for your generations," as the Lord commanded Moses. Aaron stored it near the testimony. The Israelites ate manna forty years until they came to the land of Phoenicia. Now the measure was the tenth part of three measures.

CHAPTER 16 NOTES

1 Codex Vaticanus: Sein (ⲥⲉⲓⲛ)
- LXX 25: Sina (Σινλ)
- LXX 53: Sēm (Σⲏμ)
- LXX 75: Seim (Σдμ)
- Leningrad Codex: Sîn (סִין)
- Peshitta: Syn (ܣܝܢ)
- Targum Onkelos: Sîn (סִין)
- Targum Pseudo-Jonathan: Sîn (סִין)
- Sahidic manuscript 16L: Sin (ⲥⲓⲛ)

The name Wilderness of "Sein" (Σειν) is the common translation in the Septuagint for both the Wilderness of Sîn (סִין) in *Names* and

192

the Wilderness of Sin (סִן) in Masoretic *Numbers*, which was followed by Jerome in the Latin Vulgate as the Wilderness of Sin. This suggests that the Old Aramaic version of the Torah did not differentiate between the two. As the *Book of Numbers* was likely organized into its current state during the era of King Hezekiah's reforms, and it was almost certainly written in the Phoenician script that was in use in Judah at the time, it is likely that it more accurately records the two locations as separate places. *Numbers* includes two lists of stations the Israelites stopped at during their travels from Egypt to Canaan, a shorter fragmentary list, and a longer list. It is generally accepted the two lists come from different sources, and were complied into a unified manuscript to detail the Israelites' journey.

In *Numbers* chapter 33, they are both listed in the long sequence of stops the Israelites made as they traveled from Egypt, confirming that the Hebrew translator, and probably the Judahite or Moabite compiler of the original book of *Numbers* viewed them as separate places. Sin (סִן) is identified in the verse as another name for Kadesh in Masoretic *Numbers* while in *Words* (*Deuteronomy*), Kadesh is in the Wilderness of Sin (סִן).

If the text of Names / Exodus and Numbers existed in the Canaanite language in the late Bronze Age, they would have been written in the cuneiform script. Sīn (𒂗𒍪) was the standard word for "moon" in Middle Babylonian cuneiform, based on the older Akkadian moon god ^{deity}Enzu (𒀭𒂗𒍪). The Egyptians also knew the region north of the Sinai Peninsula as the dry-land of Iȯh (⌒), meaning "moon," confirming that this was the same location. Additionally, the town in the region named after the Canaanite goddess Nikkal, supports this reading, as she was the wife of Yarikh, the Canaanite god of the moon.

If the name Sîn (סִין) was an indirect transliteration of Sîn (𒂗𒍪), it is logical that Sin (צִן) was also a transliteration of a name originally written in cuneiform. The most likely cuneiform transliteration of sin is zian (𒍣𒀭𒈾), meaning "desolate rocks," suggesting that this another way of writing ḥōrēbâ (חָרְבָה), meaning "desolation," the place were Moses encountered the wadjet, or (talking fire-plant) in chapter 3 of *Exodus / Names.* This supports the location in *Numbers* as being beyond the Gulf of Aqaba, and somewhere in the southern Jordanian highlands.

Conversely, *Exodus* shows clear signs of having been written in Akkadian cuneiform, which is likely where the pronunciation of Sin is derived, ultimately from the Akkadian spelling of Sîn (𒂗𒍪), which was spelled in Aramaic as Syn (𐤎𐤉𐤍), the direct transliteration of the Hebrew Syn (סִין). While the Aramaic spelling would have been standardized by the common spelling of the name of the moon god, there was nothing to standardize the spelling of the toponym in the Phoenician script, resulting in both toponyms being rendered phonetically by the scribes that unified the stories found in Numbers into a book circa 700 BCE.

The locations of these wildernesses have been a matter of debate for more than 2000 years, and early Christians era scholars widely debated this issue, with the majority favoring the region around Petra, in Jordan, or the Midian Mountains in northwestern Saudi Arabia. The Wilderness of Sin is identified within the Torah, as being between Elim and Mount Sinai, however, both locations are debated today. The Wilderness of Sinai is identified as including the site of Kadesh Barne, however, this location is also debated. Emperor Constantine's mother, Helena Augusta, named the Sinai Peninsula and Mount Sinai of Egypt in the 330s CE to resolve this issue, however, few scholars agree with this location today, as other

CHAPTER 16

references indicate the Israelites were wandering in northwest Saudi Arabia, Jordan, southern Syria.

Currently, Christian and Islamic scholars treating the Exodus as history, prefer Petra in Jordan, as the site of Kadesh, and Jebel al-Madhbah near Petra as Mount Sinai. This mountain has the Valley of Moses, called Wadi Musa in Arabic, which has an ancient staircase leading to the top of the mountain. It was clearly an ancient religious site, housing rain-fed cisterns, and two gigantic obelisks. At the entrance to the Valley of Moses is the Spring of Moses, which is believed to be the location that Moses struck the rock with his wand and caused water to flow. Based on the 1st century Josephus' claim that Kadesh Barnea was at Petra, the Wilderness of Sinai appears to be another name for the southern Arabah, the mostly dry valley running north from the Gulf of Aqaba to the Dead Sea. By extension, if Sinai and Sin are not two different spellings of the same place, then the location of the Wilderness of Sin would have to be the Sinai Desert, between An-Nekhel (Elim), and Hashem El Tarif (Rephidim).

2 Codex Vaticanus: Seina (ϲєιΝᴀ)

- Codex Ambrosiano: Sinai (ϲιΝᴀι)
- Leningrad Codex: Sînāy (סִינָי)
- Peshitta: Syny (ܣܝܢܝ)
- Targum Onkelos: Sînāy (סִינַי)
- Targum Pseudo-Jonathan: Sînāy (סִינַי)
- Sahidic manuscript 16L: Sin (ϲιΝ)

As this name is generally spelled as "Sinai" in English, that transliteration is used. See the previous note for a more information on Sin and Sinai.

3 Codex Vaticanus: manna (ΜΑΝΝΑ)

- Leningrad Codex: mān (מָן)
- Targum Onkelos: mān (מָן)
- Targum Pseudo-Jonathan: mannā' (מַנָּא). Translation: to count
- Sahidic manuscript 2043: manna (ΜΑΝΝΑ)

The word is related to several Egyptian words. The Egyptians used a sacred substance called mnw (𓏇𓏤𓊖), which was described similarly, however, it does not appear to have been eaten. Mnw (𓏠), commonly anglicized as Min, was also the Egyptian god of fertility, similar to the Canaanite Lehem, suggesting the original text may have been about Min or Lehem feeding the Israelites.

The source of the Egyptian substance called mnw (𓏇𓏤𓊖) isn't clear, and some researchers believe that the description of the Israelite substance falling from the sky may have originated with lecanora lichen growing on debris that fell from the sky. Large patches of lecanora lichen have been documented as appearing quickly under the right conditions and could have seemed to have fallen from the sky at night to the Israelites. Based on the Septuagint's dating of the exodus to right after the Minoan eruption, the underlying cause would have probably been the ash and ice that fell across the region creating a fertile ground for the lichen.

CHAPTER 17

All the congregation of the Israelites departed from the Wilderness of Sin, according to their encampments, by the command of the Lord, and they camped in Rephidim,[1] but there was no water for the people to drink. The people reviled Moses, saying, "Give us water, that we may drink."

Moses said to them, "Why do you hate me, and why do you tempt the Lord?"

The people thirsted there for water, and there the people murmured against Moses, saying, "Why is this? Have you brought us out of Egypt to kill us and our children and our livestock by thirst?"

Moses cried to the Lord, saying, "What will I do with this people? In a little while they will stone me."

The Lord answered Moses, "Go before these people and take with you the elders of the people, and the wand with which you struck the river, take it in your hand. Go and look, and I will stand there before you come, on the rock with a heavy plow,[2] and you will strike the rock, and water will come out from it, and the people will drink."

Moses did so before the sons of Israel, and he called the name of that place, Temptation and Reviling,[3] because of the reviling of the Israelites, and because they tempted the Lord, saying, "Is the Lord among us or not?"

CHAPTER 17

Amalek[4] came and fought with Israel in Rephidim.

Moses said to Joshua, "Choose out for yourself mighty men, and go out and set the army in formation against nomads tomorrow, and, watch I will stand on the top of the hill, and the wand of God will be in my hand."

Joshua did as Moses told him, and he went out and set the army in formation against nomads, and Moses and Aaron and Hur went up to the top of the hill. It happened when Moses lifted his hands, Israel prevailed, and when he let down his hands, nomads prevailed. But the hands of Moses were heavy, and they took a stone and put it under him, and he sat on it, and Aaron and Hur supported his hands one on this side, and the other on that, and the hands of Moses were supported until the sun went down.

Joshua routed the nomads and all their people he slaughtered with the sword. The Lord commanded Moses, "Write this as a memorial in a book, and tell to Joshua, 'I will utterly blot out the memory of nomads from under the sky.'"

Moses built an altar to the Lord, and called the name of it, 'the Lord my Refuge,'[5] for with a secret hand the Lord wages war on nomads for all generations.

CHAPTER 17 NOTES

1 Codex Vaticanus: Rafidein (ⲣⲁⲫⲓⲇⲉⲓⲛ)
- LXX 15: Rafideim (Ραφιαδμ)
- LXX 53: Rafidei (Ραφιαδ)

CHAPTER 17

- LXX 82: Rafēdein (Ραφιδιν)
- Leningrad Codex: Rəpîdîm (רְפִידִים)
- Peshitta: Rpydyn (ܪܦܝܕܝܢ)
- Targum Onkelos: Rəpîdîm (רְפִידִם)
- Targum Pseudo-Jonathan: Rəpîdîm (רְפִידִם)
- Vetus Latin manuscripts: Rapidin (Rαριδιν)
- Sahidic manuscript 16L: Rafidin (ΡαφιΔιν)
- Old Armenian manuscripts: Rafidim (Ռափիդիմ)

This location is generally associated with the Wadi Feiran, or the Feiran Oasis within it. The Wadi Feiran is an 81-mile (130 km) long wadi (seasonal river) which runs down the Jebel Musa to the Gulf of Suez. The Feiran Oasis, also called El Hesweh, is approximately 3 miles (4.8 km) long, and generally habitable year-round. The Greek geographer and polymath Claudius Ptolemy identified this as the location of Paran from the Torah, which is likely where the Arabic name came from.

The assumption that Wadi Feiran is Rephidim is again predicated on Jebel Musa being Mount Sinai, or at least in the vicinity of Mount Sinai, however, if Horeb is Sinai, then Sinai would have to be near or in Midian, as that was where Moses first encountered the fire-messenger that sent him back to Egypt, and a location in southern Sinai seems highly improbable for a Midianite shepherd, especially one trying to avoid Egyptians, who were mining in the region. If the Israelites had followed the southern road across the Sinai Peninsula en route to Mount Sinai / Horeb / Seir, they would have passed the An-Nekhel in central Sinai, and then proceeded east to the mountains of Hashem El Tarif in eastern Sinai, before following the Arabah north towards Jebel al-Madhbah. The likely location of this event along the route is at Hashem El Tarif, which did at one point have a spring flowing down from the top of the summit. The location of Rephidim at Hashem El Tarif is supported by the subsequent attack of the Amalekites, who, according to the *Book of Numbers* lived in the Negev, south of Judea, which is directly north of Hashem El Tarif.

2 Codex Vaticanus: epi tēs petras en kŏrēb (ЄΠΙ ΤΗC ΠЄΤΡΑC ЄΝΧѠΡΗΒ). Translation: on (or at, near, before) the rock (or Petra) in Horeb

- Leningrad Codex: 'al-haṣṣûr bəhōrēb (עַל־הַצּוּר בְּחֹרֵב). Translation: on (or above) the rock (or Tyre, Petra) in (or with, during, among) Horeb (or sword, war, plow)

- Peshitta: ŏl trnå bḥwryb (ܠܥܠ ܛܢܪܐ ܒܚܘܪܝܒ). Translation: on (or towards, against, about) rock (or flint) in (or at, with) Horeb (or sword, war, plow)

- Targum Onkelos: 'al ṭinārā' bəhôrēb (עַל טִנָרָא בְּחוֹרֵב). Translation: on (or towards, against, about) rock (or flint) in (or at, with) Horeb (or sword, war, plow)

- Targum Pseudo-Jonathan: bə'atrā' dətehĕmê rôšem rîgəlā' bəhôrēb (בְּאַתְרָא דְּתֶחֱמֵי רוֹשֶׁם רִיגְלָא בְּחוֹרֵב). Translation: in country (or place, region) of the seeing impression (or sketch, outline) foot (or leg, foot soldier, foot stool, hoof, base) in (or at, with) Horeb (or sword, war, plow)

- Sahidic manuscript 16L: hijn tpetra nKŏrēb (ϨΙΧΝ ΤΠЄΤΡΑ ÑΧѠΡΗΒ). Translation: upon the rock of Khoreb

The Greek translators translated the Aramaic text as "in Horeb," which is also how the Hebrew translation could be interpreted, supporting the Aramaic text as being essentially the same as the Hebrew, and reading as k̆hrb (כחרב). Unfortunately, the Greek translation does not make sense, as they were not near Mount Horeb at the time. An alternate reading of the Hebrew and Aramaic translations would be 'with a sword,' or 'with a plowshare,' neither of which probably made sense to the Greek translators, and so they opted for Horeb. Pseudo-Jonathan likely used a text that referred to a foot-plow, but did not understand the meaning, resulting in his broken translation. This appears to be a misunderstanding of the underlying Akkadian cuneiform text, in which the word kᵃrbum (𒆳𒊑𒁹𒈨𒆸) referred to a specialized heavy plow used to break up hard dry soil, as opposed to a lighter plow which was used to make furrows in fields. The name of this tool was spelled as ḥrb (חֶרֶב) in Aramaic, however, that word also meant any form of plow, sword, or spear. In this case, the Lord was apparently offering Moses a tool to breakup the hard soil and allow the water to flow. As the Greek translation is clearly incorrect, the translation of 'with a heavy plow' is imported from the Leningrad Codex.

3 Codex Vaticanus: peirasmos kai loidorēsis (ΠΕΙΡΑCΜΟC ΚΑΙ ΛΟΙΔΟΡΗCΙC). Translation: temptation and reviling (or ridicule)

• Codex Alexandrinus: pirasmos kai loidorēseis (ΠΕΙΡΑCΜΟCΚΑΙ ΛΟΙΔΟΡΗCΕΙC). Translation: temptation and reviling (or ridicule)

• LXX 15: Peirasmos kai Loidoria (Πдεασμος ιαy ΛΘΔοβιΔ) Translation: Temptation and Abuse (or Insult)

• LXX 72: Peirasmon kai (Πдεασμ℗ ιαy). Translation: Temptation and

• Leningrad Codex: massâ ûmᵊrîbâ (מַסָּה וּמְרִיבָה). Translation: trial (or temptation, miracle) and argument

• Peshitta: nså. wmrybå (ܟܐ: ܢܣܝ ܘܡܪܝܒܐ). Translation: tempted (or tested) and dispute (or quarrel)

• Targum Onkelos: nisêtâ' ûmaṣûtâ' (נְסֵיתָא וּמַצּוּתָא). Translation: standing banners (or fleeing place, existing miracle) and commandment

• Targum Pseudo-Jonathan: nisyônâ' ûmaṣṣûtâ' (נְסִיוֹנָא וּמַצּוּתָא). Translation: temptation (or trial) and commandment

• Sahidic manuscript 16L: ppeirasmos auō psohou (ⲡⲡⲉⲓ̈ⲣⲁⲥⲙⲟⲥ ⲁⲩⲱ ⲡⲥⲁϩⲟⲩ). Translation: the temptation and the curse

4 Codex Vaticanus: Amalēk (ⲀⲘⲀⲗⲎⲕ)

• Leningrad Codex: 'Ămālēq (עֲמָלֵק)

• Targum Onkelos: 'Ămālēq (עֲמָלֵק)

• Targum Jerusalem: 'Ămālēq (עֲמָלֵק)

• Targum Pseudo-Jonathan: 'Ămālēq (עֲמָלֵק)

• Sahidic manuscript 2043: Amalēk (ⲀⲘⲀⲗⲎⲕ)

In the Israelite books, the Amalek are periodically present in southern Canaan and the Sinai peninsula from the time of Moses until the time of King David, however, there is no archaeological evidence of a tribe called Amalek. They are treated as another name for descendants of Esau, who are otherwise called Edomites. The name itself is a transliteration of the Egyptian term åmw-rqî (𓄿𓄿𓂝𓏏 𓂻), which can be translated as "hostile Asiatics," "opposing Amorites," or "defiant fires."

An Egyptian named Ahmose pen-Nekhbet reported fighting at Avaris and Sharuhen in the autobiography craved into his tomb. He also noted that the Egyptians fought the šåsw (𓈙𓄿𓋴𓅱𓏏), meaning "nomads," in the Sinai peninsula during these campaigns. These nomads do not appear to have been the Israelites, who according to the Israelite texts would have been deep in the wilderness east of Edom by that point. However, the book of Numbers also places the "hostile Asiatics" in the Negev, which is where the Egyptians fought the nomads, indicating these were the same people. In the later Israelite books from the time of David, the term still refers to the nomadic tribes that lived in Midian, the Negev, and the Sinai peninsula. Therefore, this translation uses the term "nomads," as that appears to be the original meaning.

5 Codex Vaticanus: ΚS mou katafugē (ΚC MOY ΚΑΤΑΦΥΓΗ). Translation: lord my refuge

• DSS 4QpaleoExod^m: Yhwh nsy (𐤆𐤚𐤟 𐤀𐤉𐤄𐤆). DSS 4QpaleoExod^m dates to the Hasmonean Dynasty (140 to 37 BCE), and appears to be an early copy of the restored Samaritan Torah developed after General Pompey released the Samaritans from slavery under the Hasmoneans in 69 BCE.

• Leningrad Codex: Yəhōwâ. Nissi (יְהֹוָה \ נִסִּי). Translation: Yahweh. My miracle (or flag, banner, pole)

• Peshitta: mryå nsy (ܢܣܝ ܡܪܝܐ). Translation: Lord my miracle (or flag, banner, pole)

• Targum Onkelos: yəyā da'ăbad lēh nisîn (יְיָ דַּעֲבַד לֵהּ נִסִּין). Translation: Yahweh who (or that, of) serves for (or of) miracles (or banners, poles).

• Targum Pseudo-Jonathan: mêmərā' dayyā dên nîsā' (מֵימְרָא דַּיְיָ דֵּין נִיסָא). Translation: word of master that Yahweh judgment (or deliberation) sign (or symbol, constellation, appearance)

• Sahidic manuscript 2043: Sahidic manuscript 2043: joeis pe pama mpōt (ϫⲟⲉⲓⲥ ⲡⲉ ⲡⲁⲙⲁ ⲙ̄ⲡⲱⲧ). Translation: master of sky in palace that flies

The term found in the Masoretic texts and DSS 4QpaleoExod^m cannot be the original term in the verse, as nsy (נִסִּי / ܢܣܝ / 𐤆𐤚𐤟) was adopted from Persian word nišåni (𐎴𐎡𐏁𐎠𐎴), meaning "flag," or "banner." It was adopted into Judahite and Aramaic during the Persian Empire, centuries before the oldest surviving copies of this verse. Based on the context and phonetics, the original word was likely našû (𐎴𐎠𐎡), meaning to "raise up," "support," or "deliver," making the original verse read "Lord (or Yahweh) delivers," which is similar to the Greek interpretation.

CHAPTER 18

Jethro the priest of Midian, the father-in-law of Moses, heard of all that the Lord did to his people Israel, as the Lord brought Israel out of Egypt. Jethro the father-in-law of Moses, took Shiphrah the wife of Moses after she had been sent away, and her two sons, the name of the one was Gershom, when his father said, "I was a traveler in a strange land," and the name of the second Eliezer, when he said, "For the god of my father is my helper, and he has rescued me out of the hand of Pharaoh."

Jethro the father-in-law of Moses, and his sons and his wife, went out to Moses into the wilderness, where he camped on the mount of God. It was told to Moses, saying, "Look, your father-in-law Jethro is coming to you, and your wife and two sons with him."

Moses went out to meet his father-in-law, and did him reverence, and kissed him, and they embraced each other, and he brought them into the tent. Moses related to his father-in-law all things that the Lord did to Pharaoh and all the Egyptians for Israel's sake, and all the struggle that had happened to them in the road, and that the Lord had rescued them out of the hand of Pharaoh, and out of the hand of the Egyptians. Jethro was amazed at all the good things which the Lord did to them since he rescued them out of the hand of the Egyptians and out of the hand of Pharaoh and Jethro said, "Blessed be the Lord because he has rescued them out of the hand of the Egyptians and out of the hand of Pharaoh. Now know I that the Lord is greater than all gods, because of this, in which they attacked them."

Jethro the father-in-law of Moses took whole burnt offerings and sacrifices for God, for Aaron and all the elders of Israel came to eat bread with the father-in-law of Moses before God. It happened after the morning that Moses sat to judge the people, and all the people stood by Moses from morning until evening. Jethro having seen all that was done to the people, said, "What is this that you do to the people? You sit alone, and all the people stand by you from morning until evening?"

Moses told his father-in-law, "Because the people come to me to seek judgment from God. For whenever there is a dispute among them, and they come to me, I give judgment on each, and I teach them the ordinances of God and his law."

The father-in-law of Moses said to him, "You don't do this thing correctly, you will wear away with intolerable weariness, both you and all these people that are with you. This thing is hard, you will not be able to endure it yourself alone. Now then listen to me, and I will advise you, and God will be with you. You are to the people, all the things concerning God, and you bring their words to God. You testify to them the ordinances of God and his law, and you show to them the way that they will walk, and the works which they will do."

CHAPTER 18

"Do you look out for yourself out of all the people able men, fearing God, righteous men, hating pride, and you will set over them captains of thousands and captains of hundreds, and captains of fifties, and captains of tens. They will judge the people at all times, and the too burdensome matter they will bring to you, but they will judge the smaller cases, so they will relieve you and help you. If you will do this, God will strengthen you, and you will be able to pay attention, and all these people will return in peace into his own place."

Moses listened to the voice of his father-in-law and did as he advised him. Moses picked able men out of all Israel, and he made them captains of thousands and captains of hundreds, and captains of fifties and captains of tens over them. They judged the people at all times, and every too burdensome matter they brought to Moses, but every light-matter they judged themselves. Moses dismissed his father-in-law, and he returned to his own land.

CHAPTER 19

In the third month of the departure of the Israelites from the land of Egypt, on the same day, they came into the Wilderness of Sinai. They departed from Rephidim and came into the Wilderness of Sinai, and there Israel camped before the mountain. Moses went up to the mount of God, and God called him out of the mountain, saying, "These things will you say to the house of Jacob, and you will report them to the Israelites. You have seen all that I have done to the Egyptians, and I took you up as on eagles' wings, and I brought you near to myself. Now if you will indeed hear my voice, and keep my covenant, you will be for me a peculiar people above all nations, for the whole land is mine. You will be for me a royal priesthood and a holy nation, these words will you speak to the Israelites."

Moses came and called the elders of the people, and he set before them all these words, which God appointed them. All the people answered with one voice, and said, "All things that God has spoken, we will do and listen to," and Moses reported these words to God.

The Lord said to Moses, "Look! I come to you in a column of a cloud, that the people may hear me speaking to you, and may believe you forever," and Moses reported the words of the people to the Lord.

CHAPTER 19

The Lord told Moses, "Go down and solemnly order the people, and sanctify them today and tomorrow, and let them wash their garments. Let them be ready against the third day, for on the third day the Lord will descend on Mount Sinai before all the people. You will separate the people saying, 'Pay attention to yourselves that you go not up into the mountain or touch any part of it.' Everyone that touches the mountain will die. A hand will not touch it, for everyone that touches will be stoned with stones or shot through with a dart, whether animal or whether man, it will not live. When the voices and trumpets and cloud depart from off the mountain, they may come up the mountain."

Moses went down from the mountain to the people and sanctified them, and they washed their clothes. He said to the people, "Be ready and for three days don't go near a woman."

It happened on the third day, as the morning drew near, there were voices and lightning and dark clouds on Mount Sinai, and the voice of the trumpet sounded loud, and all the people in the camp trembled. Moses led the people out of the camp to meet God, and they stood by under the camp. Mount Sinai was smoking because God had descended on it in fire, and the smoke went up like the smoke of a furnace, and the people were amazed. The sounds of the trumpet were growing very much louder, and when Moses spoke, God answered him with a voice.

The Lord came down on Mount Sinai on the top of the mountain, and the Lord called Moses to the top of the mountain, and Moses went up. God said to Moses, "Go down and solemnly order the people, in case at any time they come close to see God, and a number of them fall. Let the priests that draw near to the lord of the gods to sanctify themselves, in case some are removed by the Lord."

Moses said to God, "The people will not be able to approach to Mount Sinai, for you have solemnly ordered us, saying, 'Set bounds to the mountain and sanctify it.'"

The Lord said to him, "Go, descend, and return with Aaron, but don't let the priests and the people force their way up to God, in case the Lord destroys some of them."

Moses went down to the people and said to them.

CHAPTER 20

The Lord said all these words: "I am the lord of the gods, who brought you out of the land of Egypt, out of the house of slavery."

"You will worship no other gods beside me. You will not make for yourself an idol, or an image of anything which is in the sky above, or which is in the land below, or which is in the waters under the land."

"You will not bow down to them, or serve them, for I am the lord of the gods, a jealous god, repaying the sins of the fathers on the children, to the third and fourth generation to them that hate me, and bestowing mercy on them that love me to thousands of them, and on them that keep my commandments."

"You will not take the name of the lord of the gods in vain, for the lord of the gods will not forgive him who takes his name in vain."

"Remember the sabbath day to keep it holy. Six days you will labor and will perform all your work. But on the seventh day is the sabbath of the lord of the gods, and you will do no work on it, or your son, your daughter, your servant, your slave-girl, your ox, your donkey, or any livestock of yours, or even the stranger that stays with you. For in six days, the Lord made the sky and the land, and the sea and all things in them, and then rested on the seventh day. Therefore, the Lord blessed the seventh day, and it is sacred."

"Honor your father and your mother, so it may go well with you, and so you may live long on the good land, which the lord of the gods gives to you."

"You will not commit adultery."

"You will not steal."

"You will not kill."

"You will not bear false witness against your neighbor."

"You will not covet your neighbor's wife. You will not covet your neighbor's house, or his field, or his servant, or his maid, or his ox, or his donkey, or any of his livestock, or whatever belongs to your neighbor."

All the people saw the voice, and the flashes, and the voice of the trumpet, and the mountain smoking, and all the people were afraid and stood far away, and said to Moses, "You speak to us, and don't let God speak to us, in case we die."

Moses said to them, "Be courageous, for God is come to you to try you, that his fear may be among you, that you don't sin."

The people stood far away, and Moses went into the darkness where God was. The Lord told Moses, "Say this to the house of Jacob, and report it to the Israelites, 'You have seen that I have spoken to you from the sky. You will not make for yourselves gods of silver, and gods of gold you will

CHAPTER 20

not make to yourselves. You will make for me an altar of dirt, and on it, you will sacrifice your whole burnt offerings, and your peace-offerings, and your sheep and your calves in every place, where I will record my name, and I will come to you and bless you. If you will make for me an altar of stones, you will not build them cut stones, for you have lifted your tools on them, and they are defiled. You will not go up to my altar by steps, that you may not uncover your nakedness on it."

CHAPTER 21

"These are the ordinances which you will set before them. If you buy a Habiru slave, he will serve you for six years, and in the seventh year he will go out free for nothing. If he should have come in alone, he will also go out alone, and if his wife should have gone in together with him, his wife also will go out. Moreover, if his master gave him a wife, and she had born him sons or daughters, the wife, and the children will be his master's and he will leave by himself. If the slave should say, 'I love my master and wife and children, and I will not leave,' his master will bring him to the judgment-seat of God, and then will he bring him to the door, to the doorpost, and his master will pierce his ear through with an awl, and he will serve him forever."

"If anyone sells his daughter as a slave, she will not depart like the slave-girls depart. If she is not pleasing to her master, who has betrothed herself to him, he will let her go free, but he is not at liberty to sell her to a foreign nation, because he has trifled with her. If he should have betrothed her to his son, he will do to her according to the right of daughters. If he takes another for himself, he will not deprive her of necessaries and her apparel, and her companionship with him. If he will not do these three things to her, she will go out free without silver."

"If any man strikes another and he dies, let him be certainly put to death. But as for he that did not do it intentionally, but God delivered him into his hands, I will give you a place where the slayer may flee. If anyone lies in wait for his neighbor, to kill him by craft, and he goes for refuge, you will take him from my altar to put him to death. Whoever hits his father or his mother, let him be certainly put to death. He that reviles his father or his mother will surely die. Whoever steals one of the Israelites, and prevails over him and sells him, and he is found with him, let him certainly die. If two men revile each other and strike each other with a stone or fist, and he doesn't die, but is laid up in his bed. If the man arises and walks around on his stick, he that struck him will be clear. He will only pay for his loss of time, and for his healing. If a man strikes his slave or his slave-girl, with a wand, and the party dies under his hands, he will be surely punished. But if the servant continues to live a day or two, don't let the master be punished, for he is his property."

"If two men fight and strike a woman with child, and her child is born deformed, he will be forced to pay a penalty that the woman's husband may lay on him, he will pay with a valuation. But if it is perfectly formed, he will give life for life, eye for eye, tooth for tooth, hand for hand, foot for foot, burning for burning, wound for wound, stripe for stripe."

"If one hits the eye of his slave, or the eye of his slave-girl, and put it out, he will let them go free for their eye's sake. If he should strike out the tooth of his slave, or the tooth of his slave-girl, he will send them away free for their tooth's sake."

"If a bull gores a man or woman and he or she dies, the bull will be stoned with stones, and his flesh will not be eaten, but the owner of the bull will be innocent. If the bull should have been given to goring in former time, and men should have told his owner, and he has not removed him, but he should have slain a man or woman, the bull will be stoned, and his owner will die also. If a ransom should be imposed on him, he will pay for the ransom of his mind as much as they will lay on him. If the bull gores a son or daughter, let them do to him according to this ordinance. If the bull gores a slave or slave-girl, he will pay to their master thirty silver shekels,[1] and the bull will be stoned. If anyone opens a pit or digs a cavity in stone, and does not cover it, and an ox or a donkey falls in there, the owner of the pit will make compensation. He will give silver to their owner, and the dead will be his own."

"If any man's bull gore the bull of his neighbor, and it dies, they will sell the living bull and divide the silver, and they will divide the dead bull. But if the bull is known to have been given to goring in time past, and they have testified to his owner, and he has not removed him, he will repay bull for bull, but the dead will be his own."

Chapter 21 Note

1 Codex Vaticanus: argyriou triakonta didrakma (ΑΡΓΥΡΙΟΥ ΤΡΙΑΚΟΝΤΑ ΔΙΔΡΑΧΜΑ). Translation: silver coins thirty two-drachmas

- Leningrad Codex: kesep. šəlōšîm šəqālîm (בֶּסֶף \ שְׁלֹשִׁים שְׁקָלִים). Translation: silver. Thirty shekels

- Peshitta: kspå (ܟܣܦܐ). Translation: silver

- Targum Onkelos: kəsap təlātîn sil'în (כְּסַף תְּלָתִין סִלְעִין). Translation: silver thirty rocks (or stones)

- Targum Pseudo-Jonathan: kəsap təlātîn sil'în (כְּסַף תְּלָתִין סִלְעִין). Translation: silver thirty rocks (or stones)

- Sahidic manuscript 2043: mntē nsateere nhat (ⲘⲚⲦ̄Ⲏ ⲚⲤⲀⲦⲈⲈⲢⲈ Ⲛ̄ⲄⲀⲦ). Translation: fifteen of staters of silver

The shekel was a unit of weight used throughout the Middle East for thousands of years, weighing approximately 8.6 grams of silver. The Greek drachma was a coin weighing approximately half a shekel, and therefore under Greek rule of the Middle East a two-drachma coin was used. As the Greeks clearly translated shekel into didrachma, the term shekel is restored in this translation.

CHAPTER 22

"If someone steals a calf or a sheep, and kills it or sells it, he will repay five calves for the calf, and four sheep for the sheep. If the thief is found breaking in by himself and is struck and dies, there will not be blood shed for him. But if the sun rises on him, he is guilty, he will die, and if he has nothing, let him be sold in compensation for what he has stolen. If the thing stolen is left and is in his hand alive, whether ox or sheep, he will repay them twice as much.

If anyone should feed down a field or a vineyard, and should send his animal to feed down another field, he will make compensation of his own field according to his produce, and if he will have fed down the whole field, he will pay for compensation the best of his own field and the best of his vineyard."

"If a fire has spread and caught thorns, and should also set on fire threshing-floors or ears of grain or a field, he that started the fire will make compensation."

"If anyone loans to his neighbor silver or goods to keep, and they are stolen out of the man's house, and the thief is found he will repay double. But if the thief is not be found, the master of the house will come forward before God and will swear that he has not worked deviously against his neighbor's deposit, according to every alleged injury, whether concerning a calf, or a donkey, or a sheep, or a garment, and every alleged loss, whatever it may be. The judgment of both will proceed before God, and he that is convicted by God will repay his neighbor double."

"If anyone loans his neighbor a calf or sheep or any animal to keep, and it is wounded or dies or is taken, and no one knows, an oath of God will be between both, each swearing that he is not at all guilty in the matter of his neighbor's deposit, and so his master will accept him guiltless, and he will not make compensation. If it is stolen from him, he will make compensation to the Lord. If it was killed by animals, he will take him to see the body, and he will not make compensation."

"If anyone borrows from his neighbor, and it is wounded or dies or is carried away, and it is not returned to the owner, he will make compensation. But if it is returned to the owner, he will not make compensation, but if the borrower is an employee, he will have the ruined animal instead of his employee."

"If anyone deceives a virgin that is not engaged to be married, and lays with her, he will surely take her for a wife. If her father positively refuses, and will not consent to give her to him as a wife, he will pay silver to her father according to the amount of the dowry of virgins."

"You will not save the lives of sorcerers."

"Everyone that lies with an animal you will put to death."

"He that sacrifices to any gods other than to the Lord will be killed."

CHAPTER 22

"You will not hurt a stranger, nor mistreat him, as you were strangers in the land of Egypt."

"You will not hurt a widow or orphan. If you should hurt them through ill-treatment, and they should cry aloud to me, I will surely hear their voice. I will be very angry and will kill you with the sword, and your wives will be widows and your children orphans."

"If you should lend silver to your poor brother, you will not be hard on him you will not demand interest from him. If you take your neighbor's garment for a pledge, you will restore it to him before sunset. For this is his clothing, this is the only covering of his nakedness. In what will he sleep? If then he will cry to me, I will listen to him, for I am merciful."

"You will not hate the gods, nor speak ill of the ruler of your people."

"You will not hold back the first fruits of your threshing floor and press. The firstborn of your sons you will give to me. You will do so with your calf and your sheep and your donkey. Seven days will it be under the mother, and the eighth day you will give it to me."

"You will be holy men for me, and you will not eat the flesh of animals, you will cast it to the dogs."

CHAPTER 23

"You will not receive a false report. You will not agree with the unjust man to become an unjust witness. You will not follow with the multitude into evil. You will not follow a multitude to turn aside with the majority to shut out judgment. You will not spare a poor man in judgment."

"If you find your enemy's ox or his donkey going astray, you will turn them back and return them to him. If you see your enemy's donkey fallen under its burden, you will not pass by it, but will help to raise it with him."

"You will not take away the sentence of the poor in his judgment. You will abstain from every unjust thing. You will not kill the innocent and just, and you will not justify the wicked for gifts. You will not receive gifts, for gifts blind the eyes of the seeing, and corrupt just words."

"You will not punish a stranger, for you know the heart of a stranger, as you were yourselves strangers in the land of Egypt. Six years you will sow your land, and gather in the fruits of it. But in the seventh year, you will let it rest, and leave it, and the poor of your nation will feed, and the wild animals of the field will eat that which remains. You will do this to your vineyard and your olive-yard."

"Six days you will work, and on the seventh day there will be rest, so your ox and your donkey can rest, and that the son of your slave-girl and the stranger may be refreshed."

CHAPTER 23

"Observe all things I have commanded you, and do not mention the names of other gods. They will not be heard out of your mouth."

"Hold a feast for me three times a year. Pay attention to keep the feast of unleavened bread: seven days you will eat unleavened bread, as I ordered you at the season of the month of new grain, for in it you came out of Egypt, and you will not appear before me empty. You will keep the feast of the harvest of first-fruits of your labors, whatever you will have sown in your field, and the feast of completion at the end of the year in the gathering in of your works out of your field. Three times in the year will all your males appear before the lord of the gods."

"For once I will have thrown out the nations from before you, and will have widened your borders, you will not offer the blood of my incense offering with leaven, neither must the fat of my feast remain until the morning. You will bring the first-offerings of the first fruits of your land into the house of the lord of the gods. You will not seethe a lamb in its mother's milk. And, Look, I send my messenger before your face, that he may keep you in the way, that he may bring you into the land which I have prepared for you. Pay attention to yourself and listen to him, and don't disobey him. For he will not give way to you, for my name is on him."

"If you will hear my voice, and if you will do all the things I will order you, and keep my covenant, you will be for me a peculiar people above all nations, for the whole land is mine, and you will be for me a royal priesthood and a holy nation. These words will you speak to the Israelites, 'If you will indeed hear my voice, and do all the things I will tell you, I will be an enemy to your enemies, and an adversary to your adversaries.' For my messenger will go as your leader, and will bring you to the Amorite, and Cypriot, and Perizzite, and Canaanite, and Girgasite, and Mitanni, and Jebusite, and I will destroy them. You will not worship their gods, nor serve them. You will not do according to their works, but will utterly destroy them, and break to pieces their columns. You will serve the lord of the gods, and I will bless your bread and your wine and your water, and I will turn away sickness from you."

"There will be no one on your land that is impotent or barren. I will surely fulfill the number of your days. I will send terror before you, and I will strike with amazement all the nations to which you will come, and I will make all your enemies flee. I will send hornets before you, and you will drive out the Amorites and the Mitannian, and the Canaanites and the Cypriots from you."

"I will not throw them out in one year, or the land may become desolate, and the animals of the field may multiply against you. Little by little I will drive them out from before you until you will be increased and inherit the land. I will set your borders from the Papyrus Sea to the sea of the Pelesets, and from the wilderness to the great river Euphrates, and I will give into your hand those that live in the land and will drive them out from you. You will make no covenant with them and their gods. They will not dwell in your land, in case they cause you to sin against me, and for if you should serve their gods, these will be an offense to you."

CHAPTER 24

To Moses was said, "Go up to the Lord, you and Aaron, and Nadab, and Abihu, and seventy of the elders of Israel, and they will worship the Lord from a distance. Moses alone will draw near to God, and they will not draw near, and the people will not come up with them."

Moses went in and related to the people all the words of God and the ordinances, and all the people answered with one voice, saying, "All the words which the Lord has spoken, we will do and listen."

Moses wrote all the words of the Lord, and Moses rose up early in the morning, and built an altar under the mountain, and set up twelve stones for the twelve tribes of Israel. He sent out the young men of the Israelites, and they offered whole burnt offerings, and they sacrificed young calves as a peace-offering to the gods. Moses took half the blood and poured it into bowls, and half the blood he poured out on the altar. He took the book of the covenant and read it in the ears of the people, and they said, "All things whatever the Lord has spoken we will do and listen therein."

Moses took the blood and sprinkled it on the people, and said, "Look the blood of the covenant, which the Lord has made with you concerning all these words."

Moses went up, and Aaron, and Nadab and Abihu, and seventy of the elders of Israel. They saw the place where the god of Israel stood, and under his feet was as it were a work of sapphire slabs, and as it were the appearance of the firmament of the sky in its purity. Of the chosen ones of Israel, there was not even one missing, and they appeared where God was and did eat and drink. the Lord said to Moses, "Come up to me into the mountain, and I will give you the tablets of stone, the law, and the commandments, which I have written to give them laws."

Moses rose up with Joshua his attendant, and they went up into the mount of God. To the elders, they said, "Rest there until we return to you, and look, Aaron and Hur are with you. If any man has a cause to be tried, let them go to them."

Moses and Joshua went up to the mountain, and the cloud covered the mountain. The glory of God came down on Mount Sinai, and the cloud covered it six days, and the Lord called Moses on the seventh day out of the cloud. The appearance of the glory of the Lord was as burning fire on the top of the mountain before the Israelites. Moses went into the middle of the cloud, and went up to the mountain, and was there in the mountain forty days and forty nights.

CHAPTER 25

The Lord said to Moses, "Speak to the Israelites, and take first fruits of all, who may be disposed in their heart to give, and you will take my first fruits. This is the offering which you will take of them, and gold and silver and brass, and blue, and purple, and double scarlet, and finespun linen, and goats' hair, and rams' skins dyed red, and blue skins, and incorruptible wood, and oil for the light, incense for anointing oil, and for the composition of incense, and carnelian stones, and stones for the carved work of the shoulder-piece, and the full-length robe."

"You will make a sanctuary for me, and I will appear among you. You will make for me according to all things which I show you in the mountain, even the pattern of the tabernacle, and the pattern of all its furniture: so will you make it. You will make the box of the testimony of incorruptible wood; the length of two cubits and a half, and the width of a cubit and a half, and the height of a cubit and a half. You will gild it with pure gold, you will gild it within and without, and you will make for it golden wreaths twisted around it."

"You will cast four golden rings for it and will put them on the four sides, two rings on the one side, and two rings on the other side. You will make staffs of incorruptible wood and will coat them with gold. You will put the staffs into the rings on the sides of the box, to bear the box with them. The staffs will remain fixed in the rings of the box."

"You will put into the box the testimonies which I will give you. You will make a lid, a lid of pure gold. The length of two cubits and a half, and the width of a cubit and a half. You will make two cherubs[1] graven in gold, and you will put them on both sides of the lid. They will be made, one cherub on this side, and another cherub on the other side of the lid, and you will make the two cherubs on the two sides. The cherubs will stretch out their wings above, overshadowing the lid with their wings, and their faces will be towards each other, the faces of the cherubs will be towards the lid. You will set the lid on the top of the box, and you will put into the box the testimonies which I will give you."

"I will make myself known to you from there, and I will speak to you from above the lid, between the two cherubs, which are on the box of the testimony. In all things which I order you concerning the Israelites."

"You will make a table of pure gold, two cubits in length, and a cubit in width, and a cubit and a half in height. You will make for it golden wreaths twisted around about, and you will make for it a crown of a hand-width around it. You will make a twisted wreath for the crown around about. You will make four golden rings, and you will put the four rings on the four parts of its feet under the crown. The rings will be for bearings for the staffs, that they may bear the table with them. You will make the staffs of incorruptible wood, and you will gild them with pure gold, and the table will be borne with them."

"You will make its dishes and its censers, and its bowls, and its cups, with which you will offer drink-offerings. You will make them of pure gold. You will place show-bread on the table before me continually. You will make a candlestick of pure gold, you will engrave the candlestick: its stem and its branches, and its bowls and its knobs and its lilies will be of it. Six branches proceeding sideways, three branches of the candlestick from one side of it, and three branches of the candlestick from the other side."

"Three bowls fashioned like almonds, on each branch a knob and a lily; so to the six branches proceeding from the candlestick, and in the candlestick four bowls fashioned like almonds, in each branch knobs and the flowers of it. A knob under two branches out of it, and a knob under four branches out of it. So to the six branches proceeding from the candle-stick, and in the candlestick four bowls fashioned like almonds. Let the knobs and the branches be of one piece, altogether graven of one piece of pure gold. You will make its seven lamps: and you will set on it the lamps, and they will shine from one front. You will make its funnel and its snuff-dishes of pure gold. All these articles will be a talent of pure gold. See, you will make them according to the pattern shown you in the mount."

CHAPTER 25

CHAPTER 25 NOTES

1 Codex Vaticanus: ǩeroubim (ⲭⲉⲣⲟⲩⲃⲓⲙ)

• Leningrad Codex: kərubîm (כְּרֻבִים). Translation: cherubs (or griffins)

• Peshitta: krwbå (ܟ̈ܪܘܒܐ). Translation: cherubs (or griffins)

• Targum Onkelos: kərûbîn (כְּרוּבִין). Translation: cherubs (or griffins)

• Targum Pseudo-Jonathan: kərûbîn (כְּרוּבִין). Translation: cherubs (or griffins)

• Vetus Latina manuscripts: cherubin (ⅽⱨⲉⱤⱵⰱⰹⲚ)

• Bohairic manuscripts: ǩeroubim (ⲭⲉⲣⲟⲩⲃⲓⲩ)

The word "cherub" (ܟ̈ⲣⲟ / כרוב / עעע / 𓐭) was the Semitic term for the mythical creature generally called a "griffin" today. The oldest form is recorded in the Akkadian word karibu (𒀭𒆠𒊑𒁍), meaning "one who blesses." Based on the archaeological record of Canaan, it appears that during the late Bronze Age, the "cherub" was depicted as a sphinx. During the Iron Age, the Assyrian karubu (𒀭𒆠𒊑𒁍) iconography was adopted by the Israelites. The term "cherub" appears to have been used as a substitute for śārāp (שָׂרָף) after King Hezekiah or King Manasseh's reforms to the Torah in the early 8th century BCE. Isaiah called Nəḥuštān (נְחֻשְׁתָּן) a seraph when he visited the temple in the late 9th century BCE, before it was destroyed at the beginning of the 8th century BCE. Nəḥuštān was the name or title of the Bronze Serpent statue that Moses made in *Numbers*, chapter 21. This suggests that the original "cherubs" on the Ark of the Testimony were seraphs or wadjets. Typically, wadjets were depicted in pairs in older Egyptian literature. During the Middle Bronze Age, paintings and carvings of Egyptian sacred barks, which the Ark of

234

the Testimony was modeled on, were almost always depicted with wadjets. They became less common in the Late Bronze Age, when Amen became the dominant god, and sphinx statues became more common as "guardian gods."

CHAPTER 26

"You will make the tabernacle, ten curtains of finely spun linen, and blue and purple, and spun scarlet with cherubs. You will make them with the work of a weaver. One curtain will be forty-eight cubits long, and one curtain will be four cubits wide. There will be the same measurement for all the curtains. The five curtains will be joined one to another, and the other five curtains will be closely connected to one another. You will make for them loops of blue on the edge of one curtain, on one side for the coupling, and so will you make on the edge of the outer curtain for the second coupling. Fifty loops will you make for one curtain, and fifty loops will you make on the part of the curtain answering to the coupling of the second, opposite each other, corresponding to each other at each point. You will make fifty golden rings, and you will join the curtains to each other with the rings, and it will be one tabernacle."

"You will make for a covering of the tabernacle from skins with the hair still on. You will make them from eleven skins. The length of one skin thirty cubits, and the width of one skin four cubits: there will be the same measure to the eleven skins. You will join the five skins together, and the six skins together, and you will double the sixth skin in front of the tabernacle. You will make fifty loops on the border of one skin, which is in the middle for the joints, and you will make fifty loops on the edge of the second skin that joins it. You will make fifty bronze rings, and you will join the rings by the loops, and you will join the skins, and they will be one."

"The end of the skins of the tabernacle you will fix so the half of the skin that is left you will fold over, and the extra skins of the tabernacle you will fold it over behind the tabernacle. A cubit on this side, and a cubit on that side of that which remains of the skins, of the length of the skins of the tabernacle. It will fold over the sides of the tabernacle on this side and that side, and so may cover it. You will make for a covering of the tabernacle rams' skins dyed red, and blue skins as coverings above. You will make the posts of the tabernacle of incorruptible wood. Of ten cubits will you make one post, and the width of one post of a cubit and a half. Two joints will you make in one post, answering the one to the other: so will you do to all the posts of the tabernacle. You will make posts to the tabernacle, twenty posts on the north side."

"You will make for the twenty posts forty silver sockets. Two sockets on each post on both its sides, and two sockets on the other post for both its sides. For the next side, towards the south, twenty posts, and their forty silver sockets. Two sockets for one post on each of its sides, and two sockets for the other post on each of its sides. On the back of the tabernacle at the part which is towards the west, you will make six posts. You will make two posts on the corners of the tabernacle behind. It will be equal below, they will be equal towards the same part from the heads to one joining, so will you make to both the two corners, let them be equal."

"There will be eight posts and their sixteen silver sockets. Two sockets to one post on both its sides and two sockets to the other post. You will make bars of incorruptible wood; five to one post on one side of the tabernacle, and five bars to one post on the second side of the tabernacle, and five bars to the hinder posts, on the side of the tabernacle towards the sea."

"Place the bar in the middle, between the posts, going through from the one side to the other side. You will gild the posts with gold, and you will make golden rings, into which you will introduce the bars, and you will gild the bars with gold. You will set up the tabernacle according to the pattern shown you in the mount. You will make a veil of blue and purple and scarlet woven, and fine linen spun: you will make it cherubs in woven work. You will set it on four posts of incorruptible wood coated with gold, and their tops will be gold, and their four sockets will be of silver."

"You will put the veil on the posts, and you will carry within the veil, the box of the testimony, and the veil will make a separation for you between the holy and the holy of holies. You will screen with the veil the box of the testimony in the holy of holies. You will set the table outside the veil, and the candlestick opposite the table on the south side of the tabernacle, and you will put the table on the north side of the tabernacle. You will make a screen for the door of the tabernacle of blue, and purple, and spun scarlet and fine linen spun, the work of the embroiderer. You will make for the veil five posts, and you will gild them with gold, and their chapiters will be gold, and you will cast for them five bronze sockets."

CHAPTER 27

"You will make an altar from incorruptible wood, five cubits in the length, and five cubits in the width. The altar will be square, and the height of it will be three cubits. You will make the horns on the four corners; the horns will be of it, and you will overlay them with brass. You will make a rim for the altar, and its covering and its cups, and its meat hooks, and its fire-pan, and all its vessels will you make of brass."

"You will make for it a bronze grate with netting, and you will make for the grate four bronze rings under the four sides. You will put them below under the grate of the altar, and the grate will extend to the middle of the altar."

"You will make for the altar staffs from incorruptible wood, and you will cover them with brass. You will put the staffs into the rings, and let the staffs be on the sides of the altar to carry it. You will make it hollow with boards: according to what was shown you in the mount, so you will make it. You will make a court for the tabernacle, curtains of the court of fine linen spun on the south side, the length of a hundred cubits for one side."

"The twenty columns and twenty bronze sockets from them, and their rings and their silver clasps. So there will be on the side towards the north curtains of a hundred cubits in length, and their columns twenty, and their sockets twenty of brass, and the rings and the clasps of the columns, and their sockets coated with silver. In the width of the tabernacle towards the west curtains of fifty cubits, their columns ten and their sockets ten. In the width of the tabernacle towards the south, curtains of fifty cubits; their columns ten, and their sockets ten. The height of the curtains will be fifty cubits for the one side of the gate, with three columns, and three sockets. For the second side the height of the curtains will be of fifteen cubits, and their columns three, and their sockets three. A veil for the door of the court, the height of it of twenty cubits of blue linen, and purple, and spun scarlet, and of fine linen spun with the are of the embroiderer; their columns four, and their sockets four. All the columns of the court round about coated with silver, and their chapiters silver and their brass sockets."

"The length of the court will be a hundred cubits on each side and the width fifty on each side, and the height five cubits of fine linen spun, and their sockets of brass. All the furniture and all the instruments and the pins of the court will be of brass. Do you order the Israelites, and let them take for you refined pure olive oil beaten to burn for light, that a lamp may burn continually in the tabernacle of the testimony, outside the veil that is over the box of the covenant, will Aaron and his sons burn it from evening until morning, before the Lord, and it is a perpetual ordinance to your generations of the Israelites."

CHAPTER 28

"Take with yourself both Aaron your brother, and his sons, them of the Israelites. So that Aaron, and Nadab and Abihu, and Eleazar and Ithamar, sons of Aaron, may minister to me. You will make holy apparel for Aaron your brother, for honor and glory. Speak to all those who are wise in understanding, whom I have filled with the breath of wisdom and perception,[1] and they will make the holy apparel of Aaron for the sanctuary, in which apparel he will minister to me as a priest. These are the garments which they will make: the breastplate, and the shoulder-piece, and the full-length robe, and the tunic with a fringe, and the brimmed hat, and the girdle, and they will make holy garments for Aaron and his sons to minister to me as priests."

They will take the gold, and the blue, and the purple, and the scarlet, and the fine linen. They will make the shoulder-piece of fine linen spun, the woven work of the embroiderer. The work will have two shoulder-pieces joined together, fastened on the two sides. The woven work of the shoulder-pieces which is on it will be of one piece according to the work, of pure gold and blue and purple, and spun scarlet and fine twined linen. You will take the two stones, the stones of emerald, and you will engrave on them the names of the Israelites. Six names on the first stone, and the other six names on the second stone, according to their births."

"It will be the work of the stone-engravers, as will engraving a seal on the two stones with the names of the Israelites. You will put the two stones on the shoulders of the shoulder-piece: they are memorial stones for the Israelites: and Aaron will bear the names of the Israelites before the Lord on his two shoulders, a memorial for them. You will make little shields of pure gold, and you will make two fringes of pure gold, decorated with wreathed flowers. You will put the wreathed fringes on the circlets, fastening them on their shoulder-pieces in the front."

"You will make the oracle of judgment, the work of the embroiderer: in keeping with the vest, you will make it of gold, and blue and purple, and spun scarlet, and fine spun linen. You will make it square: it will be double; of a span the length of it, and a span the width. You will interweave with it a texture of four rows of stone; there will be a row of stones, a carnelian, a topaz, and emerald, the first row. The second row, a carbuncle, a sapphire, and a jasper. The third row, a lapis lazuli, an agate, an amethyst: and the fourth row, a chrysolite, and a beryl, and an onyx stone, set round with gold, bound together with gold, and let them be in each row."

"Let there be twelve stones with the names of the Israelites engraved as seals: let them be for the twelve tribes each according to the name. You will make on the oracle woven fringes, a chain-work of pure gold. Aaron will take the names of the Israelites, on the oracle of judgment on his breast; a memorial before God for him as he goes into the sanctuary. You will put the fringes on the oracle of judgment, and you will put the wreaths on both sides of the oracle, and you will put the two circlets on both the shoulders of the vest in front. You will put the lights and perfections on the oracle of judgment, and it will be on the breast of Aaron when he goes into the holy place before the Lord, and Aaron will bear the judgments of the Israelites on his breast before the Lord continually."

"You will make the full-length tunic entirely of blue. The opening of it will be in the middle having a fringe round about the opening, the work of the weaver, woven together in the joining of the same piece that it might not be tore. Under the fringe of the robe below, you will make as it were pomegranates of a flowering pomegranate tree, of blue, and purple, and spun scarlet, and fine linen spun, under the fringe of the robe round about: golden pomegranates of the same shape, and bells around about between these. A bell by the side of a golden pomegranate, and flower-work on the fringe of the robe around it."

"Aaron will speak when he administers, when he goes into the sanctuary before the Lord and as he goes out, so he doesn't die. You will make a plate of pure gold, and you will engrave on it as the graving of a signet, Holiness of the Lord. You will put it on the spun blue cloth, and it will be on the miter: it will be in the front of the miter. It will be on the forehead of Aaron, and Aaron will bear away the sins of their holy things, all that the Israelites will sanctify of every gift of their holy things, and it will be on the forehead of Aaron continually acceptable for them before the Lord."

CHAPTER 28

"The fringes of the garments will be of fine linen, and you will make a turban of fine linen, and you will make a girdle, the work of the embroiderer. For the sons of Aaron, you will make tunics and girdles, and you will make for them brimmed hats for honor and glory. You will put them on Aaron your brother, and his sons with him, and you will anoint them and consecrate them: and you will sanctify them, that they may minister to me in the priest's office. You will make for them linen drawers to cover the nakedness of their flesh; they will reach from the loins to the thighs. Aaron will have them, and his sons, whenever they enter into the tabernacle of witness, or when they will advance to the altar of the sanctuary to minister, so they will not bring sin on themselves, in case they die. It is a perpetual statute for him, and for his seed after him."

CHAPTER 28 NOTES

1 Codex Vaticanus: pneumatos aistēseōs kai poiēsousin (ΠΝΕΥΜΑΤΟΣ ΑΙϹΘΗϹΕѠϹΚΑΙΠΟΙΗϹΟΥϹΙΝ). Translation: air (or wind, breath, life, spirit) of discernment (or perception, senses)

• LXX 53: pneumatos suneseōs (πνόυματος συνόσόωc) Translation: air (or wind, breath, life, spirit) of discernment (or perception, senses)

• LXX 58: pneuma aistēseōs (πνανμα αιϑλοσόωc) Translation: air (or wind, breath, life, spirit) of discernment (or perception, senses)

• LXX 129: pneumatos sofías kai aistēseōs (πνόυματος σοϐϕλc ιαι αιϑλοσόωc) Translation: air (or wind, breath, life, spirit) of wisdom (or Sophia) and discernment (or perception, senses)

- LXX 131: pneumatos sofías (πνόυματος σοφφας) Translation: air (or wind, breath, life, spirit) of wisdom (or Sophia)

- Leningrad Codex: rûah hokmâ (רוּחַ חָכְמָה). Translation: wind (or air, atmosphere, direction, spirit, mind, demon) wisdom (or counsel, knowledge)

- Peshitta: rwhå dhkmtå (ܪܘܚܐ ܕܚܟܡܬܐ). Translation: spirit (or specter, breath, wind, smell, pain) of wisdom (or science, philosophy, judgment, expertness

- Targum Onkelos: rûah hokmətā' (רוּחַ חָכְמְתָא). Translation: wind (or air, direction, spirit, mind) wisdom (or counsel, knowledge)

- Targum Pseudo-Jonathan: rûhā' dəhokmətā' (רוּחָא דְחָכְמְתָא). Translation: wind (or air, direction, spirit, mind) wisdom (or counsel, knowledge)

- Vetus Latina manuscripts: spiritus intellectui (sᴘɪʀɪᴛᴜs ɪɴᴛᴇʟʟᴇᴄᴛᴜɪ). Translation: spirit (or air, breeze, breath) of intelligence

CHAPTER 29

"These are the things which you will do with them. You will sanctify them so that they will serve me in the priesthood, and you will take one young calf from the herd, and two unblemished rams, and unleavened loaves kneaded with oil, and unleavened cakes anointed with oil. You will make them of fine flour of wheat. You will put them in one basket, and you will offer them on the basket, and the young calf and the two rams. You will bring Aaron and his sons to the doors of the tabernacle of the testimony, and you will wash them with water."

"Having taken the garments, you will put on Aaron your brother both the full-length robe and the vest and the oracle, and you will join for him the oracle to the vest. You will put the miter on his head, and you will put the plate, the Holiness, on the miter. You will take from the anointing oil, and you will pour it on his head and anoint him, and you will bring his sons, and put garments on them. You will gird them with the girdles, and put the brimmed hats on them, and they will have a priestly office to me forever, and you will make perfect the hands of Aaron and the hands of his sons."

"You will bring the calf to the door of the tabernacle of witness, and Aaron and his sons will lay their hands on the head of the calf, before the Lord, by the doors of the tabernacle of witness. You will kill the calf before the Lord, by the

CHAPTER 29

doors of the tabernacle of witness. You will take of the blood of the calf, and put it on the horns of the altar with your finger, but all the rest of the blood you will pour out at the foot of the altar. You will take all the fat that is on the belly, and the lobe of the liver, and the two kidneys, and the fat that is on them and will put them on the altar. But the flesh of the calf, and his skin, and his dung will you burn with fire outside of the camp; for it is an offering on account of sin."

"You will take one ram, and Aaron and his sons will lay their hands on the head of the ram. You will kill it, and take the blood and pour it on the altar and around it. You will divide the ram by his several limbs, and you will wash the inward parts and the feet with water, and you will put them on the divided parts with the head. You will offer the whole ram on the altar, a whole burnt offering to the Lord for a sweet-smelling savor. It is an offering of incense to the Lord."

"You will take the second ram, and Aaron and his sons will lay their hands on the head of the ram. You will kill it, and take of the blood of it, and put it on the tip of Aaron's right ear, and on the thumb of his right hand, and on the big toe of his right foot, and on the tips of the right ears of his sons, and on the thumbs of their right hands, and on the big toes of their right feet. You will take of the blood from the altar, and of the anointing oil, and you will sprinkle it on Aaron and his garments, and his sons and on his sons' garments with him, and he will be sanctified and his apparel, and his sons and his sons' apparel with him: but the blood of the ram you will pour round about on the altar. You will take from the ram its

250

fat, both the fat that covers the belly, and the lobe of the liver, and the two kidneys, and the fat that is on them, and the right shoulder, for this is an accomplishment."

"One cake made with oil, and one cake from the basket of unleavened bread set out before the Lord. You will place them all in the hands of Aaron, and the hands of his sons, and you will separate them for a separation before the Lord. You will take them from their hands, and will offer them up on the altar of whole burnt offering for a sweet-smelling savor before the Lord, and it is an offering to the Lord. You will take the breast from the ram of consecration which is Aaron's, and you will separate it as a separate offering before the Lord, and it will be to you for a portion. You will sanctify the separated breast and the shoulder of removal which has been separated, and which has been removed from the ram of consecration, of the portion of Aaron and of that of his sons."

"It will be a perpetual statute of the Israelites to Aaron and his sons, for this is a separate offering, and it will be a special offering from the Israelites, from the peace-offerings of the Israelites, a special offering to the Lord. The apparel of the sanctuary which is Aaron's will be his son's after him, for them to be anointed in them, and to fill their hands. The priest his successor from among his sons who will go into the tabernacle of witness to minister in the holies will put them on seven days. You will take the ram of consecration, and you will boil the flesh in the holy place. Aaron and his sons will eat the flesh of the ram, and the loaves in the basket, by the doors of the tabernacle of witness. They will eat the offerings with which they were sanctified to fill their hands, to sanctify them, and a stranger will not eat of them, for they are holy. If anything is left of the flesh of the sacrifice of consecration and the loaves until the morning, you will burn the remainder with fire. It will not be eaten, for it is a holy thing."

"So you will do for Aaron and his sons according to all things that I have commanded you. Seven days will you fill their hands. You will sacrifice the calf of the sin-offering on the day of purification, and you will purify the altar when you do sanctify it, and you will anoint it to sanctify it. Seven days will you purify the altar and sanctify it, and the altar will be most holy, everyone that touches the altar will be hallowed. These are the offerings that you will offer on the altar: two unblemished lambs of a year old daily on the altar continually, a constant offering. One lamb you will offer in the morning, and the second lamb you will offer in the evening."

"The tenth measure of fine flour mingled with a quarter of a hin[1] of beaten oil, and a drink-offering the fourth part of a hin of wine for one lamb. You will offer the second lamb in the evening, the same way as the morning-offering, and according to the drink-offering of the morning lamb. You will offer it an offering to the Lord for a sweet-smelling savor, a perpetual sacrifice to your generations, at the door of the tabernacle of witness before the Lord, and in which I will be known to you from there, to speak to you."

CHAPTER 29

"I will there give orders to the Israelites, and I will be sanctified in my glory. I will sanctify the tabernacle of the testimony and the altar, and I will sanctify Aaron and his sons, to minister as priests to me. I will be named among the Israelites and will be their God. They will know that I am the Lord their God, who brought them forth out of the land of Egypt, to be named by them, and to be their God."

CHAPTER 29 NOTES

1 Codex Vaticanus: in (ιΝ)

- Leningrad Codex: hîn (הִין)
- Peshitta: hmynå (ܗܡܝܢܐ). Translation: belt
- Targum Onkelos: hînā' (הִינָא)
- Targum Pseudo-Jonathan: hînā' (הִינָא)

The hin was ancient Samaritan and Judahite unit of measurement estimated around 3.7 liters (3.9 quarts).

CHAPTER 30

"You will make the altar of incense of incorruptible wood. You will make it a cubit in length, and a cubit wide: it will be square, and the height of it will be of two cubits, and its horns will be part of it. You will gild its grate with pure gold, and its sides around it, and its horns, and you will make for it a wreathed border of gold around it. You will make under its wreathed border two rings of pure gold. You will make it to the two corners on the two sides, and they will be bearings for the staffs, to bear it with them. You will make the staffs of incorruptible wood and will gild them with gold. You will set it before the veil that is over the box of the testimonies, in which I will make myself known to you from there."

"Aaron will burn on it fine compound incense every morning. Whenever he trims the lamps he will burn incense on it. When Aaron lights the lamps in the evening, he will burn incense on it; a constant incense-offering always before the Lord for their generations. You will not offer strange incense on it, nor an offering made by fire, nor a sacrifice, and you will not pour a drink-offering on it. Once in the year Aaron, will make atonement on its horns, he will purge it with the blood of purification for their generations. This is most holy to the Lord."

The Lord said to Moses, "If you take account of the Israelites in the surveying of them, and they will give everyone a ransom for his mind to the Lord, then there will not be among them a fall in the visiting of them. This is what they will give, as many as pass the survey, half a coin which is according to the coin of the sanctuary. Twenty gerahs[1] go into the shekel, but a half shekel is the offering to the Lord. Everyone that passes the survey from twenty years old and upwards will give the offering to the Lord. The rich will not give more, and the poor will not give less than the half shekel in giving the offering to the Lord, to make atonement for your minds. You will take the silver of the offering from the Israelites, and will give it for the service of the tabernacle of the testimony, and it will be to the Israelites a memorial before the Lord, to make atonement for your minds."

The Lord said to Moses, "Make a bronze layer, and a bronze base for it, to wash one's self, and you will put it between the tabernacle of witness and the altar, and you will pour forth water into it. Aaron and his sons will wash their hands and their feet with water from it. Whenever they will go into the tabernacle of witness, they will wash with water, so they will not die, whenever they advance to the altar to do service and to offer the whole burnt offerings to the Lord. They will wash their hands and feet with water, whenever they will go into the tabernacle of witness. They will wash with water, that they don't die, and it will be for them a perpetual statute, for him and his generations after him."

The Lord said to Moses, "Also take sweet plants, the flower of choice myrrh five hundred shekels, and the half of this two hundred and fifty shekels of sweet-smelling cinnamon, and two hundred and fifty shekels of sweet-smelling calamus and of iris, five hundred shekels to the sanctuary, and a hin of olive oil. You will make it a holy anointing oil, a perfumed ointment tempered by the skill of the perfumer: it will be a holy anointing oil. You will anoint with it the tabernacle of witness, and the box of the tabernacle of witness, and all its furniture, and the candlestick and all its furniture, and the altar of incense, and the altar of whole burnt offerings and all its furniture, and the table and all its furniture, and the layer. You will sanctify them, and they will be most holy. Everyone that touches them will be hallowed. You will anoint Aaron and his sons, and sanctify them that they may minister to me as priests. You will speak to the Israelites, saying, This will be to you a holy anointing oil throughout your generations. It will not be poured on man's flesh, and you will not make any for yourselves according to this composition: it is holy, and will be holiness to you. Whoever will make it in like manner, and whoever will give of it to a stranger, will be destroyed from among his people."

The Lord said to Moses, "Take for yourself sweet plants, stacte, onycha, sweet galbanum, and transparent frankincense. There will be an equal to equal. They will make with it perfumed incense, tempered with the are of a perfumer, a pure holy work. Of these, you will beat some small, and you will put it before the testimonies in the tabernacle of the testimony, from where I will make myself known to you, and it will be for you the holiest incense. You will not make any for yourselves according to this composition, and it will be to you a holy thing for the Lord. Whoever will make any in like manner, to smell in it, will perish from his people."

CHAPTER 30 NOTES

1 Codex Vaticanus: oboloi (ΟΒΟΛΟΙ). Translation: obols

- Leningrad Codex: gērâ (גֵּרָה). Translation: gerah

- Peshitta: zwzyn (ܙܘܙܝܢ). Translation: zuzes

- Targum Onkelos: mā'în (מָעִין). Translation: m'ahs

- Targum Pseudo-Jonathan: mā'în (מָעִין). Translation: m'ahs

The obol was a Greek coin used from around 1100 BCE, worth ⅙ of a drachma, approximately 0.72 grams of silver. The gerah was a measurement equaling one twentieth of a shekel. The zuz mentioned in the Peshitta was a coin used in the middle east from the era of the Old Akkadian empire until th Greco-Roman era, however, was valued at ½ a shekel. The mah mentioned in the Targum was the Phoenician coin equivalent to the obol, suggesting it is the term in the Aramaic text that the Greeks translated. As the Greek obol is not one twentieth of a shekel, the name gerah is imported from the Masoretic texts.

CHAPTER 31

The Lord said to Moses, "I have called by name Bezaleel the son of Uri the son of Hur, of the tribe of Judah. I have filled him with a divine spirit of wisdom, and understanding, and knowledge, to invent in every work, and as to the frame work, to labor in gold, and silver, and brass, and blue, and purple, and spun scarlet, and works in stone, and for artificers' work in wood, to work at all works."

"I have given him and Eliab the son of Achisamach of the tribe of Dan, and to everyone understanding in heart I have given understanding, and they will work in all things as many as I have appointed you, the tabernacle of witness, and the box of the covenant and the lid that is on it, and the furniture of the tabernacle, and the altars, and the table and all its furniture, and the pure candlestick and all its furniture, and the layer and its base, and Aaron's robes of ministry, and the robes of his sons to minister to me as priests, and the anointing oil and the compound incense of the sanctuary, according to all that I have commanded you will they make them."

The Lord said to Moses, "Do you also order the Israelites, saying, pay attention and keep my sabbaths, as they are a sign for me and among you throughout your generations, that you may know that I am the Lord who sanctifies you. You will keep the sabbaths because this is holy to the Lord for you, he that profanes it will surely be put to death. Everyone who will do work on it, that mind will be destroyed from among his people. Six days you will do works, but the seventh day is the sabbath, a holy rest to the Lord, and everyone who will do work on the seventh day will be put to death. The Israelites will keep the sabbaths, to observe them throughout their generations. It is a perpetual covenant with me and the Israelites, it is a perpetual sign with me."

For in six days the Lord made the sky and the land, and on the seventh day he stopped and rested. He gave to Moses when he left off speaking to him in Mount Sinai the two tablets of the testimony, tablets of stone written on with the finger of God.[1]

CHAPTER 31 NOTES

1 Codex Vaticanus: gegrammenas tō daktulō tou teou (ΓΕΓΡΑΜΜΕΝΑϹ ΤΩ ΔΑΚΤΥΛΩ ΤΟΥ ΘΕΟΥ). Translation: are written by the finger (or toe) of the god

- LXX 16: gegramménas daktúlō teoō (γόγεα μμΦΔϲ δαιττ᷂λω θόοω) Translation: are written by finger (or toe) of god

- Leningrad Codex: kətubîm bə'eṣba' 'ĕlōhîm (כְּתֻבִים בְּאֶצְבַּע אֱלֹהִים). Translation: written (or inscribed) by the fingers (or toes) of god (or gods)

- Peshitta: ktybå bṣbŏå dålhå (ܟܬܝܒܐ ܒܨܒܥ ܕܐܠܗܐ). Translation: written by finger (or toe) of the god

- Targum Onkelos: kətîbîn bə'eṣbə'ā' daYyā (כְּתִיבִין בְּאֶצְבְּעָא דַיְיָ). Translation: written with the fingers of the Yahweh

• Targum Pseudo-Jonathan: kətîbîn bə'eṣbə'ā' daYyā (כְּתִיבִין בְּאֶצְבְּעָא דַיְיָ). Translation: written with the fingers of the Yahweh

• Sahidic manuscript 2169: ptēēbe mpnoute (ⲡⲧⲏⲏⲃⲉ ⲙ̄ⲡⲛⲟⲩⲧⲉ). Translation: finger (or toe) of the god

In ancient Egypt, it was illegal to carve hieroglyphs unless one was trained as a scribe as hieroglyphs were considered sacred. The Egyptians called hieroglyphs zẖâw-mdw-nṯr (𓏞𓌃𓊹𓏪), meaning "writing god's words." The majority of the population wrote a cursive script known today as hieratic, but known to them simply as zẖâ (𓏞𓏛), meaning "writing" or "painting." Moses presenting stone tablets described as written by the finger of god, certainly means the text was carved into the stone, and was almost certainly that it was written in hieroglyphs.

CHAPTER 32

When the people saw that Moses delayed to come down from the mountain, the people combined against Aaron, and said to him, "Rise and make us gods who will lead us. For this Moses, the man who brought us out of the land of Egypt, we do not know what is become of him."

Aaron replied to them, "Take off the golden earrings which are in the ears of your wives and daughters, and bring them to me."

All the people took off the golden earrings that were in their ears and brought them to Aaron. He received them at their hands and formed them with a graving tool, and he made them a molten calf,[1] and said, "These are your gods, Israel, which have brought you up out of the land of Egypt."

Aaron after seeing it built an altar before it and Aaron made a proclamation saying, "Tomorrow is a feast of the Lord."

After rising early in the morning, he set on the altar whole burnt offerings and offered a peace-offering, and the people sat down to eat and drink and rose up to play.

The Lord said to Moses, "Go quickly, descend here, for your people whom you brought out of the land of Egypt have transgressed. They have quickly gone out of the way which you commanded. They have made for themselves a calf, and worshiped it, and sacrificed to it, and said, 'These are your gods, Israel, who brought you up out of the land of Egypt.' Now leave me alone, and I will be very angry with them and consume them, and I will make you a great nation."

Moses prayed before the Lord of the gods, "Why, the Lord, are you very angry with your people, whom you brought out of the land of Egypt with great strength, and with your high arm? Be careful or at some point the Egyptians say, 'With evil intent, he brought them out to kill them in the mountains, and to consume them from off the land. Stop from your wrathful anger, and be merciful to the sin of your people, remembering Abraham and Isaac and Jacob your servants, to whom you have sworn by yourself, and have spoken to them, saying, "I will greatly multiply your seed as the stars of the sky for multitude," and all this land which you spoke of to give to them so that they will possess it forever.'"

The Lord was prevailed on to preserve his people. Moses turned and went down from the mountain, and the two tablets of the testimony were in his hands, tablets of stone written on both their sides. They were written within and without. The tablets were the work of God and the writing of God written on the tablets.

Joshua, after hearing the voice of the people crying, said to "Moses, There is a noise of war in the camp."

Moses replied, "It is not the voice of them that begin the battle, nor the voice of them that begin the cry of defeat, but the voice of them that begin the banquet of wine do I hear."

When he drew near to the camp, he saw the calf and the dances, and Moses became very angry and threw the two tablets out of his hands, and broke them to pieces at the foot of the mountain. Having taken the calf which they made, he consumed it with fire, and ground it very small, and scattered it on the water, and made the Israelites drink it. Moses said to Aaron, "What have these people done to you, that you have brought on them a great sin?"

Aaron answered Moses, "Do not be angry, my lord, for you know the impulsiveness of this people. For they say to me, 'Make us gods, which will go before us, for as for this man Moses, who brought us out of Egypt, we do not know what is become of him.' I said to them, 'If anyone has golden ornaments, take them off, and they gave them to me,' and I throw them into the fire, and there came out this calf."

When Moses saw that the people were scattered, for Aaron had scattered them to be rejoicing to their enemies, then Moses stood at the gate of the camp, and said, "Who is on the Lord's side? Let him come to me."[2]

Then all the sons of Levi came to him, and he said to them, "The Lord God of Israel says, 'Put everyone his sword on his waist, and go through and return from gate to gate through the camp, and kill everyone his brother, and everyone kill his neighbor, and everyone kill whoever is closest to him.'"

The sons of Levi did as Moses spoke to them, and there fell of the people in that day to the number of three thousand men. Moses said to them, "You have filled your hands this day to the Lord, each one against his son or his brother, so that blessing should be given to you."

It happened after the morning had begun that Moses said to the people, "You have sinned a great sin, and now I will go up to God, that I may make atonement for your sin."

Moses returned to the Lord and said, "I pray, Lord, these people have sinned a great sin, and they have made for themselves golden gods. Now if you will forgive their sin, forgive it, and if not, blot me out of your book, which you have written."

The Lord said to Moses, "If anyone has sinned against me, I will blot them out of my book. Now go, descend, and lead these people into the place of which I spoke to you. Look, my messenger will go before your face, and in the day when I will visit I will bring on them their sin."

The Lord killed the people for the creation of the calf, which Aaron made.

CHAPTER 32 NOTES

1 Codex Vaticanus: moskon kōneuton (ΜΟϹΧΟΝΧѠΝΕΥΤΟΝ). Translation: young twig (or young animal, calf) molded

• Leningrad Codex: 'ēgel massēkâ (עֵגֶל מַסֵּכָה). Translation: young bull (or male calf) molded (or poured)

• Targum Onkelos: 'ēgel mattəkā' (עֲגֵל מַתְּכָא). Translation: calf (in Hebrew) metallic

CHAPTER 32

- Targum Pseudo-Jonathan: 'êgal mattəkā' (מַתְּכָא עֵיגֵל).
Translation: round (in Hebrew) metallic
- Sahidic manuscript 2043: noumase nouōth (ⲚⲞⲨⲘⲀⲤⲈ ⲚⲞⲨⲰⲦ̄2).
Translation: their calf (or young animal) casted

The Greek and Hebrew translations can both be read as "calf" which is the standard reading, however, this is not the only reading. The pre-Christian Greeks believed this was a statue of a donkey, not a calf. There were Greek stories about the Judahites worshiping a donkey statue, and as such the Judahite god Yhw was conflated with the Egyptian god Seth, and the Greek monster Typhon. This confusion over the statue, likely originated in a Cuneiform translation of Exodus, as the Akkadian Cuneiform word aggalu (𒀖𒃶) meant "donkey," and was almost certainly the word that would have been used, as it is the synonym of the Iron Age Canaanite âgl (𐤏𐤂𐤋), which is also documented in the Bronze Age Ugaritic texts as âgl (𐎓𐎂𐎍), both accepted as meaning "calf."

The confusion over what the word means is reflected in the targums, as neither used the proper Palestinian-Aramaic translation 'iglā' (עֶגְלָא) which means "calf." Onkelos uses is a copy of the word in the Hebrew text, while the word in the Targum Jerusalem is a homonym meaning "round," or "disc."

It is unlikely that the original statue was a donkey god, as the Egyptians did not have a donkey god until the Late Period, when Set became a donkey-headed god in some art.

If this section of text was originally in Egyptian, the word used would have been îh (𓄿𓇋𓎛), meaning "ox," "bull," or "calf." The god that Aaron was probably representing was Îôhw (𓄿𓇋𓎛𓅱), the moon-god of Heliopolis, where he had previously been a priest. Îôhw was depicted as a calf god, and was one of the major gods of the early New Kingdom era, with several Egyptian kings named after him.

CHAPTER 32

2 This battle between the two sides, "the Lord's side" and Aaron's calf-god's side is often ignored by Jews and Christians, as Aaron's calf-god had to be Yahweh, meaning Moses "Lord" was not Yahweh. Yahweh has been found depicted as a calf until the time of King Josiah's reforms, which seems to have continued the calf-god motif. Second-Temple-Era descriptions of Yahweh include horns and cloven feet, which along with his abode of fire and brimstone were adopted by the early Christians as depictions of the devil. While Aaron's calf-god shows no signs of his solar-calf descendant, he is clearly the Yahweh calf of Asherah, found on a pithos shard found at Kuntillet Ajrud, near Hashem El Tarif dated to circa 800 BCE. Moses' subsequent statement that the massacre was for the "Lord," confirms that Aaron's calf-god, was not the "Lord" at that time, yet he was a god by 800 BCE, supporting the connection to Yahweh (Iaō / Íȯ̊hw).

As Asherah was the goddess of the sky, the calf of Asherah was likely a lunar god, as many Middle Eastern and Mediterranean lunar gods were depicted as being bovine or having horns, which represented the crescent moon. Obvious examples include virtually all depictions of the Greek Selene, Roman Luna, Hurrian Kushuh, and Luwian Arma. Additionally, the earliest statue of Osiris-Íȯ̊hw discovered to date, which is accepted as representing the ancient appearance of Íȯ̊hw, has prominent horns, and appears to be almost identical to the Southern Egyptian lunar god Khonsu.

Other shards found at Kuntillet Ajrud show the Yahweh was, circa 800 BCE, part of the Canaanite pantheon, listing him with Ba'al, El, and Asherah, however, does also refer to him as the Yahweh of Samaria, and the Yahweh of the Teman, supporting the idea that he was worshiped in Samaria, as well as in Teman, which is believed to have been a town near Petra based on references in the books of Jeremiah, Ezekiel, Obadiah, Amos, Habakkuk, and

CHAPTER 32

Baruch. Eusebius reported in his Onomasticon that there was a town called Temen 15 miles from Petra, which could have been the original site of Kadesh Barnea as Petra itself had not been built yet. The radical shift of Yahweh from lunar to solar deity must have taken place between 800 and 600 BCE, during the reforms and counter-reforms in the Kingdom of Judah.

CHAPTER 33

The Lord said to Moses, "Go forward, you and your people, whom you brought out of the land of Egypt, to the land which I swore to Abraham, Isaac, and Jacob, saying, 'I will give it to your seed. I will send at the same time my messenger before your face, and he will throw out the Amorite and the Cypriot, and the Perizzite and Girgasite, and Mitannian, and Jebusite, and Canaanite. I will bring you into a land flowing with milk and honey. I will not go up with you, in case I consume you along the way because you are a stubborn people.'"

The people had heard this terrible saying, mourned in mourning apparel. For the Lord said to the Israelites, "You are a stubborn people. Pay attention in case I bring on you another plague, and destroy you. Now then take off your glorious apparel, and your ornaments, and I will show you what I will do to you."

So the sons of Israel took off their ornaments and their array from Mount Horeb. Moses took his tabernacle and pitched it outside of the camp, at a distance from the camp, and it was called the tabernacle of the testimony: and it happened that everyone that wanted the Lord went out to the tabernacle which was outside of the camp. Whenever Moses went into the tabernacle outside of the camp, all the people stood everyone watching by the doors of his tent, and when Moses departed, they took notice until he entered into the tabernacle. When Moses entered into the tabernacle, the column of the cloud descended and stood at the door of the tabernacle, and God talked to Moses.

All the people saw the column of the cloud standing by the door of the tabernacle, and all the people stood and worshiped everyone at the door of his tent. The Lord spoke to Moses face to face, as one would speak to his friend, and he retired to the camp. But his servant Joshua the son of Nun, a young man, did not leave the tabernacle. Moses said to the Lord, "Look! You told me, 'Lead these people,' but you have not shown me whom you will send with me, but you have said to me, 'I know you above all, and you have favor with me.' If then I have found favor in your sight, reveal yourself to me, that I may evidently see you. That I may find favor in your sight, and that I may know that this great nation is your people."

He replied, "I will go before you, and give you rest."

He said to him, "If you don't go up with us yourself, don't bring me up here. How will it be surely known, that both I and this people have found favor with you unless you go with us? So both I and your people will be glorified beyond all the nations, as many as are on the land."

The Lord said to Moses, "I will also do this thing for you, which you have spoken. You have found grace before me, and I know you above all."

Moses stated, "Manifest yourself to me."

God said, "I will pass by before you with my glory, and I will be called by my name, the Lord, before you, and I will have mercy on whom I will have mercy, and will have pity on whom I will have pity."

God said, "You will not be able to see my face. For no man will see my face and live."

The Lord said, "Look, there is a place by me. You will stand on the rock, and when my glory will pass by, then I will put you into a hole of the rock, and I will cover you over with my hand until I will have passed by. I will remove my hand, and then will you see my back parts, but my face will not appear to you."

CHAPTER 34

The Lord said to Moses, "Carve for yourself two tablets of stone, like the first were, and come up the mountain to me, and I will write on the tablets the words, which were on the first tablets, which you broke. Be ready in the morning, and you will go up Mount Sinai, and stand there before me on the top of the mountain. Let no one go up with you, nor be seen in all the mountain, and don't let the sheep and oxen feed near that mountain."

Moses carved two tablets of stone, as also the first were, and Moses having arisen early, went up to Mount Sinai, as the Lord appointed him, and Moses took the two tablets of stone. The Lord descended in a cloud, and stood near him there, and called the name of the Lord. The Lord passed by before his face, and proclaimed, "The Lord of the gods, pitiful and merciful, restraint and very compassionate, and true, and keeping justice and mercy for thousands, taking away iniquity, and unrighteousness, and sins, and he will not clear the guilty, bringing the iniquity of the fathers on the children, and to the children's children, to the third and fourth generation."

Moses rushed, and bowed to the ground and worshiped and said, "If I have found grace before you, let the Lord go with us. For the people is stubborn, and you will take away our sins and our iniquities, and we will be yours."

CHAPTER 34

The Lord said to Moses, "Look, I establish a covenant with you in the presence of all your people. I will do glorious things, which have not been done in all the land, or any nation. All the people among you will see the works of the Lord, that they are wonderful, which I will do for you."

"Pay attention to all things whatever I command you. Look, I throw out from before you the Amorite and the Canaanite and the Perizzite, and the Cypriot, and Mitanni, and Girgasite and Jebusite. Pay attention to yourself, in case at any time you make a covenant with the residents in the land to which you are entering, in case it becomes for you a stumbling block among you. You will destroy their altars, and break in pieces their columns, and you will cut down their Asherahs,[1] and the graven images of their gods you will burn with fire. For you will not worship strange gods, for the lord of the gods, a jealous name, is a jealous God, in case at any time you make a covenant with the residents in the land, and they go whoring after their gods and sacrifice to their gods, and they call you, and you should eat of their feasts, and you should take of their daughters for your sons, and you should give of your daughters to their sons, and your daughters should go a whoring after their gods, and your sons should go a whoring after their gods. You will not make to yourself molten gods."

"You will keep the feast of unleavened bread, seven days will you eat unleavened bread, as I have ordered you, at the season in the month of new grain, for in the month of new grain you came out from Egypt. The males are mine, everything that opens the womb, every firstborn of a calf, and every firstborn of sheep. The firstborn of a donkey you will redeem with a sheep, and if you will not redeem it you will pay a price, every firstborn of your sons will you redeem. You will not appear before me empty."

"Six days you will work, but on the seventh day, you will rest. There will be rest in seed-time and harvest. You will make for me the feast of weeks, the beginning of wheat harvest, and the feast of harvesting in the middle of the year. Three times in the year will every male of you appear before the Lord, the God of Israel. For when I will have driven out the nations before you and will have enlarged your coasts, no one will desire your land, whenever you may go up to appear before the lord of the gods, three times in the year."

"You will not mix the blood of my incense-offerings with leaven, neither will the sacrifices of the feast of the Passover remain until the morning. The first fruits of your land will you put into the house of the lord of the gods. You will not boil a lamb in his mother's milk."

The Lord said to Moses, "Write these words for yourself, for on these words I have established a covenant with you and with Israel."

Moses was there before the Lord forty days and forty nights. He did not eat bread, and he did not drink water, and he wrote on the tablets these words of the covenant, the ten sayings. When Moses went down from the mountain, and there were the two tablets in the hands of Moses, as then he went down from the mountain, Moses did not know that the appearance of the skin of his face glowed brightly,[2] when he spoke to him. Aaron and all the elders of Israel saw Moses, and the appearance of the skin of his face glowed brightly, and they were afraid to approach him.

Moses called them, and Aaron and all the rulers of the community turned towards him, and Moses spoke to them. Afterward, all the Israelites came to him, and he commanded them all things, whatever the Lord had commanded him on Mount Sinai. When he ceased speaking to them, he put a veil on his face. Whenever Moses went in before the Lord to speak to him, he took off the veil until he went out, and he went out and spoke to all the Israelites whatever the Lord commanded him. The Israelites saw the face of Moses, that it glowed brightly,[3] and Moses put the veil over his face until he went in to speak with him.

CHAPTER 34 NOTES

1 Codex Vaticanus: alsē (ⲀⲗⲤⲎ). Translation: grove (or woods, park)

- Leningrad Codex: 'ăšērāyw (אֲשֻׁרָיו). Translation: happiness

- Peshitta: ḥlthwn (ܚܠܬܗܘܢ). Translation: ossuaries

- Targum Onkelos: 'ăšērêhôn (אֲשֵׁרֵיהוֹן). Translation: asherahs

- Targum Pseudo-Jonathan: 'ăšērêhôn (אֲשֵׁרֵיהוֹן). Translation: asherahs

- Sahidic manuscript 2169: etetnarokhou (ⲉⲧⲉⲧⲚⲁⲣⲟⲕϨⲞⲨ). Translation: that which trapped them

278

CHAPTER 34

The Greek translation indicates that the word Åšrh (חﭏﭏﭏﭏ) was
used in the Aramaic translation. Asherah was the Aramaic and
Hebrew name of the Bronze Age Canaanite goddess of fertility,
who merged with the Egyptian goddess Hathor (𓉡𓏏) during the
New Kingdom Era, and became a sky goddess. In the Bronze Age,
she was one of the two wives of El, and known as Åṯrt (𒀸𒊑𒌅) in
the Ugaritic Text. In Akkadian she was a god known as ^{deity}Asdartú
(𒀭𒈹𒁯𒌈),while in Babylonian she was known as ^{deity}Ištar (𒀭𒈹).
She appears to have been worshiped by planting oak trees, like
here Middle Kingdom era Egyptian equivalent Iusaaset, who was
worshiped by planting acacia trees. Like Asherah, Atum's wife
Iusaaset was merged with Hathor during the New Kingdom Era.
This reference to the Asherahs being cut down is almost certainly a
reference to the oak trees that the ancient Canaanites used to mark
important graves.

2 Codex Vaticanus: krōmatos tou prosōpou auto (ⲭⲢⲰⲘⲀⲦⲞⲤ
ⲦⲞⲨⲦⲢⲞⲤⲰⲦⲞⲨⲀⲨⲦⲞ). Translation: skin of his face

• Codex Alexandrinus: krōtos tou prosōpou auto (ⲭⲢⲰⲦⲞⲤ ⲦⲞⲨ
ⲦⲢⲞⲤⲰⲦⲞⲨⲀⲨⲦⲞ). Translation: complexion of his face

• LXX 18: krosōton tou prosōpou auto (χℓοᴄωⲧⓅ ⲧⲱ πℓοσⲦⲠⲟⲩ
ἀⲩⲧⲟ) Translation: golden the face of him

• LXX 53: prosōpou tou prosōpou auto (ωℓᵝᴄωⲛⓅ ⲧⲱ πℓοσⲦⲠⲟⲩ
ἀⲩⲧⲟ) Translation: mask (or visage) the face of him

• LXX 509: tou prosōpou auto (ⲧⲱ πℓοσⲦⲠⲟⲩ ἀⲩⲧⲟ) Translation: the
face of him

• Leningrad Codex: qāran 'ôr pānāyw (קָרַן עוֹר פָּנָיו). Translation:
rays (or horns) of his face

• Peshitta: pth lglwlâ yhwâ (ܟܐܘܗ ܟܠܓܠܓܠ ܗܬܦ). Translation:
face light (or round, sphere) of his

279

• Targum Onkelos: səgê zîw yəqārā' də'appôhî (סְגֵי זִיו יְקָרָא דְּאַפּוֹהִי). Translation: growing (or spreading) coming out (or glowing, brightness) mass that had been burned (or baked)

• Targum Jerusalem: zîwêhôn də'appêh (זִיוֵיהוֹן דְּאַפֵּיה). Translation: full of brightness was his face (or nostrils)

• Targum Pseudo-Jonathan: 'ištabhar zîw 'îqûnîn də'anpôy (אִשְׁתַּבְהַר זִיו אִיקוּנִין דְּאַנְפּוֹי). Translation: brightness shining (or glowing) from the icons breathing

• Vetus Latina manuscripts: facies eius et color aspectus (ꜰᴀᴄɪᴇꜱ ᴇɪᴜꜱ ᴇᴛ ᴄᴏʟᴏʀ ᴀꜱᴘᴇᴄᴛᴜꜱ). Translation: his face and color appearance

• Sahidic manuscript 2043: afjieoou nhi peinex mpefho (ⲁϥϫⲓⲉⲟⲟⲩ ⲛ̄ϭⲓ ⲡⲉⲓⲛⲉ ⲛ̄ⲧⲥⲁⲣⲝ̄ ⲙ̄ⲡⲉϥϩⲟ). Translation: he became bright namely the likeness in the flesh of his face

This phrase, which repeats in the next sentence, has resulted in a number of strange translations. The Hebrew phrase in *Names* could be interpreted as Moses having horns, however, is generally interpreted as his face glowing, which is the interpretation in the Peshitta and Targum Jerusalem. During the Middle Ages many European paintings of Moses showed him with horns because of this verse. The Greek and Latin translations imply at this point he was sun burned, however, the Israelites were afraid to approach him, and he had to wear a veil for the rest of his life, which is not a common reaction to a sun burn. The Targum Onkelos interprets this as blisters or tumors that were growing from the burns, which seems the most probable original meaning. The Targum Jerusalem's usage of the Judeo-Aramaic word 'îqûnîn (אִיקוּנִין), a plural form of the Greek word eikōn (εἰκών), meaning "icon," suggests their was an Old Aramaic text that referred to Moses being burned by the breath of the gods, as 'îqûnîn was used as a translation for "false gods."

CHAPTER 34

Nevertheless, as this phrase is widely accepted as a reference to his face glowing brightly, that is the interpretation followed here. The angels (messengers of God) in the *Judahite Apocalypse of Ezra* also had glowing skin, which was caused be a salve they applied for some reason. This is similar to the glowing blue deities from the planet Vaikuntha in Hindu texts, indicating this idea of glowing messengers from the sky was widespread across southern Eurasia in the Classical Era.

3 Codex Vaticanus: oti dedoxastai (ΟΤΙ ΔΕΔΟΞΑϹΤΑΙ). Translation: it was glorified (or honored)

• LXX 52: óti dedóxastai n osis tou krōtós tou prosōpou (ᾧ᷁ ΔΟΔΟΞΔϹαͥ ν οψις τω χρωτϗϲ τω πϼοσῶπου). Translation: it was glorified (or honored) Oh, sight (or face) of the color (or skin) of the face (or visage, mask)!

• LXX 53: dedozastai to prósōpo Mōusē (ΔΟΔοϟϪϲαͥ το ϙϼ᷁ϗϾΖπο Μϙυϭρ) Translation: which had been glorified (or honored) the face (or mask, appearance) of Moses

• LXX 72: óti dedóxastai n osis tou krōmatos tou prosōpou autou (ᾧ᷁ ΔΟΔΟϾϪϲαͥ ν οψις τω χϼωμαϙτοϲ Δυτω). Translation: it was glorified (or honored) Oh, sight (or face) of the skin (or color, complexion) of him!

• Leningrad Codex: kî qāran 'ôr pənê (כִּי קָרַ֖ן ע֣וֹר פָּנָ֑יו). Translation: because shone (or horns) skin of his face

• Peshitta: lglwlå yhwå gldh (דגלולא הוא גלדה). Translation: light (or round, sphere) of his skin

• Targum Onkelos: səgê zîw yəqārā' də'appê (סְגֵי זִיו יְקָרָא דְאַפֵּי). Translation: growing (or spreading) coming out (or glowing, brightness) mass that was baked (or burned)

281

• Targum Pseudo-Jonathan: 'ištabhar zîw 'îqûnîn də'anpê
(אֶשְׁתַּבְהַר זִיו אִיקוּנִין דְּאַנְפֵּי). Translation: brightness shining (or glowing) from the icons breath

CHAPTER 35

Moses gathered all the congregation of the Israelites together, and said, "These are the words which the Lord has spoken for you to do. 'Six days will you perform works, but on the seventh day will be rest, a holy sabbath, a rest for the Lord. Everyone that does work on it, let him die. You will not burn a fire in any of your dwellings on the sabbath-day. I am the Lord.'"

Moses spoke to all the congregation of the Israelites, saying, "This is what the Lord has appointed for you, saying, 'Take of yourselves an offering for the Lord, everyone that engages in his heart they will bring the first fruits to the Lord, gold, silver, brass, blue, purple, double spun scarlet, and fine spun linen, goats' hair and rams' skins dyed red, and skins dyed blue, and incorruptible wood, and carnelian stones, and stones for engraving for the vest and full-length robe. Every man that is wise in heart among you, let him come and work all things whatever the Lord has commanded. The tabernacle, and the cords, and the coverings, and the rings, and the bars, and the posts, and the box of the testimony, and its staffs, and its lid, and the veil, and the curtains of the court, and its posts, and the emerald stones, and the incense, and the anointing oil, and the table and all its furniture, and the candlestick for the light and all its furniture, and the altar and all its furniture; and the holy garments of Aaron the priest, and the garments in which they will do service, and the garments of priesthood for the sons of Aaron and the anointing oil, and the compound incense.'"

All the congregation of the Israelites went out from Moses. In whoever's heart prompted them, and to whoever it seemed good in their mind, they brought an offering. They brought an offering to the Lord for all the works of the tabernacle of witness, and all its services, and all the robes of the sanctuary. The men, including everyone to whom it seemed good in his heart, brought from the women seals and earrings, and finger-rings, and chains, and bracelets, every article of gold. All brought ornaments of gold to the Lord, and with whatever fine linen was found, and they brought skins dyed blue, and rams' skins dyed red. Everyone that offered an offering brought silver and brass, the offerings to the Lord, and they with whom was found incorruptible wood, and they brought offerings for all the works of the preparation. Every woman skilled in her heart to spin with her hands, they brought spun articles, the blue, and purple, and scarlet and fine linen. All the women to whom it seemed good in their heart in their wisdom, spun the goats' hair. The rulers brought the emerald stones, and the stones for setting in the vest, and the oracle, and the compounds both for the anointing oil, and the composition of the incense. Every man and woman whose mind inclined them to come in and do the works, all that Lord appointed them to do through Moses, they, the Israelites brought an offering to the Lord.

Moses said to the Israelites, "Look, God has called by name Bezaleel the son of Uri the son of Hur, of the tribe of Judah, and has filled him with a divine spirit of wisdom and under-standing, and knowledge of all things, to labor skillfully in all works of precise workmanship, to form the gold and the silver and the brass, and to work in stone, and to fashion the wood, and to work by every work of wisdom."

God gave improved understanding both to him and to Eliab the son of Achisamach of the tribe of Dan. God filled them with wisdom, understanding, and perception, to under-stand to work all the works of the sanctuary, and to weave the woven and embroidered work with scarlet and fine linen, to do all work of curious workmanship and embroidery.

CHAPTER 36

Bezaleel worked, and Eliab and every one wise in under-standing, to whom was given wisdom and knowledge, to understand to do all the works according to the holy offices, according to all things which the Lord appointed. Moses called Bezaleel and Eliab, and all that had wisdom, to whom God gave knowledge in their heart, and all who were freely willing to come forward to the works, to perform them. They received from Moses all the offerings, which the Israelites brought for all the works of the sanctuary to do them, and they continued to receive the gifts brought, from those who brought them in the morning. There came all the wise men who worked the works of the sanctuary, each according to his work, which they worked. One said to Moses, "The people bring an abundance too great in proportion to all the works which the Lord has appointed them to do."

Moses commanded, and proclaimed in the camp, saying, "Let neither man nor woman any longer labor for the offerings of the sanctuary," and the people were restrained from bringing any more. They had works sufficient for making the furniture, and they left some besides. Every wise one among those that worked made the robes of the holy places, which belong to Aaron the priest, as the Lord commanded Moses. They made the vest of gold, and blue, and purple, and spun scarlet, and fine spun linen. The plates were divided, the threads of gold, to interweave with the blue and purple, and with the spun scarlet, and the fine spun linen, they made it a woven work, shoulder-pieces joined from both sides, a work woven by mutual twisting of the parts into itself. They made it of the same material according to the making of it, of gold, and blue, and purple, and spun scarlet, and fine spun linen, as the Lord commanded Moses, and they made the two emerald stones clasped together and set in gold, graven and cut after the cutting of a seal with the names of the Israelites, and he put them on the shoulder-pieces of the vest, as stones of memorial of the Israelites, as the Lord appointed Moses.

They made the oracle, a work woven with embroidery, according to the work of the vest, of gold, and blue, and purple, and spun scarlet, and fine spun linen. They made the oracle square and double, the length of a span, and the width of a span, double. There was interwoven with it a woven work of four rows of stones, a series of stones, the first row, a carnelian, topaz, and emerald. The second row, a carbuncle, sapphire, and jasper. The third row, lapis lazuli, agate, and amethyst. The fourth row chrysolite, beryl, onyx surrounded with gold, and fastened with gold. The stones were twelve according to the names of the Israelites, graven according to their names for seals, each according to his name for the twelve tribes. They made on the oracle turned wreaths, wreathed work, of pure gold, and they made two golden circlets and two golden rings.

They put the two golden rings on both the upper corners of the oracle, and they put the golden wreaths on the rings on both sides of the oracle, and the two wreaths into the two couplings. They put them on the two circlets, and they put them on the shoulders of the vest opposite each other in front. They made two golden rings and put them on the two projections on the top of the oracle, and on the top of the under part of the vest within. They made two golden rings, and put them on both the shoulders of the vest under it, in front by the coupling above the connection of the vest. He fastened the oracle by the rings that were on it to the rings of the vest, which were fastened with a blue string, joined together with the woven work of the vest; that the oracle should not be loosed from the vest, as the Lord commanded Moses.

They made the tunic under the vest, woven work, all of blue. The opening of the tunic in the middle woven closely together, the opening having a fringe round about, that it might not be tore. They made on the border of the tunic below pomegranates as of a flowering pomegranate tree, of blue, and purple, and spun scarlet, and fine spun linen. They made golden bells, and put the bells on the border of the tunic around it between the pomegranates: a golden bell and a pomegranate on the border of the tunic around it, for the ministration, as the Lord commanded Moses. They made vestments of fine linen, a woven work, for Aaron and his sons, and the brimmed hats of fine linen, and the miter of fine linen and the drawers of fine spun linen, and their girdles of fine linen, and blue, and purple, and scarlet spun, the work of an embroiderer, according as the Lord commanded Moses.

CHAPTER 36

They made the golden plate, a dedicated thing of the sanctuary, of pure gold, and he wrote on it graven letters as of a seal, 'Gift of the Holy.' They gave it a blue border, so that it should be on the miter above, as the Lord commanded Moses.

CHAPTER 37

They made ten curtains for the tabernacle, each one twenty-eight cubits long and four cubits wide. They made the veil of blue, and purple, and spun scarlet, and fine spun linen, the woven work with cherubs. They put it on four posts of incorruptible wood coated with gold, and their chapiters were gold, and their four sockets were silver. They made the veil of the door of the tabernacle of the testimony from blue, purple, and scarlet finely spun linen, woven work with cherubs, and their posts five, and the rings, and they gilded their chapiters and their clasps with gold, and they had five sockets of brass.

They made the court towards the south. The curtains of the court of fine spun linen, a hundred cubits on each side, with their twenty posts, and their twenty sockets, and on the north side a hundred each way, and on the south side a hundred each way, with their twenty posts and their twenty sockets. On the west side curtains fifty cubits long, with ten posts and ten sockets. On the east side, curtains fifty cubits long and fifteen cubits high, with three columns and three sockets. At the second back on this side and on that by the gate of the court, curtains fifteen cubits high, with three columns and three sockets. All the curtains of the tabernacle of fine spun linen. The sockets of their columns were brass, and their hooks were silver, and their chapiters were coated with silver, and all the posts of the court were coated with silver.

CHAPTER 37

The veil of the gate of the court, the work of an embroiderer, was blue, and purple and spun scarlet, and fine spun linen. Its length was twenty cubits, and its height and the width of five cubits, made the same as the curtains of the court. Their four columns, and their four sockets were brass, and their hooks were silver, and their chapiters were coated with silver. All the pins of the court around it were brass, and they were coated with silver.

This was the appointment of the tabernacle of witness, accordingly as it was appointed to Moses, so that the public service should belong to the Levites, through Ithamar the son of Aaron the priest. Bezaleel the son of Uri of the tribe of Judah, did as the Lord commanded Moses. Eliab the son of Achisamach of the tribe of Dan was there, who was chief artificer in the woven works and needle-works and embroideries, to weave with the scarlet and fine linen.

CHAPTER 38

Bezaleel made the box and coated it with pure gold both inside and outside, and he cast four golden rings for it, two on the one side, and two on the other, wide enough for the staffs so that men could carry it with them. He made the lid over the box of pure gold, and the two cherubs of gold, one cherub on the one end of the lid, and another cherub on the other end of the lid, overshadowing the lid with their wings.

He made the set table of pure gold and cast four rings for it, two on the one side and two on the other side, broad, so that men should lift it with the staffs in them. He made the staffs of the box and the table and gilded them with gold. He made the furniture of the table, both the dishes, and the censers, and the cups, and the bowls with which he would offer drink-offerings, from gold.

He made the candlestick which gives light, of gold, the stem solid, and the branches from both its sides, and blossoms proceeding from its branches, three on this side, and three on the other, made equal to each other. As to their lamps, which are on the ends, knobs like walnuts proceeded from them, and sockets proceeding from them, that the lamps might be on them, and the seventh socket, on the top of the candlestick, on the summit above, entirely of solid gold.

On it the candlestick seven golden lamps, and its snuffers gold, and its snuff-dishes gold. He coated the posts with silver, and cast for the posts golden rings, and gilded the bars with gold, and he gilded the posts of the veil with gold and made the hooks from gold. He made also the rings of the tabernacle from gold, and the rings of the court, and the rings for drawing out the veil above from brass. He cast the silver chapiters of the tabernacle, and the bronze chapiters of the door of the tabernacle, and the gate of the court, and he made silver hooks for the posts, he coated them with silver on the posts. He made the pins of the tabernacle and the pins of the court from brass.

He made the bronze altar of the bronze censers, which belonged to the men engaged in sedition with the gathering of Korah. He made all the vessels of the altar and its fire-pan, and its base, and its bowls, and the bronze meat hooks. He made an appendage for the altar of netting under the grate, beneath it as far as the middle of it, and he fastened to it four bronze rings on the four parts of the appendage of the altar, wide enough for the bars, to bear the altar with them.

He made the holy anointing oil and the composition of the incense, the pure work of the perfumer. He made the bronze layer, and the bronze base of it of the mirrors of the women that fasted, who fasted by the doors of the tabernacle of witness, in the day in which he set it up. He made the layer, that of it Moses and Aaron and his sons might wash their hands and their feet: when they went into the tabernacle of witness, or whenever they should advance to the altar to do service, they washed, as the Lord commanded Moses.

CHAPTER 39

All the gold that was employed for the works according to all the fabrication of the holy things, was of the gold of the first fruits, twenty-nine talents, and seven hundred and twenty shekels according to the holy shekel. The offering of silver from the men that were numbered of the congregation a hundred talents, and a thousand and seven hundred and seventy-five shekels, one beka[1] each, the half-shekel, according to the holy shekel. Everyone that passed the survey from twenty years old and upwards to the number of six hundred thousand, and three thousand and five hundred and fifty. The one hundred talents of silver went to the casting of the hundred chapiters of the tabernacle, and to the chapiters of the veil, a hundred chapiters to the hundred talents, a talent to a chapiter. The thousand and seven hundred and seventy-five shekels he formed into hooks for the columns, and he gilded their chapiters and adorned them.

The brass of the offering was seventy talents, and a thousand and five hundred shekels and they made of it the bases of the door of the tabernacle of witness, and the bases of the court round about, and the bases of the gate of the court, and the pins of the tabernacle, and the pins of the court round about, and the bronze appendage of the altar, and all the vessels of the altar, and all the instruments of the tabernacle of witness. The Israelites did as the Lord commanded Moses.

CHAPTER 39

From the gold that remained of the offering they made vessels to minister with before the Lord.

The blue that was left, and the purple, and the scarlet they made into garments of ministry for Aaron so that he should minister with them in the sanctuary, and they brought the garments to Moses, and the tabernacle, and its furniture, its bases and its bars and the posts; and the box of the covenant, and its bearers, and the altar and all its furniture. They made the anointing oil, and the incense of composition, and the pure candlestick, and its lamps, lamps for burning, and oil for the light, and the table of show-bread, and all its furniture, and the show-bread on it, and the garments of the sanctuary which belong to Aaron, and the garments of his sons, for the priestly ministry, and the curtains of the court, and the posts, and the veil of the door of the tabernacle, and the gate of the court, and all the vessels of the tabernacle and all its instruments: and the skins, even rams' skins dyed red, and the blue coverings, and the coverings of the other things, and the pins, and all the instruments for the works of the tabernacle of witness.

Whatever things the Lord appointed Moses, so did the Israelites make all the possession. Moses saw all the works, and they had done them all as the Lord commanded Moses, so had they made them, and Moses blessed them.

CHAPTER 39 NOTES

1 Codex Vaticanus: drakmē (ΔΡΑΧΜΗ). Translation: drachma

- LXX 15: dragmē (Δραγμὴ)
- LXX 108: drakkmē (Δραγγχμὴ)
- Leningrad Codex: beqa' (בֶּקַע)

- Peshitta: mtqlå (ܡܬܩܠܐ). Translation: scales (or shekel, beqa)

- Targum Onkelos: tiqlā' (תִּקְלָא). Translation: scales (or shekel, beqa)

- Vetus Latina manuscripts: didraghma (δıoʀ ᴀϛʜᴏᴏᴀ)

The drachma was a Greek coin used from around 1100 BCE, worth approximately 4.3 grams of silver. The beka was the half-shekel measurement used in ancient Canaan. As "drachma" was the Greek translation of beka, the term beka is restored in this translation. The Vetus Latina manuscripts deviate here, claiming is was a double-drachma, which would make it originally a shekel. The word used in the Latin translation is a transliteration of the Greek word didrakmē (δίδραχμή), indicating that the Old Latin translation was made from a Greek translation, but not a version that has survived to the present.

CHAPTER 40

The Lord said to Moses, "On the first day of the first month, at the new moon, you will set up the tabernacle of witness, and you will place in it the box of the testimony and will cover the box with the veil, and you will bring in the table and will set out that which is to be set out on it, and you will bring in the candlestick and place its lamps on it. You will place the golden altar, to burn incense before the box, and you will put a covering of a veil on the door of the tabernacle of witness. You will put the altar of burnt offerings by the doors of the tabernacle of witness, and you will set up the tabernacle around about, and you will hallow all that belongs to it around about."

"You will take the anointing oil, and will anoint the tabernacle, and all things in it, and will sanctify it, and all its furniture, and it will be holy. You will anoint the altar of burnt offerings and all its furniture, and you will hallow the altar, and the altar will be most holy. You will bring Aaron and his sons to the doors of the tabernacle of witness, and you will wash them with water. You will put on Aaron the holy garments, and you will anoint him, and you will sanctify him, and he will minister to me as a priest. You will bring up his sons and will put garments on them. You will anoint them as you did anoint their father, and they will minister to me as priests, and it will be that they will have an everlasting anointing of the priesthood, throughout their generations."

CHAPTER 40

Moses did all things whatever the Lord commanded him, so did he. It happened in the first month, in the second year after their going forth out of Egypt, at the new moon, that the tabernacle was set up.

Moses set up the tabernacle, and put on the chapiters, and put the bars into their places, and set up the posts. He stretched out the curtains over the tabernacle and put the veil of the tabernacle on it above as the Lord commanded Moses. He took the testimonies and put them into the box, and he put the staffs under the sides of the box. He brought the box into the tabernacle, and put on it the covering of the veil, and covered the box of the testimony, as the Lord commanded Moses. He put the table in the tabernacle of witness, on the north side outside the veil of the tabernacle. He put on it the show-bread before the Lord, as the Lord commanded Moses. He put the candlestick into the tabernacle of witness, on the side of the tabernacle towards the south. He put on it its lamps before the Lord, as the Lord had commanded Moses.

He put the golden altar in the tabernacle of witness before the veil; and he burnt on it incense of composition, as the Lord commanded Moses. He put the altar of the burnt offerings by the doors of the tabernacle. He set up the court round about the tabernacle and the altar, and Moses accomplished all the works. The cloud covered the tabernacle of witness, and the tabernacle was filled with the glory of the Lord. Moses was not able to enter into the tabernacle of the testimony, because the cloud overshadowed it, and the tabernacle was filled with the glory of the Lord. When the cloud went up from the tabernacle, the Israelites packed to depart again with their baggage. If the cloud did not go up, they did not prepare to depart, until the day when the cloud went up. For a cloud was on the tabernacle by day, and a fire was on it by night before all Israel, in all their preparations.

MAP

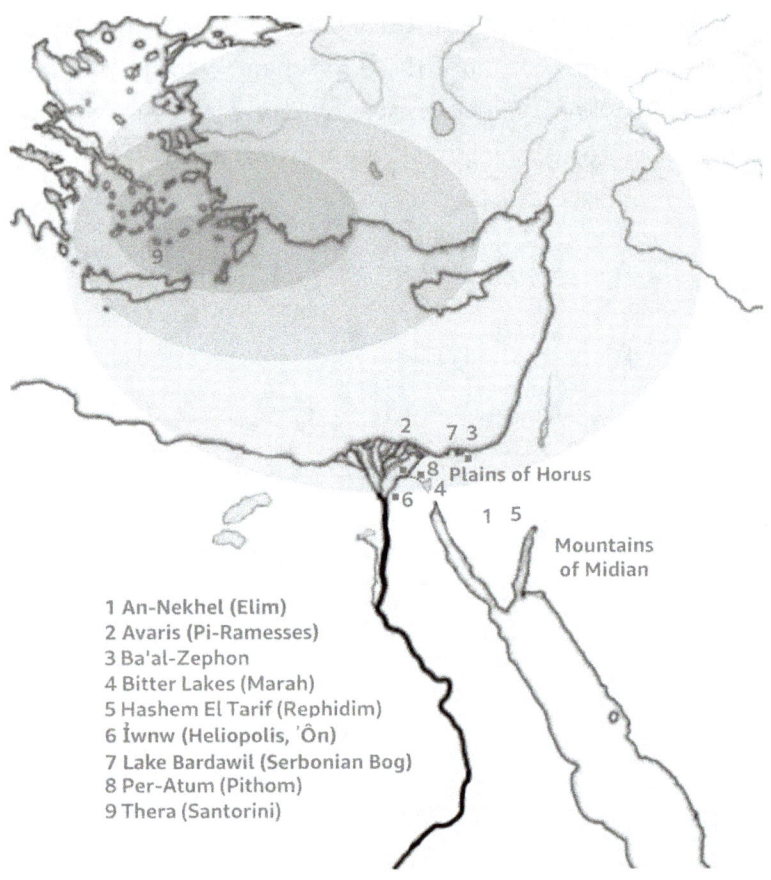

2   7 3

8 Plains of Horus

4

6

1 5

Mountains
of Midian

9

1 An-Nekhel (Elim)
2 Avaris (Pi-Ramesses)
3 Ba'al-Zephon
4 Bitter Lakes (Marah)
5 Hashem El Tarif (Rephidim)
6 Iwnw (Heliopolis, 'Ôn)
7 Lake Bardawil (Serbonian Bog)
8 Per-Atum (Pithom)
9 Thera (Santorini)

Egypt during the Minoan Eruption. The gray regions denote the range and severity of the ash fall.

Septuagint Manuscripts

The following is a list of the Septuagint manuscripts referenced in the notes for this book.

LXX A (Codex Alexandrinus) is dated to the 5th century. It is currently located at the British Library (Royal 1 D. VIII) in London.

LXX B (Codex Vaticanus) is dated to the 4th century. It is currently located at the Vatican Library (Gr. 1209) in Vatican City.

LXX F (Codex Ambrosiano A 147) is dated to the 5th century. It is currently located at the Ambrosian Library (A. 147 inf.) in Milan.

LXX 14 is dated to the 11th century. It is currently located at the Vatican Library (Vat. Palat. Gr. 203) in Vatican City.

LXX 15 is dated to the 10th century. It is currently located at the National Library of France (Coisl. Gr. 2) in Paris.

LXX 16 is dated to the 11th century. It is currently located at the Laurentian Library (v. 38) in Florence.

LXX 18 is dated to the 11th century. It is currently located at the Laurentian Library (Pal. 242) in Florence.

LXX 19 is dated to the 12th century. It is currently located at the Chigi Palace (R. VI. 38) in Rome.

LXX 25 is dated to the 11th century. It is currently located at the Bavarian State Library (Gr. 9) in Munich.

LXX 30 is dated to the 11th or 12th century. It is currently located at the Biblioteca Casanatense (1444) in Rome.

LXX 44 is dated to the 15th century. It is currently located at the Stadtbibliothek (A 1) in Zittau.

LXX 52 is dated to the 14th century. It is currently located at the Laurentian Library (Acquisti 44) in Florence.

LXX 53 is dated to 1439. It is currently located at the National Library of France (Gr. 17 A) in Paris.

LXX 54 is dated to the 13th or 14th century. It is currently located at the National Library of France (Gr. 5) in Paris.

LXX 55 is dated to the 10th century. It is currently located at the Vatican Library (Regin. Gr. 1) in Vatican City.

LXX 56 is dated to 1093. It is currently located at the National Library of France (Gr. 3) in Paris.

LXX 57 is dated to the 11th century. It is currently located at the Vatican Library (Gr. 747) in Vatican City.

LXX 58 is dated to the 11th century. It is currently located at the Vatican Library (Regin. gr. 10) in Vatican City.

LXX 59 is dated to the 15th century. It is currently located at the University Library (BE 7b. 10) in Glasgow.

LXX 64 is dated to the 10th century. It is currently located at the National Library of France (Gr. 2) in Paris.

LXX 68 is dated to the 15th century. It is currently located at the Biblioteca Marciana (Gr. 5) in Venice.

LXX 72 is dated to the 13th century. It is currently located at the Bodleian Library (Canonic. Gr. 35) in Oxford.

LXX 75 is dated to 1125. It is currently located at University College (52) in Oxford.

LXX 76 is dated to the 13th century. It is currently located at National Library of France (Coisl. Gr. 4) in Paris.

LXX 78 is dated to the 12th century. It is currently located at the Vatican Library (Gr. 383) in Vatican City.

SEPTUAGINT MANUSCRIPTS

LXX 82 is dated to the 12th century. It is currently located at the National Library of France (Coisl. Gr. 3) in Paris.

LXX 83 is dated to the 16th century. It is currently located at the Archivo da Torre do Tombo (540, 668, 669, 670, 671) in Lisbon.

LXX 84 is dated to the 10th or 11th centuries. It is currently located at the Vatican Library (Gr. 1901) in Vatican City.

LXX 85 is dated to the 10th centuries. It is currently located at the Vatican Library (Gr. 2058) in Vatican City.

LXX 106 is dated to the 14th century. It is currently located at the Biblioteca Comunale Ariostea (187 I-III) in Ferrara.

LXX 108 is dated to the 13th century. It is currently located at the Vatican Library (Gr. 330) in Vatican City.

LXX 120 is dated to the 12th or 13th centuries. It is currently located at the Biblioteca Marciana (Gr. 23) in Venice.

LXX 121 is dated to the 10th century. It is currently located at the Biblioteca Marciana (Gr. 3) in Venice.

LXX 125 is dated to the 14th century. It is currently located at the State Historical Museum (Gr. 30) in Moscow.

LXX 129 is dated to the 11th or 12th centuries. It is currently located at the Vatican Library (Gr. 1252) in Vatican City.

LXX 130 is dated to the 12th or 13th centuries. It is currently located at the Austrian National Library (Theol. Gr. 23) in Vienna.

LXX 131 is dated to the 10th century. It is currently located at the Austrian National Library (Theol. Gr. 57) in Vienna.

LXX 135 is dated to the 10th centuries. It is currently located at the University Library (A. N. III. 13) in Basel.

LXX 313 is dated to the 11th century. It is currently located at the National Library of Greece (43) in Athens.

LXX 314 is dated to the 13th century. It is currently located at the National Library of Greece (44) in Athens.

LXX 318 is dated to the 10th or 11th centuries. It is currently located at the Vatopedi (598) on Mount Athos.

LXX 376 is dated to the 15th century. It is currently located at the Royal Library (Y-II-5) in El Escorial.

LXX 392 is dated to the 10th century. It is currently located at the Abbey of Saint Mary of Grottaferrata (A. γ. I) in Grottaferrata.

LXX 426 is dated to the 11th century. It is currently located at the British Library (Add. 39585) in London.

LXX 458 is dated to the 12th century. It is currently located at the University Library (62) in Messina.

LXX 509 is dated to the 9th or 10th centuries. Sections are currently located at the Bodleian Library (Auct. T. inf. 2. 1) in Oxford, University Library (Add. 1879. 7) in Cambridge, British Library (Add. 20002) in London, and the National Library of Russia (Gr. 62) in St. Petersburg.

LXX 619 is dated to the 15th century. It is currently located at the Pelekete monastery (411) on Patmos Island.

LXX 707 is dated to the 10th or 11th centuries. Sections are currently located at Saint Catherine's Monastery (Codex Gr. 1) in the Sinai, and the National Library of Russia (Gr. 260) in St. Petersburg.

LXX 730 is dated to the 10th century. It is currently located at the Biblioteca Marciana (Gr. 15) in Venice.

LXX 799 is dated to 1280. It is currently located at the National Library of Greece (2491) in Athens.

ALTERNATIVE SOURCES

The following is a list of alternative ancient translations that were used for comparative analysis. Both the Peshitta and Coptic translations are believed to have been heavily based on the Septuagint, although do inherit relics of older Syro-Aramaic and Egypto-Aramaic translations, or imports from the Hebrew translation.

The Leningrad Codex is dated to 1008 (or 1009) CE. It is currently located at the National Library of Russia (Firkovich B 19 A) in St. Petersburg. The Leningrad Codex is the oldest complete copy of the Hebrew scriptures used within Judaism.

Peshitta: The Syriac translation of the Christian bible. The Old Testament was translated from older Aramaic and Hebrew sources during the late 2nd century CE.

The Targum Onkelos is generally accepted as having been compiled by Aquila (Onkelos) of Sinope between 100 and 120 CE, although the surviving copies are all in Babylonian Aramaic, and the text appears to have been updated linguistically in Babylon in the 4th or 5th centuries CE. Some scholars believe Aquila was reworking a now lost, older Judean-Aramaic targum from the 1st century. The Megillah (3a) tractate of the Babylonian Torah claims that the Onkelos Targum is a restoration of a version of the Torah in use before the time of Ezra the scribe in the 4th century BCE. While the idea that Aquila and Onkelos were the same person, the Talmuds mention both of them doing the same thing, creating a targum in the same era, but do not confirm they are the same person. Therefore, the Onkelos is sometimes viewed as being a continuation of an older Babylonian Aramaic translation from the Neo-Babylonian, Persian, or Greek eras.

The Targum Pseudo-Jonathan has historically been misidentified as the Targum Jonathan, and is also called the Targum Jerusalem in some literature, although this is not the same document as the

Targum Jerusalem listed below. It is written in Palestinian-Aramaic, and generally dated to sometime between the 4th and 11th centuries. Some scholars believe it originated in the 4th century and was modified after the Islamic conquest of Palestine, as it includes some Arabic names generally found in Islamic sources. It existed before the crusades, as it was documented at the time.

The Targum Jerusalem, sometimes called the Targum Jerusalem II or the Fragments Targum, is a collection of fragments from one or more targums written in Judean Aramaic that surfaced in Italy during the medieval era. It contains a number of heretical concepts, such as Judean-polytheism, suggesting some are a relic of a polytheist Israelite sect from before the Maccabean Revolt. The oldest Targum Jerusalem fragments date to the medieval period or later, and are copies of a manuscript reworked in the 5th century CE. However, the Targum is written in a form of Judeo-Aramaic that supports its origin in the Persian, Hellenistic, or Hasmonean eras.

The Vetus Latina manuscripts are Old Latin manuscripts translated from Aramaic and Greek sources between the 3rd century BCE and 4th century CE. Surviving manuscripts are copies that were made much later. The earliest surviving manuscripts that include Exodus date to the 5th century CE.

The Coptic manuscripts are translations of the Septuagint into Coptic, the Classical form of Egyptian. Translations of the Septuagint were made into at least five of the Coptic dialects, however, complete copies only survive in Bohairic and Sahidic. These dialects were written slightly differently, and therefore words transliterated into Coptic retain slightly different pronunciations, reflecting the different source texts used.

Sahidic manuscripts are translations of the Septuagint into Sahidic (also known as Thebaic), one of the six dialects of Coptic, the classical era form of the Egyptian language. Sahidic was the dominant form

308

of Coptic used before the 11th century, and is believed to have originated in the region around Hermopolis, at the boundary between Upper and Lower Egypt. Translations of the Septuagint into Sahidic are known to have existed by the 4th century, however, early non-dialect specific translations are generally accepted as having been made as early as the 1st century CE, with some scholars suggesting the 1st century BCE. The early non-dialect specific forms of Coptic are generally grouped with Sahidic, as Sahidic did not have a standardized spelling until the 6th century.

Sahidic manuscript 16L is a Sahidic Coptic and Arabic parallel text dated to earlier than 1443. It is currently located at the Biblioteca Apostolica Vaticana (Borg. copt. 109, cass. XXIII, fasc. 99) in Vatican City.

Sahidic manuscript 2000 is a late Sahidic manuscript dated to the 4th century. It is currently located at the Bibliotheca Bodmeriana (Papyrus Bodmer XVI) in Cologny.

Sahidic manuscript 2002 is a late Sahidic manuscript dated to the 9th century. It is currently located at the Universitätsbibliothek Leuven (Copt. Lov. 2) in Leuven.

Sahidic manuscript 2043 is dated to the 7th or 8th century. It is currently located at the Bibliothèque nationale de France (Copte 129) in Paris, the British Library (Or. 8810) in London, and the Österreichische Nationalbibliothek (K 2600, K 9869) in Vienna, and the Biblioteca Apostolica Vaticana (Borg. copt. 109, cass. I, fasc. 4) in Vatican City.

Sahidic manuscript 2148 is dated to the 11th century. It is currently located at the Bibliothèque nationale de France (Copte 129) in Paris, the British Library (Or. 3579 A) in London, and the Österreichische Nationalbibliothek (K 9879, K 9875, K 9876, K 9877, K 9878) in Vienna, and the Biblioteca Apostolica Vaticana (Borg. copt. 109, cass. X, fasc. 32) in Vatican City.

ALTERNATIVE SOURCES

Sahidic manuscript 2169 is dated to the 7th or 8th century. It is currently located at the Bibliothèque nationale de France (Copte 129) in Paris.

Fayyumic manuscripts are translations of the Septuagint into Fayyumic (also known as Bashmuric), one of the six dialects of Coptic. Fayyumic was mainly spoken in the Faiyum Oasis, west of the Nile Valley. Fayyumic manuscripts are known dating to the 3rd through the 10th centuries, however, all are incomplete.

Bohairic manuscripts are translations of the Septuagint into Bohairic (also known as Memphitic), one of the six dialects of Coptic. Bohairic originated in the western Nile Delta of northern Egypt. The earliest Bohairic manuscripts date to the 4th century, however, the majority of texts come from the 9th century or later. Bohairic is the dialect used today as the liturgical language of the Coptic Orthodox Church, although Sahidic was used before the 11th century.

The Armenian bible was translated from the Septuagint in the 5th century, replacing the older Armenian bible that had been translated from Aramaic texts, however, includes some of the older names.

DEAD SEA SCROLLS

The following is a list of the Dead Sea Scrolls mentioned in the notes for this book. Most are held by the Israel Museum in Jerusalem.

DSS 1Q2 (1QExod) is dated to the Roman rule of Judea (6 to 390 CE).

DSS 2Q2 (2QExod^a) is dated to the Herodian Dynasty in Judea (37 BCE to 6 CE).

DSS 2Q3 (2QExod^b) is dated to between 50 BCE and 1 BCE by paleographic experts. In 2025, the Enoch AI provided a wider range of 40 BCE to 130 CE.

DSS 4Q1 (4QGen-Exod^a) is dated to the Hasmonean Dynasty in Judea (140 to 37 BCE).

DSS 4Q11 (4QpaleoGen-Exod^l) is dated to the Hasmonean Dynasty in Judea (140 to 37 BCE).

DSS 4Q13 (4QExod^b) is dated to between 50 BCE and 1 BCE by paleographic experts. In 2025, the Enoch AI provided a slightly later range of 40 BCE to 20 CE.

DSS 4Q14 (4QExod^c) is dated to the Herodian Dynasty in Judea (37 BCE to 6 CE).

DSS 4Q17 (4QExod-Lev^f) is dated to the Maccabean Revolt in Judea (165-140 BCE).

DSS 4Q22 (4QpaleoExod^m) is dated to the Hasmonean Dynasty in Judea (140 to 37 BCE).

DSS Mur1 is dated to the Roman rule of Judea and Palestine (6 to 390 CE).

ALSO AVAILABLE

ALSO AVAILABLE

- Septuagint: History, Volume 2

- Octateuch: The Original Orit

ENOCH AND METATRON SERIES:
- Books of Enoch Collection

- Books of Enoch and Metatron Collection

- Books of Metatron Collection

- Secrets of Enoch

OTHER TRANSLATION:
- Apocalypses of Ezra

- Arabic Maccabees

- Hebrew Maccabees

- Life of Adam and Eve

- Memories of the New Kingdom

- Septuagint's Esther and the Vetus Latina Esther

- Septuagint's Ezekiel and the Ba'al Cycle

- Septuagint's Job and the Testament of Job

- Septuagint's Proverbs and the Wisdom of Amenemope

- Syriac Maccabees – Deuterocanonical Books

- The Amarna Letters

- Testaments of the Patriarchs Collection

- Tobit and Ahikar

- Ugaritic Texts: Ba'al Cycle

- Wisdom of Ahikar

www.ingramcontent.com/pod-product-compliance
Lightning Source LLC
Chambersburg PA
CBHW061557120626
46550CB00004B/1527